AFGHANISTAN

For Bapa, who is no more.

AFGHANISTAN ———

The Labyrinth of Violence

AMALENDU MISRA

polity

Copyright © Amalendu Misra 2004

The right of Amalendu Misra to be identified as Author of this Work has been asserted in accordance with the UK Copyright, Designs and Patents Act 1988.

First published in 2004 by Polity Press

Polity Press
65 Bridge Street
Cambridge CB2 1UR, UK

Polity Press
350 Main Street
Malden, MA 02148, USA

A catalogue record for this book is available from the British Library.

Library of Congress Cataloging-in-Publication Data

Misra, Amalendu.
Afghanistan : the labyrinth of violence / Amalendu Misra.
     p. cm. (Hot Spots in Global Politics)
   Includes bibliographical references and index. ISBN 0-7456-3114-2 (hb : alk. paper) – ISBN 0-7456-3115-0 (pb : alk. paper)
    1. Afghanistan-History. I. Title.
DS361.M55 2004
958.104′6 – dc21

                      2003012991

Typeset in 10.5 on 12 pt Sabon
by SNP Best-set Typesetter Ltd., Hong Kong
Printed and bound in Great Britain by TJ International, Padstow, Cornwall

For further information on Polity, visit our website: www.polity.co.uk

Contents

Acknowledgements

Thanks to my constant critics and companions Bhikhu Parekh and Noël O'Sullivan; to Beverley Milton-Edwards for her generosity; to my intrepid editors Louise Knight, Sue Leigh and Jean van Altena at Polity for much helpful advice, encouragement and support throughout the writing and production stage; to Shahid Qadir of *Third World Quarterly* and Richard Jones of *Conflict Security and Development* in whose journals I tried out some of my ideas; to Shane O'Neill for providing a happy academic environment in which to work; to Reginald Cormier and Matthew Fielden for going through various chapters of the manuscript; to Gurharpal Singh, Karin Fierke, Adrian Guelke, Bob Eccleshall, Abel Rivera Sanchez, S.G. Pandian, Timothy Curry, Cathal McCall, Davide Muroni, Rogelio Alonso, Trilok Nath Mishra and Aga Zahid Ali Hilali for their friendship and kindness over the years; and to Bou for letting me live by my own rules. Any errors in this work are solely my responsibility, of course.

Introduction

Medieval is Afghanistan on a good day.

Anatol Lieven, *Afghan Statecraft*, 2002

In contemporary international society, Afghanistan is a country like no other. A relatively unknown actor in global politics, Afghanistan unwittingly became a catalyst in the last great ideological war of the twentieth century, which saw the demise of communism and the triumph of liberalism. While the international community acquired a victory of sorts following the end of this confrontation, the state and the society that had served as a front line in this conflict found itself in complete ruin. Their success assured, the self-serving external powers who had used Afghanistan for their own designs conveniently forgot about its needs. A devastated country and its distraught people were left in mire.[1] Nevertheless, at the century's end, Afghanistan had reinvented itself under an enigmatic leadership the actions of which were so decisive that they were responsible for defining the nature of international relations in the early twenty-first century and once again putting the country at the centre stage of world politics.

To recount the story of Afghanistan's place in the world is to reconstruct a microcosm of international Cold War politics, in which Soviet domination, American intervention,

Pakistani reassertion, Iranian double-dealing, vicious muja-hidin offensive and the Afghan experience all find their place. This narrative, however, captures only the nature of the international system during the Cold War years and falls short of explaining the genesis of Afghanistan's overall misfortune.

The crisis in Afghanistan raises several intriguing conceptual questions pertaining to the nature of the international system. Is the conflict organically linked to the bipolarity of the Cold War years? Is it among the symptoms of the changing international order characterized by the rise of a new ideological bipolarity between resurgent radical Islam and the West? Is it a localized conflict, which was subsequently exported to the outside world via forces of globalization? Taken independently, no single issue fully explains the crisis in Afghanistan.

Taken as interrelated variables, however, they lend credence to the argument that a multitude of factors contributed to the breakdown of the Afghan state. From a definitional perspective, the conflict in Afghanistan was 'neither an inter-state war nor a classic civil war. In fact, the conflict has moved through several phases and might now be characterized as part regional proxy war and part civil war' (Atmar and Goodhand 2001: 1). Given that the international society is much more interlinked (homogenized) than at any other time in human history, the conflict in Afghanistan simply spilled over beyond its borders, and consequently affected the international community as a whole.

Although sympathetic to the prominence of the above-mentioned factors in Afghanistan's civil war dynamics, I none the less argue that it was state failure primarily that created conditions for various attendant elements to contribute to the conflict. Drawing on the 'failed state' theory, I highlight how Afghanistan was on a course of natural decline ever since its inception as a self-governing territory. At no time in its history was the Afghan state able to 'comprehensively penetrate' all areas of its territory. It existed more as an idea than as a viable political unit. The country remained divided into various tribal groups, which controlled carefully demarcated fiefdoms.

Each tribal chief exercised day-to-day government by tribal support and force. What we know as 'Afghanistan' was far from being a single ethnic, cultural or even political idea in any period of its history. Its definition as a state, therefore, was more of an external attribute, and did not take into account the underlying divisions. The 'idea of nation' that various regimes and rulers tried to develop did not mean anything to most Afghans. Only a minority of political staff and intellectuals in the capital Kabul subscribed to the suggestion of a mainstream identity (Centlivres and Centlivres-Demont 2000: 424).

In Afghanistan, tribe pre-dates the state both as an anthropological and as a political phenomenon. The country stood united as one when it enjoyed the good will of its tribes. When that goodwill dissipated, chaos followed. The state in effect was caught in a double jeopardy: it could enjoy legitimacy only when the constituent tribes were rewarded with benefits; but it could not provide these services if the citizenry did not contribute to the coffer. Caught in this vicious circle, Afghanistan could never emerge as a viable state. Studying this aspect of the country's political culture, scholars have argued that 'tribal societies like that of Afghanistan are by nature unfit to act as the basis for the formation of modern state, the needs of which are in direct opposition to their traditions of "ordered anarchy" '(Lieven 2002: 27). State failure in Afghanistan is likely to have been 'preceded and inaugurated by complex and conflict-ridden processes of deterioration, decline and erosion of institutional functions' (Doornbos 2001: 5).

A failed state is one which 'cannot or will not safeguard minimal civil conditions, i.e., peace, order and security domestically' (Jackson 1998: 2). A state can gain this ignominious status if it fails to maintain the rule of law, promote human rights, and provide effective governance and deliver public goods to its citizenry, including education, health care and basic economic growth. According to the proponents of 'failed state' theory, because of the civil strife, economic collapse and breakdown of the welfare system, the inhabitants of a failed state are likely to (a) flee to neighbouring countries as refugees; (b) organize themselves along ethnic and tribal lines and establish independent fiefdoms; (c) engage in illicit economic practices, including smuggling of arms and contraband, mining, drugs production and drug trafficking; and (d) threaten the stability of their neighbours (Helman and Ratner 1993: 7–8). Faced with these challenges, a failed state may become its own worst enemy and lose its continued coherence (Olson 1993: 5).

Under conditions such as these, many states easily fall victim to a whole array of outside interferences. Viewed from outside, a ' "failed state" is one that is utterly incapable of sustaining itself as a member of the international community' (Helman and Ratner 1993: 3). States unable to maintain their political and territorial integrity or provide a semblance of law and order within often fall victim to the designs of external powers and become breeding grounds for dangerous non-state actors. As a response to state failure, an external power (concerned with its own security or wishing to expand its territorial and political hegemony) may attack such a state. But most alarming of all, a failed state may provide an environment in which mercenaries, social rejects, religious fanatics, ideologically blind politicians and criminals colonize its physical space and use it to promote their own particular vision or consolidate and expand their interests and operations.[2]

According to one theoretical interpretation of the origins of nations, many modern states are inventions (Anderson 1984). The identity of a group of seemingly different individuals is transformed from a mosaic of parochial affiliations to a greater and all-embracing national community through a process of national integration. Although European colonialism was primarily exploitative, it none the less 'spurred the creation of nascent national identities' (Anderson 1984: 34) among the colonized that were critical in the formation of many modern non-European states.

Unlike many of its Asian counterparts, Afghanistan was never fully colonized by any European or outside powers. In order to avoid a direct confrontation between them, both Russia and Britain arrived at an informal agreement that created Afghanistan's border arbitrarily and imposed statehood upon it. The artificiality of the nation-state in this setting, and its incommensurability with Afghan social and political realities, deepened inherent contradictions within the country (D. B. Edwards 1996: 3). Therefore, as has been argued by many scholars, Afghanistan was essentially an artificial state from its inception (Piacentini 1996: 29).

Since Afghanistan escaped colonization, in effect it missed the opportunity to develop a coherent sense of nationhood. The state creation here was artificial. Therefore, when Afghans encountered their modern polity they had difficulty relating to it as they did not have a corresponding degree of national solidarity. The tragedy of Afghanistan is in essence a result of its political and moral incoherence. As one critic puts it, 'the fundamental artificiality of the Afghan nation-state is the absence of a moral discourse of statehood shared by a majority of its citizens' (D. B. Edwards 1996: 3). Landlocked, isolated and economically backward, the country escaped the modernization process that many developing and underdeveloped countries witnessed at the end of colonialism. Absence of any effective interaction with the outside world and a deeply entrenched tribal culture contributed to Afghanistan's failure to emerge as a viable modern state.

It was held together not through consensus or the ideal of civic nationalism, but merely by ethnic and tribal dominance of one group over the rest of the constituent partners (often mediated by the exertion of brute force). Since national consolidation was marshalled through force, control of the central authority or government on the whole of the physical territory remained tenuous. Moreover, coalitions of tribes and ethnic groups regularly rose up to defend themselves against any central government rulings that aimed to introduce a unifying set of rules or policy undertakings.

The citizenry saw such interventions as intrusion into their lives. Consequently, the authority of the state over its citizenry remained patchy, and the state did not penetrate all areas. Afghanistan entered the modern age incapable of projecting power and asserting authority within its own borders, leaving its territories governmentally empty. In essence, 'Afghanistan has never been a homogeneous nation but rather a collection of disparate groups divided along ethnic, linguistic, religious and racial lines and forced together by vagaries of geopolitics' (Goodson 2001: 14). Given this inauspicious inheritance, Afghanistan's continued tryst with conflict is no surprise.

One way of countering this dearth in national spirit is to introduce a form of benign government that is transparent and reflective of the interests of all communities and constituent units. Beset by intrigues, infighting and political assassinations, the state in Afghanistan slipped into the hands of self-serving regimes that worked exclusively for themselves. The main casualty of this misadministration was trust. After the deposition of King Muhammad Zahir Shah in 1973, Afghans could never develop a sense of mainstream political community. Unsurprisingly, they remained barely loyal to the state. Lacking this commitment from its own citizenry, Afghanistan hung perpetually in a transition to a 'viable state', and eventually failed.

It is suggested that 'state failure is often progressive, without clear turning points, warning signals, threshold, or pressure spots' (Zartman 1995: 9). In the case of Afghanistan, however, the indications of state failure were all too stark and vivid. The growth of state failure in Afghanistan dates back to the 1970s. Within a very short period, a series of *coups* and counter-*coups* and political assassinations robbed the country of most of its vital governing institutions. According to some theorists, 'when states fail to satisfy the basic preconditions of the right to state autonomy they also lose their immunity' (Parekh 1997: 51). When the Soviet Union invaded Afghanistan in 1979, the Afghan state was effectively disintegrating. Although the Soviet invasion of Afghanistan had strong ideological and strategic underpinnings, Moscow's intervention could be seen as a direct attempt to stop state failure in Afghanistan, and can be compared with the international community's intervention in 2001. Therefore, one could argue that the overall aim of Soviet intervention in Afghanistan was to rescue the country and prevent its demise. For the disintegration of Afghanistan posed a direct threat to the Soviet Union's own borders.

Afghanistan never had an indigenous economic foundation – often a key to viable state formation. Construction of an infrastructure was hampered by the absence of natural resources, the dearth of any industries or commerce, and its rudimentary agricultural sector. In addition, given the autonomous nature of its tribal territories, the central government could never impose, let alone extract, any kind of revenue from its citizenry. Put simply, lacking meaningful or realistic economic means of redress, the central government in Kabul could not exercise the legitimacy of the state over its citizenry. An aggressive tax-collecting system could have facilitated the power and authority of the state to some degree.

However, dependent on revenue and aid from external sources, and faced with internal opposition, successive governments simply discounted any policy implementation which would require a comprehensive taxation system throughout the country. Predictably, this rendered the state weak and kept it dependent on external assistance. In the opinion of some critics, from its very inception Afghanistan survived as a 'rentier state' – i.e. a state that depended on external aid for its continued existence (Rubin 1995a). When such aid was not forthcoming, the citizenry and tribal leaders resorted to plunder, which led to the rise of warlordism and the depletion of central authority.

Unsurprisingly, this form of state failure had disastrous consequences. A failed state with deep-seated intertribal rivalry, absolutely no economic strength, and an extremely important geostrategic location made Afghanistan a perfect arena for regional and world powers to try out their power projection in the region. For Afghanistan was not only a state created by outside actors; these actors also regularly sponsored rival factions in order to prevent it from emerging as a viable polity (Rubin 1995a; L. Dupree 1997). Chapter 1 analyses the geopolitical predicament of Afghanistan, and explains how political geography was responsible for stifling its nation-building initiatives.

It is widely believed that 'violence consciously initiated by individuals, communities or social groups emerges only under conditions of a growing inauthenticity of the political and social order' (Senghaas 1987: 6). A section of the citizenry is forced to engage in such activities, as what should be the supreme guarantor of order – i.e. the state – fails to live up to its role. State failure or malperformance inevitably creates conditions such that various actors or the citizenry respond in accordance with their selfish and survival needs. Although reduced to a satellite during the Soviet occupation (1979–89), the Afghan state continued to exist on the margins, and was able to respond to some existential demands. The Soviet pull-out, however, plunged the country into absolute chaos, and whatever little semblance of order had survived dissipated almost overnight. Violence against civilians increased mightly as rival groups contested for power, and no legitimate central government emerged. This ordered anarchy was in fact a direct outcome of state failure. In chapter 2, I highlight the dynamics of ethnic mobilization during this phase and assess its impact on the overall situation.

It is argued that most failed states could have a legal, but not much political, existence (Takeyh and Gvosdev 2002: 100–1). Afghanistan under the Taliban regime unfortunately had neither. Unrecognized by the entire international community (except Saudi Arabia, the United Arab Emirates and Pakistan), its pariah status added to its citizens' woes. Without this crucial external, international, legal scaffolding, and unable to sustain itself economically within, Afghanistan slipped into the grip of Islamic radicals from outside the country. They not only provided the much-needed economic assistance, but also promised the elites of the society a grand Islamic confederation at whose centre would be Afghanistan.

Wedded to this utopia, the Taliban set about organizing an internal revolution that would consume itself and destroy whatever little social and economic fabric had survived two decades of civil war. Driven by regime insecurity, it preyed on its own citizens (Rotberg 2002a: 86). It survived only through its ability to exert internal violence. For it is an undeniable reality that 'dying states resort to gross violence against their own populations in last gasp efforts to maintain power' (R. Peters 1995: 22). Chapter 3 narrates the story of the Taliban's inheritance of a failed and dying state. It argues that, unable to construct a viable state, the Taliban regime simply destroyed it.

If left unattended, 'failed states' can become 'sanctuaries for unwanted actors' (Hamre and Sullivan 2002: 85). Compared to a 'viable state', a 'failed state' is often at a disadvantage when it comes to defending itself from corrupt and destabilizing forces or ideas. Stripped bare of resources, and existing on the margins of international society, failed states are often vulnerable to invidious influences. For in such a situation external forces can easily penetrate the boundaries of the state and use it for their own self-serving vision. 'Failed states hold a number of attractions for non-state actors and terrorist organizations' (Takeyh and Gvosdev 2002: 98). The relative ease with which the al-Qa'ida operated from Afghanistan suggests that conditions of 'state collapse' existed under the Taliban.

Taking advantage of this state of affairs, al-Qa'ida easily exploited Afghanistan's vulnerability. It helped the Taliban enter into an informal alliance with it where each looked after the other's needs. In this symbiotic arrangement, the Taliban provided a safe haven for Osama bin Laden, his high command and his network, and the latter, in return, provided financial and professional assistance to the Taliban (Record 2002: 5). Chapter 4 highlights how non-state actors such as al-Qa'ida took advantage of Afghanistan's physical isolation, perpetual civil war, crumbling state structure, and the prevalence of a medieval outlook among a section of its elite and citizenry to launch a world-wide campaign of terror.

States are the fundamental units of the international system, and are responsible for maintaining both order and justice. As a result, when they develop any complications, they become a liability. Failed states are a threat not only to themselves but to the interests of their neighbours, region and the international community as a whole. Seen in this light, Afghanistan under the Taliban had clearly become a threat to world peace and stability. What should be the response of the international community to a conflict-ridden political unit such as Afghanistan? Do great powers have any responsibility concerning a 'failed state' if that state is a calamity for its population and a liability to its neighbours (Jackson 1998: 3)? The widely held answer to these questions is that the international community has to respond to 'human suffering and rescue failing states' (Vincent and Wilson 1993). If there is a moral, legal and strategic obligation, how ought we to proceed in our intervention? Chapter 5 explores the dynamics of the international armed intervention in Afghanistan within the framework of the United Nations Charter and according to the principle of 'just war'.

Further, it analyses the attendant problem of 'state-building' and the long-term challenges it poses. The chapter highlights the fact that the involvement of the international community or external powers could partly counter the pessimistic or grim forecast of many policy analysts that the likelihood of the citizenry returning to a civil war in a 'failed state' is potentially very high. Seen in conjunction with civil war theory, the fundamental problem of 'failed states' is that 'they do not simply go away; they linger; and the longer they persist, the greater the potential challenges to neighbouring states, regional stability and international peace' (Horf 1996: 18–19). This chapter also raises several contentious aspects of the conflict, and asks whether it is realistic to expect that the international community will remain committed to Afghanistan in the long haul.

Failed states are clearly a calamitous reality for their populations (Jackson 1998: 3). Without a legally recognized juridical government, citizens in a failed state are more likely to come under the influence of regional leaders or warlords. A strong tradition of tribal hierarchy aided the disruption of the Afghan state. Since the authority of the state remained contested, warlords could easily declare their individual fiefdoms and coax those living within the demarcated territory to work for their own self-serving narrow interests. Citizens in a failed state are far more likely than their counterparts elsewhere turn to criminalized economic practices for their survival. The 'anti-state actors' such as warlords often take advantage of this situation, and enlist their supporters in the farming of an illegal crop, or engaging in gun-running or narco-trafficking (R. Peters 1996: 21). The issue of poppy cultivation, discussed in chapter 6, can be seen in this context.

In a globalized world, it is argued, 'when states fail, other states are needed to put them back on their feet' (Holm 2001: 13). Preventing state failure and reviving states that do fail have become a strategic as well as a moral imperative (Rotberg 2003). The international community's and individual state's commitments to the restoration of war-ravaged societies or polities are a step in that direction. Chapter 7 takes a rather cautionary view of post-conflict reconstruction in Afghanistan. It argues that the presence of external actors cannot guarantee Afghanistan's return to normalcy.

As has been suggested by scholars assessing peace operations in many other conflict-ridden societies, militias, warlords and non-state actors who benefit during conditions of anarchy will 'make themselves enemies of everything and make it extremely difficult for a peace support force to be impartial; if the force is there simply to restore order, those who favour disorder will not see it as impartial' (Horf 1996: 23–4). Consequently, these self-serving, ideologically driven actors with little to lose in a traumatized land may treat foreigners and peacekeeping forces whose presence is identified with the West as a possible or even desirable target, as were the US marines at the height of the Lebanese civil war and later in Somalia (Weinberger 2002: 273).

In the light of our discussion of Afghanistan as a failed state, the most crucial aspects of the new debate about the 'capable state' concern 'what it means for citizens' participation in politics, freedom of expression and the creation of a professional non-corrupt civil service to serve citizens' needs'(Hird 1997: 61). A civil war peace settlement requires 'consolidation of the previously warring factions into a single state, build a new government capable of accommodating their interests, and create a national, non-partisan military force' (Walter 1999: 43). To what extent have these goals been met in Afghanistan? Prevention of state failure depends exclusively on internal will and external assistance.

The conclusions drawn from this analysis relate not only to the relationship between external and internal factors, with implications for the future occurrence of conflict, if any, but also to three possible future scenarios for Afghanistan: namely, a gradual reduction in tension, the emergence of a basic state structure, or a return to civil war dynamics. The continuation of any of these scenarios will be shown to have divergent explanations, with important consequences for understanding of the strengths and the weaknesses of each of the variables in differing contexts.

The Curse of Geopolitics

> For good or bad Afghanistan's geographic position has con-
> tributed the single most important element to the shaping of
> its history, its ethnic diversity, its economy and its political
> situation in the region and increasingly in the world.
>
> Magnus and Naby, *Afghanistan,* 1998

Introduction

Throughout its history, Afghanistan has been subject to intervention by external powers. Forces operating from outside its
geographical confines have continually determined its overall
politics, social structure and consequently its place in the
world. Being at the crossroads of Central Asia, it was subjected to an uninterrupted stream of offensives and conquests
from the earliest times.

The first recorded foreign invasion of the country took
place in sixth century BC, when Darius I of Persia brought it
under his control. This was followed by another spectacular
invasion by Alexander the Great in 328 BC. Alexander's conquest formally opened up the society to Indo-European commerce, culture and religious ideas. In the following centuries,
Sakas (Scythians), Parthians and Kushans (who were practis-
ing Buddhists), all tracing their roots to Central Asia, kept
the country successively under their control. Interestingly,

this pattern continued well into the seventh century AD. During this phase, Hephthalites, or White Huns, ruled over Afghanistan in the fifth and sixth centuries AD.

Conquest of another form took place in Afghanistan in the seventh century AD, when invading Arabs introduced Islam into the country. From a peripheral territory lying in the outlying areas of various emperors and their empires, Afghanistan briefly became the seat of an empire when Mahmud of Ghazni made it the centre of Islamic power, glory and civilization in the eleventh century. Invading Mongols from the north, however, destroyed much of Mahmud's creation, and from the thirteenth until the sixteenth century Afghanistan's fortunes were created, destroyed and recreated by Timur-i-Lang (Tamerlane), Babur (the founder of the Mughal dynasty in India) and the Safavid rulers of Persia.

Afghanistan entered the modern age with the introduction of European colonialism in Asia. Unlike many of its Asian counterparts, Afghanistan escaped full-scale colonization. However, its internal politics and the right to conduct its affairs with the outside world with absolute freedom were severely curtailed. Its accursed geography once again came to determine the fate of the Afghan people and their larger political processes. The 'strategic location of Afghanistan made it important for the control of the Indian subcontinent, defensively as well as offensively' (L. Dupree 1997: 343).

'The Great Game'

European imperialism entered a new phase when Germany was united under Bismarck, and the new unified nation tried to acquire colonies to gain respectability as a power to be reckoned with. This altered Russian and British geopolitical thinking in Central Asia and Afghanistan. Lord Curzon (viceroy of India, 1899–1905), a great believer in 'British Forward Policy', saw imperialist fervour in Europe as a great opportunity to acquire new territories by way of rescinding all earlier treaties with Afghanistan.

According to Curzon, Turkistan, Afghanistan, Transcaspia, Persia, etc. are pieces on a chess-board upon which is being played out a game for dominance of the world. Of all these places, Afghanistan was closest to the British India geographically, and appeared within its reach. British India had already fought two wars with Afghans in order to fulfil this ambition. Under Curzon's leadership there was a revival in British expansionism. Soon the British were pushing their outposts into tribal territories well within Afghanistan. But there was one obstacle.

From the seventeenth century, Tsarist regimes in Russia coveted the warm water ports to the south of their land borders. Peter the Great (1682–1725) was the first to introduce this idea among his fellow citizens. Russia coveted warm water ports to the south, either on the Dardanelles, in the Persian Gulf or in the Indian Ocean (L. Dupree 1997: 363). Many Russians considered it a national duty and their historic mission to find ways to move forward in this direction. Obstacles to the fulfilment of this national goal, however, were many. This ambition was curtailed by the presence of Persia (modern-day Iran) and Afghanistan, which stood as a barricade to Russia's southward expansion. Persia, owing to its powerful empire and solid military base, was almost impregnable by the Russians. Afghanistan, however, was a different matter.

The decline of the Safavids in Persia and of the Turkish Ottoman Empire, coupled with marginalization of Central Asian khanates in the nineteenth century, produced a power vacuum in and around Afghanistan. This new uncertain political atmosphere created conditions for other powers to step into the vacuum. Tsarist Russia found it to be an opportune moment to bring Afghanistan into its sphere of influence, and nurtured the hope of merging it subsequently with the Russian Empire. But this expansionist design was a direct threat to the interests of British India. In addition, Russian or British gain or loss in Asia had direct implications for those nations' strength and standing in Europe (Yapp 1980; Klass 1990; Hauner 1990). Afghanistan, in other words, held the key to the future success or failure of two powerful empires in Asia and Europe. Whilst both were aware of Afghanistan's strategic geography, neither was prepared to engage in a direct military confrontation leading to a conclusive result.

Instead, both tried to test their prowess indirectly. And Afghanistan became a cockpit for their battle skills. Their diplomatic and military offensives were enacted in this no man's land. This cat and mouse game between imperial Russia and British India was termed as 'the Great Game' by the English poet and novelist Rudyard Kipling. During the Great Game, both Russia and British India would invade a part of Afghan territory and retreat afterwards. In this imperial game of chess, various regions of northern Afghanistan fell to Russian incursion at one point or another, and the British controlled parts of southern Afghanistan on several occasions throughout nineteenth and early twentieth centuries.

British occupation of southern Afghanistan – namely, the vital Khyber Pass – prompted Tsarist Russia to respond in a similar manner. It interpreted the British invasion of the country as a direct threat to its interests. Under Great Game politics, the Russians suspected the British of hatching a diabolical scheme to create an anti-Russian confederacy consisting of the khanates of Bukhara, Khiva and Kokand (Hopkirk 1994; Meyer and Brysac 2000). The British, in turn, suspected the Russians of similar designs by trying to incorporate these states into their forward defence of Turkestan through Afghanistan and then India (Hauner 1990: 80). In quick succession, imperial Russia gobbled up one territory after another in Central Asia, either through the imposition of a system of political and economic vassalage or through control of trade, until it reached the doors of Afghanistan. The British under the 'Forward Strategy' would extend their military stronghold close to the Persian border by establishing the impregnable outpost in Herat.

Although Afghanistan's impassable vastness, and this quirky colonial engagement, enabled it to avoid complete occupation by either Tsarist Russia or imperial India, the Great Game nevertheless severely restricted the country's political process, plunging its future into darkness and

turning Afghanistan into a nation ever suspicious of outsiders. The British for their part perpetually accused various
Afghan ruling houses as Tsarist sympathizers, and held them
responsible for not doing enough to stop Russian incursion
into Afghanistan. Armed often with very little or no sub-
stantive evidence to support their accusations, the British
instigated various military campaigns against the country.
These were known as the Anglo-Afghan wars: the first in
1839–42, the second in 1878–80, and the third in 1919.
These campaigns were doomed from the start. According to
a contemporary study, the first invasion of Afghanistan was
'the most complete humiliation in the history of the British
Empire – a cocktail of viceregal arrogance, diplomatic stu-
pidity, and military ineptitude leading to the annihilation of
the invading army on its way back' (Meyer and Brysac 2000:
72).

Having failed to conquer or even subdue the Afghans in
the first two Anglo-Afghan wars, the British were forced to
subsidize an Afghan ruler (powerful enough to be accepted
by his own people and recognized outside) to serve as a buffer
between an ambitious Tsarist Russia and British India. For
this, 'the British sought a ruler who could establish a government stable enough to make Afghanistan a barrier to the
Russians while not posing a threat to India' (Magnus and
Naby 1998: 35). Ultimately, the choice fell on Abdur Rahman
Khan, a nephew of Amir Sher Ali, who lived in exile in
Tashkent. The British, who 'respect even those monarchs who
betray them' (Kapuściński 1985: 190), invited the renegade
Abdur Rahman to take power in Afghanistan, simply because
no one else could do it (Klass 1990: 2).

For his part, Abdur Rahman had a very sound appreciation of the politics of the Great Game. His first-hand experience of Russian politics during his exile in Tashkent and
direct dealings with the British made him realize that these
powers harboured strategic visions completely opposed to
each other. He concluded that while the Russian posture was
offensive, conditioned by its resolve to find access to warm
water ports in the Indian Ocean, the British interest in
Afghanistan was purely defensive and motivated by the

resolve to stop the Russian advancement at all costs. Confronted by these antagonistic camps on both sides Abdur Rahman Khan would muse: 'How can a small power like Afghanistan which is like a goat between these lions (Britain and Tsarist Russia), or grain of wheat between two strong millstones of the grinding mill, stand in the midway of the stones without being ground to dust?' (Khan 1900: 280).

Yet, by playing off these powers against each other, he secured Afghanistan's continued independence. In order to avoid a direct confrontation between them, Russia and Britain came to respect Afghanistan's borders. While Afghanistan was useful to the great empires for sustaining the balance of power, the rulers in Afghanistan received enough resources from the neighbouring powers to sustain control and internal stability (Stobdan 1999: 723).

Strange as it may seem, the Great Game was ultimately responsible for the emergence of the modern Afghan state. The Anglo-Russian competition in Central Asia led to the demarcation of Afghanistan's ethnically divisive borders, and facilitated a process that culminated in the creation of a state structure in the modern sense of the term (Goodson 2001: 31). Prior to Russian and British inching towards Afghanistan, the latter had a chaotic political culture. There was no centralized Afghan state, no overarching authority, and only a very loose definition of Afghan identity among its inhabitants. Like most of India and much of Central Asia, Afghanistan was a hotbed of political intrigues, where competition between small local tribes, khanates and various ethnic groups was as natural as night following day. Thanks to both formal and informal agreements between the two imperial powers, Britain and Russia, Abdur Rahman Khan had to spend his energy and vision on consolidating his country.

Having been forced to exist in the shadow of two powerful empires with expansionist tendencies (Goodson 2001: 23), that throughout the twentieth century came to dominate the country's internal as well as external politics, Afghans developed an idiosyncratic attitude. These encounters with Russia and Britain made Afghans hardened isolationists and fiercely independent. Strange as it may seem, 'at a time when virtually the entire Islamic world had come under the rule or indirect control of one or another European imperial power', Afghanistan retained its sovereignty (Magnus and Naby 1998: 38). In the grand scheme of the imperial chess-board, Afghanistan served as a no-go area. Its status as a buffer state was further consolidated during the leadership of Abdur Rahman Khan.

United as a result of foreign incursions, Afghanistan attained international recognition in 1919, following the conclusion of the third and last war with British India, and gained complete independence the same year. Soon after gaining international recognition, in 1926, the new king Amanullah launched Afghanistan on various diplomatic initiatives in the region, especially in Central Asia. As a part of this undertaking, an Afghan military contingent was sent to save the Bukharan Khanate from the Soviet Red Army. Kabul also mooted the idea of an Islamic Confederation in the region, comprising the khanates of Merv, Kushk, Panjdeh and Bukhara. Such a flurry of activities, however, yielded nothing. As the Soviet Union consolidated its authority over the whole of the Central Asian region, Afghanistan was pushed out of the regional decision-making process. What followed was complete isolation for Afghanistan.

During World War II, Afghanistan briefly became 'the Switzerland' of Central Asia in a new game of intrigue, as Allied and Axis coalitions jockeyed for position in the region (Bearden 2002: 39). For the Nazis, Afghanistan was important for two reasons. The first one was racial, and the second, geopolitical. The ideologues and politicians of the Third Reich believed Afghanistan to be the cradle of the Aryan heartland, and this belief led to increased co-operation with Afghanistan. The Nazi leader Adolf Hitler had greater ambitions. Like previous European conquerors, notably Alexander the Great, Hitler wanted to advance after defeating Russia in the direction of India through Afghanistan (Hauner 1990: 177–8). The attention paid to Afghanistan was short-lived, however. After the war, the country settled back into its natural state of isolation.

From the end of World War II until 1979, when the Soviets invaded it, the West and the international community blissfully ignored Afghanistan. Various factors contributed to this lack of interest. First, Afghanistan was not a major player in local and regional, let alone international, politics. Second, its contribution to world trade and commerce was almost negligible. Third, its inhospitable terrain and closed culture deterred potential tourists from visiting the country, which meant that it gained little or no publicity abroad. Fourth, its land-locked position, flanked by a secretive Soviet Union in the north and the mighty Himalayan range to the south, effectively sealed off its territory, creating a proverbial no man's land. Scholars, too, ignored Afghanistan, and it was regarded as 'a historic appendage that had outlived any significance' (Klass 1990: 6). Unlike the rest of the world community, the newly created Union of Soviet Socialist Republics (USSR) found it hard not to engage in Afghanistan. Although it rid itself of the Tsarist regime, it did not relinquish the Tsarist dream of bringing Afghanistan into the Russian orbit of influence, thereby to further its long-term interest in Asia.

The long betrayal

Abolition of the Tsarist regime and the emergence of the Soviet Union in 1917 revived a renewed Russian interest in Afghanistan. Enthused by their success in Russia, the Bolsheviks switched to the pursuit of anti-colonial subversions and uprisings in Asia. Thanks to its strategic location, Afghanistan once again was a natural choice as a transit route to export this ideology to rest of Asia – that is, British India (Hopkirk 1994; Meyer and Brysac 2000). One of the foremost Russian military strategists, Andrei Evgenievich Snesarev (1865–1937), who was favoured by both the Tsarist regime and its successor, the Communists, was of the opinion that the only way the Bolsheviks could extend their world domination and destroy the evils of capitalism was by a forward march to British India (Hauner 1990: 78). This venture, of course, was dependent on finding a passage through Afghanistan.

Though ambitious, the Bolsheviks lacked the resources and a viable operational strategy to implement this policy framework. Therefore they remained indecisive on their forward policy for Asia and the place of Afghanistan in it in the initial years of their consolidation. Just as the Bolsheviks were unsure about their long-term treatment of Afghanistan, so 'the British vacillated between two extreme policies, and ended up adopting neither' (L. Dupree 1997: 405). Of these two, the first aimed at including those areas gained as a result of military expeditions into British India. The second was an extreme one, which included within it the proposal to retreat from Afghanistan completely and leave the country 'strictly to itself'.

In the post-World War I period the British position in India weakened considerably. Forced to worry about the rising level of dissent against its rule in India, the British Raj could not remain actively engaged in Afghan affairs. As mentioned earlier, following the end of the third Anglo-Afghan war in 1919, the British retreated from Afghanistan completely. Taking advantage of this new development, the Soviet state made gradual political incursions into Afghanistan through a series of treaties that would eventually force Afghans to stay within the Soviet sphere of influence. In 1921, King Amanullah signed a Soviet–Afghan treaty of friendship, which facilitated the presence of Soviet military and civilian advisors in Afghanistan. Within five years, Moscow managed to extract from the Afghans a non-aggression pact. The 1926 treaty also established Afghanistan's neutrality. Between the two World Wars, through various treaties, pacts, diplomatic arm-twisting, low-level military incursion and participation in internal power struggles while choosing one side over the other, the Soviets came to monopolize the political process in Afghanistan and its place in the world to their own advantage.

In spite of being a founding member of the United Nations and the Non-Alignment Movement (NAM) Afghanistan found it hard to repel the pervasive shadow of the USSR.

Once again, geography played a decisive role in preventing the country from assuming a completely independent stance. Following disputes over border demarcation, Pakistan sealed its frontiers for transit trade in the 1950s, and thereby forced Afghans to explore other alternatives. Land-locked, shunned by its southern neighbour, Pakistan, and under the heavy influence of its powerful northern neighbour, the USSR, Afghanistan had no choice but to turn to the Soviets just to stay afloat.

Taking advantage of this cartographic misery, the Soviets offered far too many economic concessions for Afghans to refuse. In the year 1955 alone, a series of treaties were signed between the two that facilitated Afghan–Russian barter trade. And in the same year, Soviet Premier Nikita Khrushchev visited Afghanistan and provided it with a US $100 million development loan. Among the other, less publicized issues covered during this visit was secret Soviet military aid, promises to repel the threat from Pakistan, and extension of the 1931 friendship treaty between the two countries for another ten years.

The hardened Afghans, however, tried to offset this overt reliance on the Soviet Union. They realized fully that, without the powerful British presence to balance Soviet pressures to the north, their freedom would be undermined and that they would be easily crushed by Moscow. Drawing from their experience of Great Game diplomacy, they attempted to negotiate another set of deals with the United States to counterbalance their dependence on Soviet Union. With this aim in view, in 1954 the government of Prime Minister Mohammed Daoud approached the Eisenhower administration in Washington for limited military aid to update its vintage and often obsolete military hardware.

The US strategists, for their part, viewed Afghanistan as of negligible importance to long-term American interests, and did not feel compelled to respond to its requests. The possibility of any meaningful military interaction dissipated when Washington insisted that Kabul join one of the US-sponsored military treaty organizations in the region, such as the Baghdad Pact or the South-East Asia Treaty Organization

(SEATO), immediately settle its border dispute with the key US ally in the region, Pakistan, and reorient its external policy in order to qualify for any arms shipments. A traditionally neutral and non-aligned Afghanistan could not reconcile itself to these conditions, and was forced to stay within the Soviet orbit.

The inability of American strategic thinkers to foresee Afghanistan as a place of future geopolitical importance was reflected in Washington's attitude to the country as 'strategically negligible, a relic of out-dated imperialist strategies, and the Afghans as annoyingly intractable, their independent stance verging on the uppity' (Klass 1990: 4). Post-World War II American strategic thinkers were of the opinion that those mountain ranges and the passes that had guarded the Indian subcontinent for 3,000 years had been rendered obsolete by the air age. According to this argument, Afghanistan's geography was of limited strategic importance, as it could be mitigated by superior air power. Since the USA was already treaty-bound with Pakistan on military co-operation, it did not feel the need to nurture Afghanistan.

Such a mind-set was further reinforced by Kabul's professed non-aligned beliefs during the early years of US–Soviet rivalry, which implied that it posed little or no threat to superpower interests. The Afghan government, however, saw a clear need to build up its military strength in order to avoid any external incursion into its territory and any undermining of its national interests. Since it shared a history of border disputes with its southern neighbour, Pakistan, various regimes in Afghanistan felt the need for a powerful ally. And the Soviet Union was a natural choice.

Every power has its own dynamics, its own domineering, expansionist tendencies, its bullying obsessive need to trample the weak (Kapuściński 1985: 176). With Afghanistan consolidating itself against its southern neighbour, there was a revival in the Soviet Union of the Tsarist vision of Russian expansionism in Asia. The Eurasian Heartland Thesis propounded by two twentieth-century geopolitical theorists, Sir Halford Mackinder and Karl Haushofer, of Britain and Germany respectively, immensely influenced Soviet geostrategists in this matter. According to these theorists, whoever controlled the Eurasian heartland, comprising south-eastern Europe, Central Asia and Afghanistan, with access to the Indian Ocean, held the key to world domination.

With the British out of India in 1947, and an increasingly internally unstable Afghanistan, the Soviets saw their chance for world domination. Thus began a series of Soviet overtures towards the country. As stated earlier, through various diplomatic, economic, military and political pacts, the Soviet Union maintained a permanent presence in Afghanistan. 'Capitalising on factional strife inside this land-locked country, Moscow invested its troops there, while simultaneously putting itself in a better position to move toward "warm waters" through the systematic build-up of transportation infrastructure' (Hauner 1990: 113–14). Moscow's policy planning and various programmes aimed at Afghanistan were designed to improve the long-term strategic value of the country if and when Soviet occupation should take place (Poullada 1990: 46). With the United States fighting a losing war in Vietnam in the 1960s and 1970s, Afghanistan stayed within the close embrace of the Soviet Union, whose pre-eminence in the region remained unchallenged.

Although geopolitical considerations continued to dominate Soviet foreign policy postures, these underwent further transformations in the 1960s. Under Nikita Khrushchev the foreign policy projection was a composite of three key factors: strategic interests, ideology and opportunity. This policy framework remained unchanged until Leonid Brezhnev succeeded Khrushchev in 1964.

The Soviet Union

While strategically important, Afghanistan was also a liability for the Soviet Union. The geographical proximity of the two countries and Moscow's close association with Kabul meant that it could not remain oblivious to the internal and external developments in and around Afghanistan. The prevalent thinking in Moscow in the first quarter of the twentieth century was that 'if the Afghans cannot keep their house in order, the Russians will be liable to do it for them' (Byron 1981: 246).

In fact, this attitude was not only confined to a certain phase but characterized Soviet perception throughout. Sensing the rise of an incipient Communist movement in Afghanistan in the 1960s, the Soviet Union encouraged its growth, and by the mid-1970s the leftist factions within the People's Democratic Party of Afghanistan (PDPA) had gained a foothold in the country's political process. For Afghanistan's then Prime Minister Mohammed Daoud, these were worrying developments. In order to isolate the Communists, he adopted a series of policy initiatives to shrug off Moscow's domineering presence in Kabul. With this aim in mind, Daoud appeared in various international forums, and openly declared his intention to return Afghanistan 'from its pro-Soviet orientation to genuine non-alignment'.

Daoud's initiatives came to an early end when he was killed in a bloody Communist *coup* on 27 April 1978. As the Afghans came to realize that they had been taken over by the Communists, they revolted *en masse*. In order to placate this dissent, the Saur Revolution (as this *coup* came to be known) instantly started new land redistribution policies. The new regime immediately began signing hundreds of new agreements with Moscow and Soviet satellite states, bringing the country completely within the orbit of the world Communist movement. In addition, it gave up control over economic and military affairs.

As mentioned earlier, the Soviet contribution to the *coup* in Afghanistan and the subsequent Soviet invasion of the country in order to maintain the Communists in power, although they had an ideological underpinning, were also coloured by strategic interests and designed to benefit from the opportunity this confusion offered. Prior to the Saur Revolution, there was a growth of Islamic militancy in the country. Moscow was genuinely afraid that this might spread to Soviet Central Asia and create instability on its eastern flanks. A Communist takeover was ideal from Moscow's point of view to isolate this impending threat. Soviet fear gained further credence in 1979 when an Islamic revolution took place in Iran, a country on the borders of both the Soviet Union and Afghanistan.

A parallel was drawn to an earlier Communist domino effect theory, which was replaced by an Islamic domino effect, and Moscow tried its utmost to avoid such an occurrence. The Soviets did not want to see a repetition of the Iranian story in Afghanistan, and were not prepared to give in to any form of Islamic radicalism. Military intervention in Afghanistan was considered a vital security measure for Moscow, and it became one of the more urgent arguments for sending troops into the country. Intervention, in other words, held the possibility of keeping Afghanistan a buffer state between fanatic Iran, Islamic Pakistan and Moscow's own restive Central Asian Islamic flank (Garthoff 1994: 1036).

The Soviet invasion of Afghanistan can be seen simultaneously as a culmination point, a watershed, and the beginning of a new phase in Moscow's foreign policy perspective. Invasion of Afghanistan was Moscow's first direct use of force in support of its objectives outside the Soviet bloc since World War II (Krakowski 1990: 165). Moscow, however, could not retreat from Afghanistan after a quick surgical intervention. Using Afghanistan's geopolitical situation, the United States began a series of offensives against its rival and arch-enemy Soviet Union.

Unable to retreat in the face of this proxy war, Moscow was dragged deeper and deeper into the Afghan quagmire. And it would be another ten years before it could finally withdraw from the country after a humiliating defeat. As the chief architect of US proxy intervention in Afghanistan, Zbgniew Brzezinski put it, Moscow's Afghan adventure 'brought about the demoralisation and finally the break-up of the Soviet Empire' (Brzezinski 1997).

● The United States

The US involvement in Afghanistan had a complex character. Self-serving diplomats, generals and politicians with short-term goals and very little understanding of the dynamics of the conflict initiated it. The main architect of US policy toward Afghanistan was Zbgniew Brzezinski, the National Security Advisor to President Jimmy Carter. Brzezinski, a lifelong anti-Communist of Polish origin, was driven by both an ideological and a personal mission. Following the Soviet intervention in Afghanistan, he saw his chance to rival Henry Kissinger as a heavyweight strategic thinker and diplomat. In Brzezinski's scheme of things, it was not enough to create a front to expel the Soviet forces from Afghanistan; the conflict presented an opportunity to export the ideology of nationalism and radicalism to Central Asia which would greatly undermine the Soviet state and the political order. Prior to the Soviet invasion of Afghanistan, Brzezinski was involved in starting a civil war in Afghanistan.[1] Following the invasion, 'Brzezinski was posing for photographs in a Pathan turban on the Khyber Pass and shouting "Allah is on your side", while Afghan fundamentalists were being feted as freedom-fighters in the White House and Downing Street' (Ali 2000: 134).

Once involved in the Afghan imbroglio, top US diplomats, generals and technocrats came to defend their stance on strategic grounds. In their view, Soviet incursion into Afghanistan was a direct threat to US oil interests in the Persian Gulf region (Cooley 2000: 17). Until 1979, the United States enjoyed favourable hegemonic conditions in the oil-rich Persian Gulf region. The fall of the Shah's regime in Iran in 1979 robbed Washington of a key ally, and presented an unsettled future for US interests. The old idea of Russian attempts to reach the warm water ports on the Indian Ocean was revived and played out loud in the corridors of power in the United States. Self-seeking diplomats such as Brzezinski introduced the US administration to the idea of controlling the Central Asian region, as that would be the 'ultimate arbiter' of American interests in the future (Brzezinski 1997).

In response to this strategic threat, the United States utilized the intelligence services of Egypt, Pakistan and Saudi Arabia to create, train and finance an international network of Islamic militants to fight the Russians in Afghanistan. To fulfil this objective, the United States aided radical Islamists with traditional forces and encouraged Arab and Islamic states to support their own anti-Soviet proxies (Khalilzad and Byman 2000: 66). Apart from indirect military intervention, the United States also fought a propaganda war against the Soviet Union in Afghanistan and the whole of what is now known as the Central Asian region. The operations introduced by the Carter administration were pursued earnestly by the Reagan administration that succeeded it. In fact, the Reagan government was far more committed to the cause than its predecessor was. It continued with an intensive propaganda war through radio campaigns (by using its mouthpiece Radio Free Europe and Radio Liberty) to arouse and heighten religious passion among Afghans and Central Asians.

This move, it was believed, would create ethnic and religious consolidation among the inhabitants of the region, and help them rise up against the then Soviet state. Working closely with Saudi Arabia and Pakistan, the Central Intelligence Agency (CIA) co-ordinated the war efforts in the region on several fronts. But one of the glaring contradictions of this mission was the promotion of Islamism throughout the region, on the one hand, and a sustained opposition to a successful Islamic country – namely, Iran – on the other.

In spite of this contradiction, the United States continued to wage its campaign against the Soviet Union through its proxy war in Afghanistan. In other words, Afghanistan provided the perfect battleground for the United States to unleash its power dynamics against Soviet Union. Washington succeeded in attaining its objectives when in 1988 the then Soviet leader Mikhail Gorbachev announced his government's decision to facilitate troops' withdrawal from Afghanistan. As a result, a complete pull-out of Soviet troops had taken place by 1989.

Once its strategic and ideological goals had been achieved, the United States came to regard Afghanistan as a liability. Washington was 'largely disinterested in the post-Soviet order of Afghanistan. Staying true to a script written back in the early years of the Cold War, having expediently used their Pakistani allies and the mujahidin to serve their ends, they simply turned their backs on the country' (Krishna 2002: 77). Predictably, it was abandoned in just the same way it was embraced by the United States when the Soviet tanks rolled into the country. With its strategic value gone, Washington would unplug itself from the developments there for 11 long years. Between 1989 and 2001, Afghanistan went from being one of Washington's top foreign policy priorities to one of the areas least important to it (Khalilzad and Byman 2000: 65).

Pakistan

Pakistan's contribution to the 24-year-old conflict in Afghanistan has been immense. During the Soviet presence in the country, Pakistan assumed front-line status by default, and became the transit route for the supply of arms, ammunitions and military aid to Afghans fighting for their homeland. Pakistani generals and its secret service, the Inter Services Intelligence (ISI), worked in unison with US generals and the CIA towards a common goal. War strategies against the Soviets were planned, unveiled and implemented from here. Throughout this period, it served as the base for various disgruntled Afghan factions. Afghan political parties operated from here. Leaders were chosen or selected with the approval and blessing of Pakistan's generals and politicians.

Islamabad kept the mujahidin divided 'to the level where they would be coordinated enough to ease the need for Pakistani influence and control' (van de Goor and van Leeuwen 2000: 25). Pakistan received millions of Afghans displaced by the civil wars. It provided them with succour, and indoctrinated them with radicalism. When the Soviets retreated, it helped some of these radicals take over the country. The Taliban – as this group came to be known – received recognition from Pakistanis when the whole world shunned them. The current history of Afghanistan is intimately linked to Pakistan. No discussion of Afghanistan is complete without an analysis of the Pakistani contribution to war and peace in the region.

Thanks to its geographical, cultural and religious proximity to Afghanistan, Pakistan featured prominently in almost all UN, regional and bilateral peace initiatives. It was a natural partner in any discussion on Afghanistan's future. However, Pakistan was responsible for doing more harm than good. Unsurprisingly, it remained a potential threat to all peace proposals. Many an opportunity for settlement of conflict was marred due to Islamabad's obdurate role.

In the beginning, Islamabad's involvement in the Afghan conflict was a reflection of its domestic considerations. General Zia ul Haq, the Pakistani general who overthrew the popularly elected democratic government of Zulfikar Ali Bhutto, was desperate to create a popular base for his regime. The conflict in Afghanistan was an excellent opportunity for General Zia to shore up support for his regime. Pakistan's campaign in Afghanistan provided political legitimacy to Zia ul Haq's military rule. He gave a religious dimension to an external political issue in order to placate the extremist religious elements within the country. He succeeded in his endeavours by allowing the Muslims to take up the cause of the displaced, exiled Afghans in Afghanistan (Wriggins 1984; Wirsing 1991). The Pakistani ISI officially operated seven training camps where around 100,000 mujahidin fighters were trained to fight against the Soviet occupational force. Furthermore, ISI's involvement contributed massively to the smuggling of arms across the region and to trafficking of narcotics on a 'colossal scale' (Urban 1988; Kaplan 2001).

Pakistan not only shares a border with Afghanistan; it also has a significant Pashtun population in its northern areas. Since Pashtuns are an ethnic majority in Afghanistan, they have always interacted with their counterparts in Pakistan. Pakistan for its part has influenced Pashtun politics in Afghanistan through its own Pashtun population. This symbiotic relationship, however, has always been used to Pakistan's advantage. In other words, whenever the Pakistani government realized that its own interests were in danger, it masterfully manipulated the situation to its benefit. Fearful of Afghan irredentism on the issue of Pashtunistan, President

General Zia ul Haq introduced the concept of 'Strategic Depth', which not only included acquiring military decision-making authority in Afghanistan, but also helped to undermine a larger Afghan nationalism emerging there which could have threatened Pakistan's own ethnic patchwork by promoting Pashtun separatism.

Host to Pashtun refugees fleeing Afghanistan, Pakistan was instrumental in initiating them into Islamic fanaticism and warmongering in its countless madrasahs, or religious schools, as we shall see in the chapter on the Taliban. By 1992, however, these students had become too numerous for Pakistan to handle. The Chief Minister of the North-West Frontier Province was of the opinion that unless sent across the border, 'the juvenile fanatics in the madrasahs would certainly destabilise what was left of Pakistan' (Ali 2000: 135).

Political opportunism was one of the key features of Islamabad's approach to the conflict in Afghanistan, and it remains so. By 'exercising its leverage over the country's landlocked status, as well as exerting its historical influence, Pakistan played a vital role in shifting Afghanistan's political and military dynamics' in favour of itself (Ahmed 2001: 84). Islamabad nurtured, supported and promoted political parties, ethnic factions, religious groups, warlords and political leaders if they appeared to be subservient to Pakistan's long-term interest. In other words, Pakistan actively pursued a policy of strategic offence against any group or faction which was inimical to Pakistani interests. It created leaders, then pulled the carpet from under their feet if they tried to be independent of Islamabad. Pakistan's involvement in the conflict was underlain by geostrategic considerations.

Pakistan hoped that consolidation of the mujahidin victory over the Soviets would provide it with a secure northern corridor, and potentially ward off any co-ordinated attack from its arch-rival India and the Soviet Union, which were bound by a friendship treaty going back to 1971. In addition, Pakistan's interventionist policies in Afghanistan in the 1990s were steeped in a wide range of objectives, including attempts to gain access to the oil and gas resources of Central Asia via

Afghan territory, to undermine Iran's influence in South-west and Central Asia, and to gain strategic depth against India in its proxy war in Kashmir (Ahmed 2001: 86).

In the end, Afghanistan's tragedy was Pakistan's gain. A cost–benefit analysis of the conflict suggests that Islamabad received close to US $8 billion from the United States and Saudi Arabia during this campaign. This economic largesse not only spruced up its defence establishment *vis-à-vis* the arch-rival India, but the aid also contributed to the country's fiscal growth and had an effect on the larger socio-economic development (Wirsing 1991; Kaplan 2001).

Iran

Afghanistan and Iran share an overlapping history, geographical terrain and language. The cultural influence of Iran over Afghanistan is immense. A significant minority in Afghanistan – namely, Tajiks and Hazaras – speak a variant of Persian known as Dari. Besides this cultural factor, Iran is linked to Afghanistan by a key religious consideration. Almost 15 per cent of the ethnic Hazaras belong to the Shi'a sect, making them the fourth largest Shi'a community in the world after Iran, Iraq and Lebanon. Teheran views the fate of Hazaras in Afghanistan with extreme anxiety. Understandably, its response to the conflict in Afghanistan is driven by this key concern. From time to time, it supported and propped up various Shi'a political factions, in order to give them a voice in the political process in the country.

This support ranged from moral, economic, political and, on occasion, limited military aid. Interestingly, Iran also established alliances and strategic partnerships with all those non-Shi'a factions that revolted against any ethno-religious conformism. For example, during the early years of civil war, it promoted an umbrella organization called Hizb-i-Wahadat Islamii Afghanistan (the Islamic Unity Party of Afghanistan, HWAI). However, when its influence in the political process waned, it shifted its support to another political front, called Jamiat-i-Islami.

The shifting nature of Teheran's diplomatic overtures is partly a reflection of its failure to find a viable solution to the Shi'a minority question. Teheran devoted considerable energy and effort to persuading the mujahidin leadership to allow substantial autonomy, and conceded as much as 25 per cent of the representation in the proposed interim Afghan government that came into being after the Soviet withdrawal. Nevertheless, no such concession was allowed. Having failed to arrive at a settlement, Teheran now made overtures to the Moscow-backed regime of President Najibullah. Fortunately, Najibullah's government gave assurances to Teheran that it would not interfere with the *de facto* autonomy of the Hazarajat, a region over which it had little or no control. But this sat ill at ease with the mujahidin alliance that was trying to build a united coalition against Najibullah's government. Naturally, once Najibullah was deposed, the persecution of Hazaras began in earnest.

Although the issue of Shi'a minorities was among its priorities, Teheran also had greater geopolitical ambitions. Following the breakup of the Soviet Union and the emergence of the Islamic Central Asian Republics, opportunities for Iran to provide a sea route for Central Asian trade loomed large. The success of this plan, from planning to operational stage, was dependent on Afghanistan providing a land corridor for goods to be ferried from Bandar Abbas, the Iranian port on the Indian Ocean. Iran's regional trade ambitions, however, undermined Pakistan's own objectives in the same region. Iran's move to reach out to Central Asia was thwarted by Pakistan.

Arguably, Iran's 'assets', such as its historical, cultural, ethnic and religious links, enabled it to play an important role in the political developments in Afghanistan (Tarock 1999: 818). In diplomacy, and especially in its involvements in the issue of Hazarajat, Iran has amply demonstrated that it has, and will always have, a significant stake in the political process in Afghanistan. Thanks to Teheran's renewed interest in the Shi'ite population in Afghanistan, a new Hazara nationalism is coalescing in the central regions of the country. Iran would like to see the emergence of a federal Afghanistan where the rights of the Shi'a population are respected and secured.

Saudi Arabia

Saudi Arabia's involvement in the conflict in Afghanistan can be divided into two phases. The first phase covered the years of Soviet occupation of the country until the rise to power of the Taliban. Whereas the involvement in the first phase was indirect, in the second phase it was upgraded to a direct interaction. This was made possible following the Saudi recognition of the Taliban regime and the establishment of diplomatic relations with it, while the entire international community shunned it.

Saudi Arabia had long been a bulwark of anti-communism, its rulers playing the role of major contributors of anti-leftist forces around the world – be it in Angola, Mozambique, Portugal or Italy. The fact that Afghanistan had an almost 100 per cent Muslim population was an additional incentive to Riyadh (Hiro 1999: 2). During the mujahidin offensive against the Soviets, Saudi Arabia assumed the role of a major contributor to the war efforts. Saudi Arabia was brought into the alliance against the Soviets because of its willingness to match US funds to the mujahidin (Hartman 2002: 478). The dividend for the Saudis following their partnership in this alliance was immense. Saudi Arabia formed a strategic partnership with the United States and Pakistan to undermine Soviet authority and gain influence in the region. It is estimated that the US–Saudi–Pakistani alliance's financing, training and arming of the mujahidin cost some US $40 billion, and Saudi Arabia contributed almost half of this amount. Saudi involvement in this campaign, however, was not confined to its opposition to communism alone.

The conflict in Afghanistan was a momentary opportunity for Saudi Arabia to export its brand of Sunni Wahabi Islam in the face of Iranian effort to bolster Shi'a ideology in the region (Saikal 1998). Alongside Saudi government assistance, unofficial parallel involvement by private individuals in Afghan affairs played a crucial role in determining the future of Afghanistan. This led to the arrival of a growing stream of freelance activists and groups arriving in Afghanistan and Afghan refugee camps in Pakistan with a mission to convert people to Saudi religio-political doctrine with fervent zeal. These soldiers of religious fortune often fought alongside mujahidin forces, and engaged in extreme violence against those who opposed them. But their influence in the political process was limited. However, their fortunes took a dramatic turn for the better when the Taliban forces marched into Afghanistan from Pakistan and took with them the doctrinaire views espoused by the Saudis.

For both strategic and ideological reasons, Saudi Arabia supported the Taliban's contest for power in Afghanistan. As mentioned earlier, when the Taliban wrested authority from the retreating mujahidin, Saudi Arabia was among only three countries to recognize the new regime. First, the ideological explanations: the Taliban's interpretation of Islam was close to the heart of the Saudi religious outlook. Both subjected women to male domination. Shari'a, the system of Islamic law, was applied in the two societies. Each strictly followed rules regarding social mores and customs as prescribed by the Qur'an and Hadith. Second, from a strategic perspective, Saudis embraced the Taliban in order to isolate Iran.

Ever since the emergence of Islamic republics in the Central Asian region in the 1990s, Teheran had tried hard to build bridges to further Iran's ideological and strategic interests in the region. Furtherance of such influence, however, was directly in opposition to Saudi Arabia, which nurtured similar visions. The domestic lobbies in both countries were equally vigorous in forcing their respective governments to take a firm stand in relation to Afghanistan. Many Saudi financiers had spent considerable effort and energy on the proposed oil and gas pipeline through Afghanistan. That economic imperative was a further incentive to the Saudi government to remain engaged in the unfolding political process in Afghanistan.

Non-state actors

A little known aspect of the conflict in Afghanistan is the corporate battle for control over this strategic land mass in the post-Cold War era. While various states vied with each other and fought proxy wars in Afghanistan for power projection, influence or glory, many corporate houses (mainly American oil companies) joined the fray to facilitate and further their business interests. Two interrelated factors account for their attempt to have a stake in Afghanistan's future.

First, the 1990s were marked by the Gulf War. This incident reduced the area of operation of these companies. Second, the Palestinian–Israeli imbroglio created massive anti-Americanism in the region, and in turn compromised the interest of these corporate houses. These events necessitated the search for alternative sources of oil. Fortunately, the conflicts in the Middle East coincided with the emergence of several newly independent states in the Caucasus and Central Asian region. With proved gas and oil reserves, this region became an effective substitute for Middle Eastern oilfields.

To many US oil corporations, exploitation of this vital resource depended on its export to the energy-hungry West. There were two possible routes to channel the oil and gas reserves from the Caspian Sea and Central Asia: one going through the volatile and unstable Caucasus region, the other through Afghanistan and Pakistan. Of these two routes, the second was argued to be the most viable.

While the US administration followed 'a hands off policy' on Afghanistan in the aftermath of Soviet withdrawal from the country, American oil companies were seriously exploring the possibilities of building oil and gas pipelines through Afghanistan in order to transport Central Asian and Caspian Sea oil. With that objective in mind, an unofficial channel was opened in the US administration that sought to broker a deal with the new Afghan government. Interestingly, two key figures in current Afghan politics – namely, President Hamid Karzai and the US Special Representative for Afghanistan, Zalmay Khalilzad (both then working for the US oil conglomerate UNOCAL) – were at the forefront of brokering a deal with the Taliban regime. Any serious progress in this direction, however, was stalled by the Taliban regime's international isolation and allegations of involvement in the export of terrorism.

Although these non-state actors failed to construct the targeted pipeline through Afghanistan, they were none the less successful in convincing the US administration of the future economic significance of the region. Following the events of 11 September, Afghanistan once again regained its strategic importance. These twin factors – oil and strategic geography – convinced the USA that Afghanistan held the key to its future role as the security and resources manager in the region. In the current geostrategic arrangement, Afghanistan has become directly or indirectly entangled in what is ubiquitously termed by scholars 'pipelinistan politics'. In the new geography of conflict over resources, control of Afghanistan is like controlling the sea route to India during the Age of Discovery. Indeed, the United States would be very reluctant not to take advantage of Afghanistan's location for the furtherance of its own interest.

Afghan strategic culture

The Afghans have indeed had a tragic fate, and a sense of sadness, of the historical wrongs and misfortunes that accompany them, is encoded deep within their consciousness. Yet, during the past 200 years of their modern history, Afghans have always managed eventually to outwit anyone with the impudence to try controlling their fate. The grim and brutal recollections that Afghans hoard in their national memory in turn produced a strategic culture, which has remained unique to this day.

Judging by their tortuous and chequered history, it would be safe to argue that Afghans represent the only society of its kind with a long line of unbroken involvement in guerrilla warfare. Their frequent marshalling of various armed tactics to further their cause indicates the importance that Afghans attach to their independence. Their unresponsiveness to centralized control, their ability to subsist on little, and their continuous warfare among themselves have made them formidable enemies. Unsurprisingly, when confronted with an external enemy on their own ground, the Afghans make use of their strategic inheritance, warrior skills and superior knowledge of the landscape 'to fight fierce and cunningly' (Keegan 1985: 98).

External invasions in fact produced a culture of intense strategic sophistication among various tribes in the country. They not only excelled in the art of guerrilla warfare, but gained formidable mastery in forging political alliances, treaties and what might be called a 'balance of power' throughout the country's ancient and modern political history. And they liberally engaged in political duplicity if it proved to their advantage. The stark manifestation of this strategy is the construction of 'short-term alliances between traditional enemies in the face of a common external threat' (Goodson 2001: 26). From the time of Alexander the Great to the Soviets, all major external powers who tried to compromise Afghans' freedom and independence faced a hitherto fractional enemy coming together almost overnight and forgetting all their ancient feuds in order to face the challenge posed by the alien invader.

According to one critic, 'two Afghan tribes might fight each other to death for control of power or resources, but the mere presence of an external force in their frontier would weld them together in a common cause i.e. the protection of the Afghan state and its *izzat* or honour' (L. Dupree 1997: 330). All great rulers and military men, including the great Persian warrior Darius, the Greek military genius Alexander the Great, the Saka emperor Kanishka, and the formidable Islamic strategist Tamerlane, who at one time or another tried to control Afghanistan or made attempts to include it in their empire came to realize that the inhabitants of this land would never give in to complete subjugation or imposition of an alien rule. Arrian, the chronicler of Alexander the Great's military campaigns in Asia, highlights how, after several unsuccessful attempts to introduce his own method of governance,

Alexander conceded to the inhabitants the retention of their local autonomy.

The clamour for communal, tribal or regional autonomy survives to this day. This is reflected not only from an external perspective, but is equally true of internal power sharing and power projection. Afghan opposition to any form of dominance by one tribal or ethnic group over another is legendary. For instance, 'no Pashtun likes to be ruled by another, particularly someone from another tribe, sub-tribe or section' (Kaplan 1994: 63). All forms of expansionist overture by one tribal group or another have faced fierce opposition.

This suspicion of all forms of power projection is not confined to ethnic and tribal boundaries, but equally affects regional ones. For instance, 'over most of the country outside the cities and towns, where at least nine-tenths of the population live, the inhabitants have traditionally run their own affairs, with little outside interference and the state has never been strong enough to establish effective control throughout the countryside' (Ewans 2001: 8). Although culture plays a key part in this attitude, geography none the less is a significant factor in this way of thinking.

Conclusion

Throughout its troubled and chequered history, Afghanistan reveals the story of 'a piece of real estate trying to become a nation-state, its external patterns uncontrollably linked with those outside its territory' (L. Dupree 1997: 415). So long as geography plays a role in history, Afghanistan will remain what it has been since prehistoric times: the defence perimeter of the Indian subcontinent, crucial to access from the Eurasian land mass to the Indic plains, the Persian Gulf and the Indian Ocean (Klass 1990: 6). On the other hand, geography will continue to hamper Afghan attempts to build a strong political system and a viable economic state (Gopalakrishnan 1982: 50).

While the conflict in Afghanistan was an ideological war, the players involved in it had their own specific interpretations of the conflict, and therefore did not fully appreciate the long-term objectives of each other. In the case of the Soviets and the Americans, it was primarily a tug of war over the extension of their own Communist and capitalist visions, respectively. And Afghanistan happened to be the testing ground to gauge each other's strength. For all those Afghan and Islamic resistance fighters, however, the conflict was a war of liberation: liberation from the nefarious designs of the non-Islamic world. In their involvement in the conflict in Afghanistan, Islamic resistance fighters realized for the first time that their own sacred geography was being violated not only by the Soviets but also by the United States and its allies throughout the Islamic world.

The war against the Soviet occupational army created a sense of nationhood among Afghans, but this wartime wedding had its obvious limitations. The war temporarily buried antagonistic designs of various ethno-religious and tribal factions, but fell far short of producing an effective mainstream identity. Therefore, the withdrawal of the Soviets from Afghanistan did not necessarily mean the end of their objective. On the contrary, it presented them with a new set of tasks that involved identifying other Islamic territories where forms of external non-Islamic domination were in existence.

2 Ethnic Rivalry and _____ the Death of the Afghan State

The only chance small countries from the Third World have of evoking a lively international interest is when they decide to shed blood.

Kapuściński, *The Soccer War*, 1990

Introduction

While the role of external actors in fermenting chaos and eventually contributing to the civil war in Afghanistan cannot be understated, one also needs to bear in mind that this was possible only because of deep-seated divisions existing within the society. Therefore, any explanation of the background to the conflict in Afghanistan needs to start with an assessment of its ethnic composition. In Afghanistan, the issue of ethnicity is complex. One of the first ethnographic maps of the country, published in 1955, categorized 16 ethnic groups (L. Dupree 1997). Another study, conducted in the mid-1980s, identified 55 ethnic entities (Centlivres and Centlivres-Demont 2000: 419–20).

However, the entire population of the country can be divided into eight major ethnic groups. In order of their numerical strength, these are Pashtuns, Tajiks, Hazaras, Uzbeks, Baluchis, Turkmens, Aimaqs and Kirgiz (L. Dupree 1997; Ewans 2001). These major groups often have sub-ethnic or sub-tribal divisions within them. Apart from inter-ethnic rivalry, intra-ethnic divisions on the basis of sub-categories have been a source of perpetual conflict.

Although acrimonious in their interaction, these groups traditionally managed to reach an accommodation through an informal balance of power. Given the fact that Afghanistan remained primarily an authoritarian monarchy for most of its history and the reach of the central government was tenuous in the outlying areas, as a matter of expediency various regimes and ruling houses allowed regional autonomy that often coincided with ethnic or tribal autonomy. While this worked well for some time, Afghanistan's exposure to the outside world put strains on this arrangement. Unsurprisingly, at the time of national crisis or external threat, Afghans found themselves in opposite camps and ended up fighting each other.

In the contemporary period, Afghanistan is the only country in Asia to have experienced an uninterrupted civil war for almost 25 years. Unlike other existing civil war-affected states such as Sri Lanka or the Philippines, the conflict has not been confined to one particular part of the country. The conflict in Afghanistan affected every citizen, and spread over the entire length and breadth of the country. As highlighted already, the civil war in Afghanistan was primarily a product of state failure.

The civil wars that characterize failed states usually stem from, or have roots in, ethnic, religious, linguistic or other inter-communal enmity (Rotberg 2002a: 86). Our under-standing of the conflict in Afghanistan, therefore, requires us to explore questions pertaining to ethnicity and the communal divide there. I do this by examining the history of the conflict in terms of various variables and suggesting how each variable was significant in terms of ethnic and tribal contests for power and authority and how they contributed to the unfolding conflict.

Ethnic multiplicity

Generally a national awareness is built in relation to an external otherness, especially the external stranger (Centlivres and

Centlivres-Demont 2000: 419). Identity formation in Afghanistan, however, did not follow this pattern. Throughout the ages, the inhabitants of the country identified themselves primarily according to their ethnic background, which was constructed in relation to other tribes or ethnic categories within the country. As an identity marker, 'external otherness' was replaced by 'internal division'. Traditionally, 'Afghan' denoted only a particular ethnic group: namely, Pashtuns (Kakar 1974: 13). In fact, the idea of Afghans as a single people was introduced from outside, and aimed to define the people living within a single geographical and political unit. The name 'Afghanistan' itself is a British construction. It was introduced into the official and public domain on the eve of the Anglo-Persion Treaty of 1801. To all intents and purposes, this was an external political interpretation, and did not inspire a sense of common identity or nationhood on the part of the citizenry.

This was partly due to the tradition of autonomous tribal spirit, but was also in reaction to ethnic hegemony expressed by various rulers. King Abdur Rahman Khan (reign 1880–1901), who is credited with consolidating the country, was also responsible for creating ethnic discontent. In his nation-building efforts at the end of the nineteenth century, he mercilessly crushed all forms of ethno-tribal division and replaced them by a unitary system of law and administration that made a clean break with the earlier division of power and autonomy according to ethnicity. Although progressive in spirit, the new arrangement was not completely devoid of traces of ethnicity. In effect, this move strengthened ethnic divisions. The Emir was a Pashtun, and all those who succeeded him were Pashtuns. This Pashtunization of the country in effect established an ethnic hegemony, and thereby put a wedge between the major ethnic group and rest of the minorities.

Thus, while the central government tried to impose its own vision of a united Afghanistan, its reach was confined to the capital Kabul and other big cities. Devoid of communication networks, and in the absence of any major infrastructural facilities in the outlying areas, most ethnic groups went about living under their own tribal laws, sustained themselves through specific economic practices, and upheld their own unique autonomy. Because of Kabul's inability to administer directly in the north and west, Tajiks and Uzbeks, in particular, remaining effectively isolated from any talk of a national mainstream identity, maintained virtual self-rule (Magnus and Naby 1998: 23).

The 1964 and 1977 Constitutions described Afghanistan as a 'unitary and indivisible state', and required that 'the word Afghan shall apply to each and every individual' living within this political unit. This move, however, did not find a wide acceptance. Individuals and communities continued to define themselves against other ethnic or tribal groups. Since 'the creation of a strong unitary state in which Pashtun elites would remain dominant constituted the essential policy goal of every Afghan ruler' (Poullada 1974: 40), the new constitutional arrangement was seen as another attempt by the Pashtuns to assert majoritarian hegemony (Centlivres and Centlivres-Demont 2000: 422). This attitude, as we shall see during the course of our discussion, would have serious implications for conflict in the country. In this chapter, I argue that ethnic division was key to state failure and, consequently, to the continuation of the civil war in Afghanistan.

Pashtuns, who constituted the majority, with some 40 per cent of the population prior to 1979, have been the state-forming ethnos. Yet sub-ethnic divisions within the Pashtuns were instrumental in creating chaos prior to the Soviet invasion and its subsequent occupation of the country for ten long years. The elite among the Pashtuns, belonging to a sub-category called the Durrani tribe, held power for most of the country's modern history. Because of their education, wealth and exposure to modernity, they were a liberated lot; but they were often estranged from the ground realities of local societies.

The 1964 and 1977 constitutional changes were made according to the Durrani world-view, which was far removed from the traditional ideals held by bulk of the Pashtun population. The progressive, egalitarian, secular and often socialist principles present in these two amendments led to the coalescence of the non-Durrani Pashtun opposition, which feared a loss of identity and marginalization of Pashtun interests because of Durrani overtures towards other ethnic minorities.

For by 1978 the Durrani elite and leadership had not only introduced new revolutionary ideas, but had opened the country's bureaucracy and army to Tajiks, Uzbeks and Hazaras.

This inter-ethnic solidarity instigated by the Durranis galvanized the tradition-bound rural Pashtun majority to take up arms against the reform programmes. Throughout the 1970s, numerous Pashtun insurrections aimed to undermine the socialistic leanings of the ruling People's Democratic Party of Afghanistan (PDPA). As the opposition against the PDPA grew, so did its terror campaign against all those who did not subscribe to its key ideals.

In retrospect, one could argue that the PDPA could have emerged victorious and marginalized its opponents. But the party was beset by internal ethnic infighting, and it was not long before the PDPA's modernizing impetus was lost, and it lapsed into factionalism (Ewans 2001: 124). The PDPA was under the control of two hostile factions: the *Khalq* ('Banner') and the *Parcham* ('Masses'). While the *Parcham* was made up of an assortment of non-Pashtuns, the *Khalq* was primarily a hard-line tribal Pashtun faction. And neither could agree on a power-sharing arrangement and policy decisions. Owing to such ethnic divisions within each faction, their approach to, and interpretation of, Afghanistan's political process differed significantly. Devoid of any unitary ideal, each tried to undermine the other. Since ethnic affiliation was paramount in this factional division, it is no surprise that both tried to use it to further their cause.

In this power struggle, the Khalqi leaders used the notion of ethnic supremacy to eliminate their political rivals. Once the non-Khalqi rivals had been eliminated from important governmental positions, the notion of ethnic supremacy dominated the political environment of the PDPA (Nojumi 2002: 65). Although Pashtun in origin, the Khalqi leadership did not hesitate to wipe out their Pashtun counterpart: namely, those belonging to the progressive Durrani sub-group. During its consolidation drive, the Khalq also massacred thousands of educated Tajiks who were sympathetic to the Durranis.

However, used to its own logic of sub-ethnic internal division, the Pashtun Khalqi leadership could not stay united, and there emerged another leadership contest. Two groups, led by Noor Mohammed Taraki and Hafizullah Amin, jockeyed for supremacy within the Khalq after undermining the Parcham. Eventually Noor Mohammed Taraki was killed by his rival Hafizullah Amin's henchmen. With the Parcham neutered and Taraki eliminated, Hafizullah Amin launched a campaign of ethnic cleansing with the explicit aim of Pashtun consolidation. In this campaign, thousands of Pashtuns were recruited to the country's Special Police Academy, and these recruits were used to fight against other ethnic minorities – the Hazaras and Tajiks.

Prelude to an invasion

Afghanistan's immediate neighbour and ideological godfather of the time, the Soviet Union, watched these developments in Kabul with apprehension. It (a) felt that the Amin government was not true to the country's professed socialist principles; (b) feared that the ethnic war launched by the government was inimical to Afghanistan's future stability; (c) considered the continuation of the Amin regime inimical to Afghanistan's and the Soviet Union's interests. In order to facilitate peace in the country and the region, Moscow orchestrated a *coup*, which brought to power Babrak Karmal, the leader of Parcham faction within the PDPA. Interestingly, Karmal happened to be the second non-Pashtun ruler in the country's history. As expected, there was widespread hostility to a non-Pashtun holding power. This opposition made Karmal's government extremely vulnerable. In order to stop the country sliding further into chaos, the Soviet Union invaded Afghanistan on 24 December 1979. Under the tutelage of the Soviet Union, the country declared itself the Democratic Republic of Afghanistan (DRA).

However, given Afghans' obsession with tribalism and ethnic rivalry, the DRA could not stay above these divisions. Once the Parcham was in power (with Soviet backing and under the leadership of President Karmal), a non-Pashtun terror campaign began against prominent Pashtuns who were members of Parcham's earlier arch-rival, the Khalq. Assassination squads began to appear throughout the country, and especially Kabul, and took a toll of leading Khalqi members. Meanwhile the regime also engaged in an orgy of violence, arresting and executing anyone who did not owe his or her full allegiance to the new government (Ewans 2001: 153). This policy programme of the DRA proved to be a disaster for Afghans in general and the Soviets in particular. On the one hand, to avoid the new terror campaign, hundreds of thousands of non-Pashtuns joined the now coalescing mujahidin to fight the government and its backer, the Soviet Union. On the other, in order to protect its protégé (the Karmal regime), the Soviet Union was dragged into an internal conflict.

The consequence

The Soviet invasion and subsequent occupation was a serious deathblow to whatever little inter-ethnic solidarity existed in the society. Moscow's incursions not only strengthened the old tribal and ethnic divisions, but also further fragmented the ethnic hatred. Although initially the Soviet Union did not explicitly support one ethnic group over the other, as opposition to its presence grew, it became partial in its treatment. As it came to incur increasing hostility, it too started using the ethno-tribal dimension to confront its enemies. A key feature of this strategy was recruitment of special units along ethnic and regional lines and, critically, the introduction of 'ethnic militias' to curb opposition to its occupation (Giustozzi 2000).

As a damage-limitation strategy, Karmal's government tried to broaden its support base by introducing the idea of a National Fatherland Front and asking all Afghans to join this new forum. But there were few takers. In the early 1980s, some remaining Khalqi members and sympathizers resurfaced, and publicly questioned the Parcham's role in the Soviet presence in the country.

Although a committed ally of Moscow, Babrak Karmal was a failure in terms of winning the support of various ethnic groups to his regime. Being a non-Pashtun, he was at a disadvantage in trying to reach out to the Pashtuns. His regime was considered illegitimate, not only because of his role in the Soviet presence in the country, but also because of his non-Pashtun background. Keeping this intricate ethno-tribal dynamics in mind, Moscow replaced him with Mr Mohammed Najibullah, a former head of the country's secret service KhAD, appointing him the new PDPA Secretary in May 1986. Najibullah's attempt to ease the raging civil war through a policy of national reconciliation did bear some results, and many hard-line Pashtuns reduced their offensive against the state. But by and large the country remained divided, even at the height of the mujahidin offensive against the Soviet forces.

The Soviets followed a divide-and-rule policy in Afghanistan. They pitted the minority Tajiks and Uzbeks against the majority Pashtuns, and often accorded preferential treatment to various ethnic groups, depending on their commitment to the Soviet presence. Under this policy, the Tajiks and Uzbeks, who constituted the bulk of the trading and bureaucratic classes in the society, were allowed to continue with their way of life, while the Pashtuns were punished for not opening themselves to reform. Unsurprisingly, the complete loss of inter-ethnic harmony was reflected in inter-ethnic war.

A divided opposition

Civil war often gives way to those affected coming together under one umbrella when the offensive is against a foreign aggressor or enemy. To a majority of Afghans, the Soviet presence in the country was a dishonour to their very identity. Yet this sentiment was not reflected when Afghans embarked on confronting their external adversary. Although, in true Afghan spirit, almost the whole country rose up with arms against the 'Little Satan' under the flag of Islam, there existed very little cohesion among Afghans who chose to confront 'the enemy'. The war of liberation, as fought by the mujahidin forces, did not involve a combined opposition, but a fragmented coalition (Rashid 1990; Bux 1994; Giustozzi 2000). United in a common objective, they none the less remained a fractious lot, who were fragmented into tribal, regional and ethnically exclusive groups.

Why the Afghans remained a divided house is a question that is very often asked by students and observers of contemporary Afghan politics. There are several possible explanations. But the most important one, and the one relevant to our current interpretation, is the absence of inter-ethnic cohesion and the prevalence of deep-seated communal antipathy that goes back for centuries. According to Magnus and Naby, the paradoxical condition of heightened inter-ethnic distrust at a time of external aggression has the following dimensions.

First, guerrilla warfare requires considerable trust among the participants for a successful offensive. Since the society had not undergone sufficient homogenization and integration prior to Soviet invasion, those who took part in the offensive could not reach out to their fellow warriors – i.e. mujahidin – with absolute confidence. In the absence of this vital line of communication ethic groups coalesced within their own region, and co-operation became more marked across traditional and Islamist mujahidin groups within the same region than among Islamists who belonged to different ethnic groups (Magnus and Naby 1998: 141).

Second, some mujahidin groups were more successful in attracting external funding and attention than other fellow fighters. This not only created jealousy, but was also an opportunity for many disgruntled and dejected mujahid commanders and their faithful to raise the *status quo ante*. The attention paid to Tajik commander Ahmed Shah Mas'ud by the international community, and the subsequent military aid that he received from the USA and its allies, 'drove a further wedge of distrust among mujahidin' (Giustozzi 2000: 246). The Pashtuns, because of their historic animosity to the Tajiks, felt that they were being undermined, and so nurtured ethnic hatred.

Third, the combined Islamic resistance did not treat all mujahidin fronts as equal. It was divided along sectarian lines. The war of resistance by Shi'a Hazaras was largely dismissed by fellow mujahidin belonging to the non-Shi'a camp. Thanks to their own rivalry with Iran, external donors such as the United States, Saudi Arabia and Pakistan excluded Hazaras from receiving any military and financial aid. In other words, they promoted Pashtun mujahidin over their Hazara counterparts. Caught in this internal sectarian and external ideological divide, the Hazaras remained over-reliant on Iran for their cause. Unsurprisingly, this cemented their 'outsider' status within the combined resistance movement.

Fourth, those living in the northern regions of the country, mainly Tajiks and Uzbeks, maintained their own separate front, because to them a combined opposition meant accepting Pashtun hegemony. In terms of resistance strategy, they were by far the most organized and effective. Their motivation and dedication to the resistance movement was spurred by their vision of claiming a central role in post-Soviet Afghanistan and replacing the rival Pashtuns.

Finally, as one critic put it, in Afghanistan during the Soviet occupation, the sole Islamic duty of the Muslims had been to participate in jihad, or holy war, in which the person pursues his duty as a mujahid, or holy warrior. By subscribing to this Islamic ideal, it was expected that the mujahid would voluntarily give his life and property for the sake of the brotherhood (in this case every ethnic group in the country). While the average Afghan did not have a problem with the general concept of jihad, he was at his most vulnerable when confronted with the issue of leadership. Since every Afghan came from one particular ethnic group with its own specific narrative on social hierarchy, every mujahid subscribed to or had a vision of his own preferred leadership. This was expressed primarily along ethnic lines. Hence none could agree on a common leadership, and none would allow others to claim this title (Nojumi 2002: 91).

Similarly, as Magnus and Naby have argued, 'the best hope for mujahidin unity, based on a specifically non-ethnic and non-regional Islamist perspective, failed on the triple dangers of ethnic rivalry, envy and distrust' (Magnus and Naby 1998: 142). All things considered, it is easy to see why a successful guerrilla movement could not evolve into a cohesive political force. The designs and agendas of external powers, coupled with the ambitions of self-serving mujahidin warlords and leaders, effectively blocked any attempt at national consolidation (Mishra 2001: 20). In short, Soviet invasion not only strengthened the old tribal and ethnic loyalties, but helped ethnic solidarity to be used for inter-ethnic wars. This would have significant bearing on the period following the Soviet withdrawal.

Afghanistan after the Soviet withdrawal

In the end, the Afghan battle tactics dispirited the mighty Soviet Army and forced them to an unceremonious retreat. For Afghans have and had 'no tradition of waging conventional war and no shame about preferring irregular tactics of which they are masters' (Keegan 1985: 95). Yet with Soviet withdrawal came its dark side.

> The day the Soviet troops left Afghanistan, the tune changed. The image of the mujahidin became one of reactionaries, fighting amongst themselves and unable to form a government. The situation was suddenly complex. It was difficult to understand who was fighting whom, and why. The media lost interest, and it seemed as though the rest of the world no longer had an interest in what happened in this remote corner. (Marsden 1999: 114)

Suddenly the Afghan nation that had stood united against the external enemy became a fragile thing: the sense of camaraderie and community spirit and the social contract that had built up during the resistance years disappeared.

The PDPA managed to hold on to a fading institutional framework – namely, the Afghan state – with the support of the Soviet Union. However, as the Soviets withdrew, so the PDPA's capacity to maintain that framework diminished. As the state vanished, so did the citizens' sense of commitment to their state.

As the Soviet troops departed, so a vicious civil war spread throughout Afghanistan. Once the Moscow-backed regime of President Najibullah fell, the country was plunged into chaos, anarchy, breakdown of the state, and fragmentation of authority, and the civil war began in earnest. The *de facto* alliance of the USA, Saudi Arabia, Pakistan and Iran that had backed different mujahidin factions soon disintegrated. The umbrella opposition that had emerged to counter the Soviets was now divided along ethnic and sectarian lines. Pashtuns, Tajiks, Uzbeks and the Shi'a Hazaras now found themselves in different, warring camps. The civil war reduced a once united force to numerous alliances.

The United States for its part saw little rationale for staying put in Afghanistan. So it handed the overall decision-making on Afghanistan to Pakistan. Pakistan for its part did not want any broad-based government to emerge, as that would have undermined its own interest. Therefore, with the tacit approval of its allies, the USA and Saudi Arabia, Pakistan propped up its own puppet regime headed by Gulbuddin Hekmatyar. The course of war in this shifting alliance politics was not hard to comprehend. From the fall of Najibullah's regime in 1992 until the incursion of the Taliban in 1996, every major group had both allied with and fought against every other major group at one time or another (Giustozzi 2000; Kaplan 2001).

During the Soviet occupation of the country, Afghanistan received some US$5.7 billion worth of arms and military equipment. To offset the balance and gain an edge over their rivals, the United States and its allies supplied $5 billion worth of sophisticated weaponry to various mujahidin factions. It is now estimated that the light arms shipments alone that Afghanistan received during the Cold War years rivalled those of the combined total held by Indian and Pakistani military establishments. The presence of this huge cache of military hardware could be argued to have been another factor behind state failure in Afghanistan.

Strange as it may seem, both the Soviet Union and the United States dispensed their armaments among Afghans as a humanitarian organization would distribute food aid during famine. Since the country lacked a credible central government, most of the arms went to groups fighting one another. These arms remained in the hands of individual Afghans and warlords even after the Soviet withdrawal. With no central authority to enforce a ban or implement arms decommissioning, civil war was imminent. With no centralized authority now, the factions used the arsenal procured earlier to contest for power and authority.

The consequence

It is argued that failed states are 'deeply conflicted, dangerous, and bitterly contested by warring factions' (Rotberg 2002a: 85). Unlike Somalia, however, Afghanistan escaped the fate of a truly collapsed state. Instead of the total absence of authority that typifies a collapsed state, there emerged multiple authorities throughout Afghanistan between the years of Soviet withdrawal and the Taliban's consolidation of power. Afghanistan remained a single geographical idea with multiple power centres but not a single unifying authority. The central government existed only on paper. The authority and functioning of various ruling regimes during this period remained short-lived, and did not extend beyond the perimeters of the capital, Kabul.

Thanks to the chaos, the tussle for power between the various warring factions, and the equally fractious state of the international community, a succession of regimes held power following the withdrawal of Soviet forces on 14 February 1989. President Mohammed Najibullah's Soviet-backed regime, which came to office following the downfall of the PDPA in May 1986, managed to hold on to power initially, as confrontation between Iran- and Pakistan-based leaders over power sharing between the majority Sunni and minority Shi'a prevented the mujahidin from wresting control. Najibullah's government finally collapsed on 19 April 1992, however, and a coalition of anti-Soviet, Peshawar-based mujahidin groups headed by President Burhanuddin Rabbani took over. But the mujahidin suffered from weak leadership and were beset by internal bickering.

Additionally, it confronted numerous logistical, political, social and economic problems, including a collapsed communications infrastructure, lack of a centralized bureaucracy, complete disregard for law and order among the citizenry, an empty treasury, and no means of implementing government decrees. As Rabbani and mujahidin commander Gulbuddin Hekmatyar – one of the most formidable enemies of the Islamic government – competed for power, the coalition gradually disintegrated into warring factions based on ethnic, clan, religious and personality lines. (Hekmatyar refused to discuss power sharing with other political parties, and launched several unsuccessful attempts to capture the seat of government by force.)

Consequently, the country was divided up, and came under the control of five regional armed political forces. The north was in the hands of Dostum; the south-east (Paktia) was under the command of Mawlawi Haqhani and groups loyal to Hekmatyar; the leadership of Ismail Khan remained intact in Herat in the west; Haji Abdul Qadir established his authority in the east; and Kabul and areas north of the capital were under the tenuous rule of Ahmed Shah Mas'ud. Under Ahmad Shah Mas'ud's offensive, tens of thousands of Afghans were killed, and Kabul was laid waste when he fought rival warlords like Burhanuddin Rabbani and Gulbuddin Hekmatyar.

External and proxy interventions by Pakistan, Saudi Arabia, the former Soviet Union and the USA made a bad situation worse. While the Soviet Union sided with the government, the other three nations backed the mujahidin rebels. From the start of the Soviet invasion until 1991, each of these countries remained loyal to the same side (Giustozzi 2000: 245). Things changed after 1992, when the external powers noticed growing disunity and infighting among the mujahidin.

Unsurprisingly, they 'switched from one faction to the other with extreme opportunism' (Giustozzi 2000: 245). For instance, Russia at times supported Jamiat-i-Islami[1] and/or its arch-rival, Jumbeshi-i-Milli-i-Islami, led by Abdul Rashid

Dostum. Saudi Arabia at first backed Jamiat-i-Islami and later switched to the Taliban, while Iran (a consistent player throughout the Soviet occupation) initially lent its support to Hizb-i-Wahadat,[2] then to Jamiat-i-Islami, and finally to the Uzbek warlord, Dostum. Pakistan's role was murkier still: it propped up Hizb-i-Islami, and then the Taliban – sometimes both.[3] Little wonder that one of the most significant peace initiatives – within the framework of Six Plus Two, unveiled in 1999 – yielded no result.[4] The duplicitous role of the Pakistani Foreign Office, which facilitated the peace effort via shuttle diplomacy while simultaneously remaining engaged in the civil war through its military and Inter-Services Intelligence (ISI) agency, reinforces the point.

'In the absence of a powerful central government, peripheral forces emerged stronger, resulting in the rise of suppressed ethnic/tribal animosities. Notwithstanding the frequent shifts in power relations within and outside Afghanistan, the regional/ethnic power blocs fighting since the end of PDPA regime failed to agree for a unified institution to govern the country' (Stobdan 1999: 719–20). As a political community, Afghans lost their sense of national pride and communitarian spirit, and felt vulnerable and marginalized. This domestic anarchy produced the perfect condition for competing groups to eke out power and dominance.

That such a fate awaited the country was clearly spelled out by one of the foremost mujahidin commanders, Ahmed Shah Mas'ud of the Northern Alliance. He was convinced that there would be clashes between major ethnic and linguistic groups in the country, in the run-up to a free Afghanistan. According to Mas'ud, Afghanistan was made up of different nationalities. Since various groups had participated in the resistance movement, they were justified in demanding a fair share in the future government. But since each group had a specific notion of its place in the power structure, a prolonged conflict was likely (Gall 1994: 141–2). Thus, as the 1990s began with great hope elsewhere in the world, Afghanistan remained committed to state failure, and spun into anarchy (Bearden 2002: 43–4).

Some scholars hold that the proxy war between the Soviet Union and the United States in Afghanistan created 'pervasive social disorientation among conflicting groups and the population at large, creating conditions for state failure' (Doornbos 2001: 7). Subsequently, non-state forces with their own ethnic, cultural, ideological and political agendas filled the vacuum created by the collapsed state. Afghanistan after the Soviet withdrawal and prior to the Taliban's rise was a failed state. The civil war that raged in the country between 1989 and 1996 reduced Afghanistan to a mere geographical entity. In sum, the breakdown of the rule of law, the destruction of all forms of governing institutions, and the universalization of violence and fear became the dominating features of Afghanistan (Fielden and Goodhand 2001). Under such conditions, sub-state actors took over parts of the territory and started consolidating their authority.

Political economy of state failure

One aspect of Afghanistan's misfortune that has not received adequate attention is the political economy of state failure. As briefly highlighted in the introductory chapter, the absence of a viable economic base was one of the prime factors that led to state failure in Afghanistan. From the mid-1970s (following the deposition of King Muhammad Zahir Shah in 1973), the country came increasingly under Soviet economic influence. As the pressure on the government in Kabul to deliver increased, it became ever more dependent on external economic aid to cater to the needs of its citizenry and the state. In effect, prior to the Soviet invasion in 1979, the country had assumed all the characteristics of an economic satellite of Moscow.

This relationship, which some have termed the 'rentier model' (Rubin 1995a), continued in earnest during the Soviet occupation of Afghanistan. Understandably, given the civil war situation in the country and a perpetual offensive between Soviet troops and the mujahidin, the atmosphere was not conducive for any form of economic activity. With an already decaying, or even non-existent economy, the Marxist government in Kabul had to depend entirely on the Soviet Union for both military and economic sustenance. Thus between 1979 and 1989 to all intents and purposes Afghanistan assumed the characteristics of a 'rentier state'. Long accustomed to a rentier economy, Afghanistan had always relied heavily on outside sources of income, but during the war this reliance increased dramatically (Goodson 2001: 101).

Although the state was heavily dependent on external aid, many Afghans living in inaccessible rural areas sustained themselves by primitive agrarian practices. The war, however, changed all that. It destroyed the traditional social and economic system, damaged the economic self-sufficiency of many local communities, and made them dependent on external aid (Nojumi 2002: 73). Whereas the Marxist government in Kabul and its supporters (in effect, the Afghan state) survived on Soviet economic hand-outs, those opposing the regime were given sustenance by their external benefactors – in this case the United States and its allies. This process continued until the end of the Soviet presence in the country. Once the Soviets decided to pull out, their main Cold War adversary, the United States, did not see any benefit in maintaining the earlier 'alternative rentier model'. This created a severe challenge to the country and its future.

Soviet withdrawal created not only a political but an economic vacuum too. The state, with no foreign reserves, no infrastructural base, no agricultural output, no viable industries and no external economic largesse, could not sustain itself and the civil servants who facilitated its continued existence during the most difficult years in the country's recent history. Although a puppet Marxist regime under the leadership of President Mohammed Najibullah survived nominally, its power and reach over the war-weary citizenry remained tenuous. The Soviet Union, which had disintegrated by this time (and was succeeded by Russia), could not sustain Afghanistan economically, as it was undergoing its own economic austerity measures. Abandoned by its two main erstwhile benefactors, the orphaned state simply plunged into an abyss.

As is natural in such circumstances, an informal economy emerged in its place to cater to individual needs. Since this economy grew out of state failure, it was by its very nature unregulated, illicit, anti-state and extremely predatory. The second phase of war in Afghanistan had its origin in the extreme economic uncertainties faced by the country. True, external powers such as Pakistan, Saudi Arabia and Iran provided limited economic and military aid to various factions in the civil war. In the event of one of these groups consolidating its authority, one or other of those powers could perhaps have helped rescue Afghanistan's economy. But, since there were no clear winners in this conflict, they all withdrew from any long-term economic commitment.

As has been suggested by many critics, this form of economic deprivation often results in the corrosion of the state itself. Faced with dwindling economic conditions, which seriously affect the livelihood of a large majority of the population, fragile states suddenly lose their relevance, and in some instances their very legitimacy (Doornbos 2001: 10; Rotberg 2002b: 131). This condition, as pointed out earlier, is best described as state failure. Owing to the perpetual power struggle, and in the absence of a 'rentier system' between 1989 and the emergence of the Taliban in 1996, Afghans went back to their predatory economic past of the medieval times.

The economic and political disintegration of the state was responsible for individuals, armed gangs and warlords engaging in banditry, looting and plunder of life and property across Afghanistan's physical space. An apparent climate of lawlessness and disorder provided wide opportunity to sub-state actors to intervene and take over (Rotberg 2002a: 90). This 'pervasive socio-economic disorientation among conflicting groups and the population at large' (Roy 1995: 79), as we will see in the next chapter, was ultimately responsible for the emergence and consolidation of a non-state force – namely, the Taliban – in Afghanistan's political process.

Conclusion

Though nationalism, great power rivalry, and a dependent economic system explain much of the origins of the war in Afghanistan, this conflict was laced throughout with the contest between rival tribal groups and their attempts at hegemonic control of the power base. With the unsettled atmosphere of post-Cold War politics thereafter, regional powers such as Iran and Pakistan muddied the waters of any prospect for peace in the country as they became self-proclaimed kingmakers and power-brokers through their military and economic support of one ethnic faction over another.

As Robert Kaplan, one of the very few Western journalists who stayed throughout the conflict in Afghanistan, mused, 'Because the Afghans lacked the material wealth that people in the West are terrified of losing, they were psychologically able to go on fighting and suffering. . . . The very underdevelopment of the Afghan economy made it difficult to destroy. In the end what "worked" on Afghanistan was not reason or negotiation or the advent of perestroika but the Afghans' willingness to die' (Kaplan 1989: 27). Bereft of political institutions that functioned effectively and an economy that functioned at all, the Afghans became inured to the everyday violence that rose all around them (Goodson 2001: 103).

The Soviet pull-out in 1989 assured a sort of victory for everyone except the common Afghan. The ignominious retreat allowed Islam to reclaim its lost ground; Afghanistan recovered its sovereignty; and the West, with a victory under its belt, lost interest in the country for the next decade (Nugent 2002: 15). While a prominent issue during the Cold War years, the Afghan conflict took a different turn in the post-Soviet-era unipolar world. It was no longer considered important by the international community. Those who had remained committed to Afghanistan for the pursuit of their own self-serving designs or otherwise (for almost a decade and half) made a quiet and hasty retreat.

For Russia, the successor state to the Soviet Union, Afghanistan suddenly became a distant territory – physically, emotionally and ideologically. Busy in its attempt to cajole newly emerging ex-Soviet satellites in Eastern and Central Europe, Washington conveniently ignored Afghanistan. As has been suggested by many critics, Washington adopted a 'hands off' policy with regard to the conflict in Afghanistan, while leaving all key decision-making authorities to its strategic ally in the region, Pakistan.

All things considered, it is easy to argue that the Soviet invasion of Afghanistan changed the future of both countries for ever. The Soviet offensive in Afghanistan was ultimately responsible for the breakup of this mighty Communist empire. Moscow's political and military adventurism in this land-locked terrain finally compromised its own power projection in the international arena; and after a brief interlude, it lost its superpower position. In Afghanistan the whole colouring and understanding of Afghan political culture changed; a backward, isolated country was ripped open; its sacred frontiers were effortlessly breached time and time again by outside forces; ancient villages and urban settlements were plundered, scattered and reduced to ghost towns; a once proud people was reduced to destitution; six million Afghans were displaced from their homes and ended up in refugee camps; and another million died of bullet wounds, mortar fires or starvation.

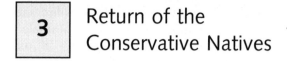

3 | Return of the Conservative Natives

The Taliban, who have emerged from the masses of the people, have started their struggle to deliver their compatriots from pain and hardship by creating a powerful Islamic government in Afghanistan.

Voice of Shari'a, Kabul, 5 November 1996

Introduction

Within five years of Soviet withdrawal, Afghanistan was carved up and divided among various factions, with many mujahidin commanders who fought together in the past fighting against one another. As the warlordism continued, the stories of looting, extortion, terrorization of aid agencies, hijacking of international humanitarian staff, rape and trading of girls and boys between commanders, and killing of innocent civilians became far too frequent. The United States, which was the key actor in Afghan politics for almost a decade, abandoned the country to its fate, once the Soviet troop withdrawal was complete.

Far from helping to ease the civil war in the country, regional powers such as India, Iran and Pakistan actively encouraged factional infighting, and vied with each other for power and dominance in this chaotic atmosphere. By the year 1994, Afghanistan had become really and truly an anarchical place. The idea of Afghanistan as a coherent polity had dissipated completely. Its definition as a country was held together by images of lawlessness, the destitution of the people living within it, and the extreme violence that everyone experienced there.

Afghanistan, at this juncture, truly manifested the classic symptoms of a failed or failing state. For under conditions such as these, the state itself becomes a potential target for internal or external disruption and insurgences (Horf 1996: 19). The prevalent anarchy was extremely conducive for a transnational or sub-state actor, operating from within and outside the troubled country to seek to exploit conditions in order to promote its own agenda (Cooley 2000; Bergen 2001).

It was against this dark, unfortunate background that the Taliban emerged. Although the civil war had dispersed former mujahidin into various factions, camps and regions, there were still a few veterans who had remained neutral and were consumed by a sense of loss. Mullah Mohammed Omar Akhunzadeh was one such disillusioned former mujahid. A veteran of the war against the Soviets, Mullah Omar returned to his village in Kandahar following the Soviet pull-out and concentrated on teaching students in a religious school called a madrasha. The young men who called themselves students or Taliban coalesced around Mullah Omar on account of his apparent resolve to bring peace to this chaotic landscape.

An opportunity presented itself in January 1994, when some of Mullah Omar's followers attacked the headquarters of a regional warlord responsible for gross atrocities against local inhabitants. The students or the Taliban returned from this small campaign successful. This unexpected victory, and the prospect of making changes in the political process, spurred the Taliban's resolve to undertake similar campaigns wherever and whenever an opportunity presented itself. Between February and October 1994 the Taliban, operating from Mullah Omar's village of Singesar in the Arghestan district of Kandahar province, had mounted several offensives against various regional militias and warlords, and had come out victorious. So effective was the Taliban's campaign that governments outside Afghanistan had come to take serious notice of their progress.

Ever since the demise of the Soviet Union and the emergence of Central Asian republics, Pakistan had nurtured greater economic ambitions. Islamabad wanted to reach out to Central Asia to revamp its own economy through intra-state trade. Unfortunately, Afghanistan was a major obstacle, standing there literally between Pakistan and Central Asia. Added to this geographical predicament was the human factor: that is, the civil war and competition among various factions for national authority marred the prospects of long-term Pakistani economic objectives. 'For its part, Islamabad was becoming desperate for a solution, since it regarded the opening of trade routes into Central Asia to be a priority national interest' (Magnus and Naby 1998: 180).

By October 1994 the government in Islamabad had worked out the arithmetic of long-term gains to Pakistan should the Taliban become the new rulers. With this objective in mind, it started orchestrating an offensive that would plunge Afghanistan into another three years of internecine war and eventually consolidate the Taliban's authority over most of the country. Pakistani tradesmen who were impatient to secure trade routes to Central Asia assumed the position of new financiers in a new round of war plans for Afghanistan. By financing the advancing Taliban, they hoped to use the country as transit route for intra-regional trade (Davis 1998: 43).

But an assessment of the role of 'student army' from Pakistan is crucial in understanding the fortunes of the Taliban. While in Pakistan, many poor Afghan refugee families were forced to send their children to the madrashas, because they knew they would be fed and looked after there. Satiation of hunger, however, came at a price: the children were required to spend their days learning the Qur'an. The schools taught a more ideological and austere brand of Islam than the ones practised in the mountains of Afghanistan.

Thus they ended up praying, learning to hate all non-Muslims, and receiving little in the way of a formal education. They left the schools with a rudimentary knowledge of the world, but a fanatical belief in the supremacy of Islam and their responsibility to fight and ensure its spread (Reeve 1999: 225–6). They had little or no understanding of Afghanistan's complex history and heritage. They could not recount their tribal and clan lineages. They possessed no interest in myths and legends from the country's past. These youths were devoid of nostalgia, because they could not relate to the land of Afghanistan. But they were consumed by a passion to reclaim the country.

As the country fell apart in an orgy of lawlessness, young Afghans who had grown up in the refugee camps of Pakistan, with solid, uncompromising and orthodox indoctrination in Islamic values, came in contact with people within Afghanistan who were frustrated by this dark state of affairs. Together these two groups formed an alliance across the frontier. Pakistan – always a catalyst in its neighbour's travails – meanwhile encouraged these students to march across the border and claim a stake in the power vacuum. When they returned to Afghanistan, these students became the core of the Taliban movement. The aim of the angry, alienated, deprived youth that formed the core of the Taliban was to destroy a system they believed had become dysfunctional and was rotten to the core. 'By disarming their foes, the Taliban also brought peace to most of Afghanistan, but at a high price' (Nugent 2002: 14–15).

Was the Taliban a product of eccentricities in a society that was visibly bewildered by a world that had left it behind? What was the rationale behind the Taliban's interpretation of Islam in Afghanistan's political process? Why was a Third World state with a rudimentary infrastructure used as a pawn during the heyday of the Cold War and later by mindless Islamic fanatics, mercenaries and their ideologues? How could a failed state without a coherent political life make an arresting impact on the larger international scene? And have we seen the end of reactionary Islamism with the overthrow of the Taliban?

What is important about the Taliban's political thinking is not so much any novel theoretical contribution to our understanding of, say, orthodox Islam or the place of an Islamic polity in contemporary international society, but its remarkable ability to misinterpret sacred religious texts, make inconsistent and double-standard policy decisions, and fashion violent counter-narratives of the rest of the non-Islamic world from shards of self-selected evidences for the consumption of both an isolated and an insulated mass. From a liberal perspective, the Taliban's claim to authority was suspect on two counts. First, its interpretation of Islam was flawed. Second, the Taliban did not represent the legitimate national will in Afghanistan. However, beyond these ontological debates, the question that looms large and requires a coherent explanation concerns the evolution and working of the Taliban. The Taliban remain an enigma, even after their overthrow. They pose more questions than they answer.

The Taliban and their surrogates

Although there are clear indications that Islamic radicalism in Afghanistan coincided with the Soviet invasion of the country in the late 1970s, its roots can be traced back to a much earlier period. In the first quarter of the twentieth century there were conscious attempts by various ruling houses in Afghanistan to introduce a particular variant of Islam propagated by a radical Indian cleric named Maulana Madoodi. Similarly, in the 1950s, there existed a flourishing Islamic movement in Kabul (Roy 1986). Around this time, many Afghan intellectuals in the Kabul University's faculty of theology established links with the Islamic Brotherhood movement in Egypt, and envisioned a total Islamic revolution (Rubin 1997: 182). Interestingly, the Taliban's preference for this particular variant of Islam was a mere reintroduction of the Deobandi school of thought, which was tried almost a century ago.[1]

In the 1970s King Zahir Shah's liberalization drive alienated many Islamists, who saw his reformations as too leftist in their orientation. In fact, around this time the disgruntled religious elements within the country for the first time penetrated most government organs and established 'Islamic cells' within the army. Mohammed Daoud, who succeeded Zahir Shah by orchestrating a *coup* against the king in 1973, was even more leftist in his political beliefs. Mohammed Daoud's regime was instrumental in sending many of his political opponents into exile. In their exile, these dissidents compared Daoud's government with an infidel regime and 'a godless force seeking to extend its dominion into the countryside and to subvert religious and tribal traditions', and vowed to unseat it through a religious war. Thus emerged the concept of mujahidin or holy warriors. Religion was indeed the sole motivating factor behind the original mujahidin uprising (Kaplan 1988: 13).

More recently, radical Islamization of Afghanistan began as a CIA-initiated move to unite the Muslims of the country against the occupying Communist force. As mentioned earlier, under the Reagan Doctrine,[2] an estimated $3.5 billion was invested in the Afghan war efforts (Cooley 2000; Griffin 2001). Although Washington stopped its arms supply to Afghanistan following the Soviet withdrawal in 1989, it did not sever strategic linkages with Afghan mujahidin who occupied the power vacuum left behind by the retreating Soviet occupational force and later the Taliban.

Between 1994 and 1996, Washington maintained a shaky and ambivalent relationship with the Taliban and provided them with vital political support through its traditional allies in the region – namely, Saudi Arabia and Pakistan. The Taliban provided a handy tool for the West to contain Iran (Stobdan 1999: 721). The militia's rise was also seen in the context of Iran's positive overtures in strategically important Central Asia. Therefore, it became imperative for the United States, Saudi Arabia and Pakistan to commit themselves to any new power configuration in Afghanistan which could deny Iran any strategic advantage in the region which it had acquired in the immediate aftermath of the collapse of Soviet Union. By propping up the Taliban, policy-makers in Washington thought they could create an anti-Iranian and anti-Shi'a movement that would severely limit Iran's influence in the region.[3] The Taliban, which had not yet tasted real power, tempted the United States to believe that:

The movement disliked Iran, that it would curb poppy cultivation and heroin production, that it was opposed to all
outsiders remaining in Afghanistan and including the
Arab-Afghans and it had no desire to seize power or rule the
country. As a matter of fact, some U.S. diplomats who had
opened up contact with the Taliban saw them as messianic
do-gooders – like born-again Christians from the American
Bible Belt. (Rashid 2000: 182)

As early as 2000, the US co-ordinator for counter-terrorism,
Michael Sheehan, was reported to be of the opinion that 'the
Taliban was not hostile to the US'. This was supposedly a
reaction to the Taliban's claim that they wanted good relations with the USA, and the latter considered it a 'sincere
desire'.

Once they assumed power, the Taliban ignored all their
promises and, to the horror of the United States, went about
publicly ridiculing it. According to one critic, 'owing to the
interests of American Oil Company UNOCAL, Washington
was not just muted about, but was dismissive of, the social
and judicial excesses of the Taliban rule' (Ewans 2001: 184).
As things got worse, the United States simply handed over
the responsibility for dealing with the Taliban to its one-time
ally in the region, Pakistan. Without Pakistan's help, the
Taliban would never have seized power. Pakistan's continuing support of the Taliban regime was embedded in its larger
geopolitical designs in South Asia. Like its predecessor civilian government, the military regime in Islamabad recognized
the importance of a strategic ideological partnership with the
Taliban, while keeping in view the issue of Kashmir (Stern
2000).

But somewhere along the line, the Taliban adopted
an Arcadian pre-modern, and in some cases anti-Islamic,
vision which did not reflect the CIA's original enterprise in
Afghanistan. And Pakistan found itself in the middle of international criticism for recognizing and promoting the interest
of a regime in Afghanistan which the CIA considered Fascist,
fundamentalist and terrorist. What went wrong? According
to one observer, 'not for the first time where Afghanistan
was concerned, the vagaries and inconsistencies of American

policy worked against their own best interest in the region'
(Ewans 2001: 184).

While the civil war continued, the Taliban were the only
force capable of keeping the masses together in a fast-
disintegrating state where nationalism had truly and fully dissipated. There was plenty of scope to allow Afghans to escape
the civil war and the Fascist Taliban regime. Perhaps the
events following 11 September would never have happened.
Although the United States was quick to enlist Afghanistan
in the wider conflict of the Cold War, it was far from committed to steering the country back into the folds of normalcy.
It is generally agreed that the onus at this point rested solely
on the United States to help Afghanistan recover from the ills
of a long-drawn-out war. In the end, only the United States
and Pakistan could have averted the systematic vandalization
of Afghanistan. But both these powers pursued a policy in
Afghanistan that aimed primarily at perpetuating their self-
seeking narrow national interests and wilfully ignored the
interests of Afghans (Giustozzi 2000).

Clearly, there was no forgiveness on the part of the new
regime of the United States, which had brought death and
destruction while settling scores with another superpower.
Once they stepped into the chasm of Afghan politics, the
Taliban merely replicated the strategic thinking of their one-
time intellectual gurus from the CIA. During the Soviet
occupation, the United States encouraged the recruitment of
non-Afghan Islamic mercenaries to fight against the Soviets.
The Taliban 'pursued the same method, but the only difference this time around was that it was waged against the
United States and its allies' (Griffin 2001: 93). Indeed, 'the
Taliban and its cohorts were not slow to identify a new
godless infidel enemy in the CIA' (Cooley 2000: 236).

The rhetoric this time had a wider appeal, because it was
laced with some highly evocative messages. Evidently, in its
attempt to raise the spirit of the mujahidin against the Soviet
occupational force, the CIA had liberally used the analogy of
the lost honour of Islam before the godless Communists. The
Taliban effectively summoned the conscience of the Islamic
community as a whole, and demanded that they respond to

the evil designs of the West. Osama bin Laden's rallying cry that 'Muslims are starving to death while the United States and the west are stealing their wealth and honour' infused a spirit of resistance akin to the mujahidin defiance of the Soviets.

An antiquated vision

I do not wish to belabour the central ideology of the Taliban. Yet there was very little that the regime proposed to tell the outside world about itself or its national agenda of action. It had an official website, though, on which the regime claimed to have brought security, peace and prosperity to the country. Its twenty-odd A4-page manifesto was also a deliberate critique of the working of international society. According to many commentators on the Taliban, they were a group of Fascists, a bunch of fanatics, a cabal notorious for their extremism, and so on.

While I do not wish to contradict these characterizations, what I seek is the answer to the question: Who really were the Taliban? For almost two years after their overthrow, it is not yet clear who in Afghanistan belonged to the Taliban and who did not. There is indeed a justifiable confusion. Our slender knowledge of the Taliban comes from what they wanted the outside world to know about them. From the perspective of structural bureaucracy, the Taliban were notoriously difficult to pinpoint.

The Taliban administration was deliberately informal, personal and non-transparent. Apart from the top leadership, which included ministers and mullahs, the identity of the rest of the hierarchy was never known. It was also not clear how the overall administration of the state was conducted with regard to the exercise of power and authority throughout the country. It now emerges that the administration of areas beyond Kabul and the strategic support to the regime were based on a strategy of informal networks. This included loyal regional warlords, tribal and religious heads, local militia and, on occasion, drug traffickers with significant economic clout in their area of operation. These agents did not always pursue the policy recommendations of the central high command. But the Taliban managed to unite these assorted groups of power-brokers through strict dictat of religion, and often with the help of the terror tactics of al-Qa'ida and Takfir wa'l hijra, who operated within the country as the eyes and ears of the regime.

One might be tempted to argue that when the Taliban insisted on the right to absolute impunity in matters relating to internal issues, they lacked a critical vision and had thrown themselves into such an ideological construct without thinking about the repercussions. But not quite. Their repudiation of the idea of a conventional and modern society, as we know it, was a conscious and perceptive action undertaken by the Taliban.

The story that the Taliban proposed to tell was that Afghanistan under their rule assumed the character of an archetypal and self-conscious community based on Qur'anic principles. They further argued that this community was a product of will, where individual members had chosen as a form of self-dedication to abhor the professed rationalism and modernity of the world around them. This nostalgia for an ideal type had little to do with Islam. Contrary to their claims, the Taliban's authority was not rational Islamic communitarianism mediated by a contract. The appeals they made on behalf of Islam were historically grounded in Pashtun tribal behavioural patterns, values and norms which were either pre-Islamic or had little to do with the code of conduct laid down in the Qur'an and the Hadith. The interpretation, distortion and use of Islamic religious texts by the Taliban were therefore arbitrary and made to incorporate their own narrow vision.

I am prepared to risk here a large generalization and suggest that the Taliban did not have any intellectual curiosity. Despite the parade of orthodoxy, there still remained plenty of ambiguity in their interpretation of Islam. As a close observer of Afghan politics writes, the Taliban were 'neither radical Islamists inspired by *Ikhwan* [a Muslim brotherhood founded in Egypt in 1928], nor mystical *Sufis*, nor traditionalists . . . The Taliban represented nobody but themselves and recognised no Islam except their own' (Rashid 2000: 87–8).

The Taliban were far from effective administrators. They inherited a state by pure accident. A series of good fortunes and the assistance of Pakistan helped them consolidate. They had little experience of running a government; nor did they see this as a priority when they took power (Marsden 1999: 45). Instead, they channelled their time, energy and effort into military campaigns, with the single-minded vision of victories against opponents and the establishment of absolute law and order in the face of anarchy that was like an open and running sore.

Although they promised to establish an egalitarian order based on the principles of Islam, the relationship in the socio-religious and political arena was dominated by a vertical arrangement. In its preoccupation with the promotion of virtue and the abolition of vice, the Taliban had either thrown overboard issues such as political rights and minority cultures or relegated questions of national importance to a secondary space. In this hierarchical order, the consequentialist view of means and ends had a special place indeed.

The Taliban imposed religiously satisfying cultural narratives constructed to conform to traditional orthodoxy and the expectations of the clerics, and to satisfy various conservative elements in the society. The Talibanization of Afghanistan could be interpreted as an adventure with itself. The Taliban introduced the idea of a puritanical Islamic state in order to postpone the transition to a normal civilian rule after the Soviet withdrawal. Thanks to the globalization of radical Islam, Afghan mujahidin were taken on board and found such conflict zones as the Balkans, north Caucasus and Kashmir extremely fertile (Cooley 2000; Griffin 2001). Yet the number of war-loving Afghan mujahidin making it to these far-flung places was a trickle. Thus, devoid of a cause and to vent their habitual warmongering, they turned their hatred and anger inward. The result was a spectacular backlash against everything associated with what we call facets of modernity.

The economic, political and finally religious atomization of Afghan society went through various phases. In the first phase, the contest was between the urban elite and the rural poor. During this, their rural counterparts treated a politically conscious enlightened urban mass as religiously emasculated beings. Therefore a vigorous campaign to eliminate everything related to the urban way of life became a fundamental duty for the Taliban forces, who originally belonged to the periphery of society. Having *de*modernized society, in the second phase the Taliban went about restricting the freedom of women. Since the remnants of an earlier non-Islamic civilization represented a semblance of secular identity, in the third phase the regime took upon itself the task of its systematic elimination. Interestingly, like Stalinist Russia or Cambodia under the Khmer Rouge, the Taliban-initiated revolution in Afghanistan was controlled from above, and was not egalitarian in its approach.

It is an established truth that Afghanistan is a 'man's country' (Newby 1981: 75). This idea of male superiority has both a tribal and a religious origin. The coercive measures undertaken by the Taliban, which reduced women to second-class citizens, were to some extent designed to reinforce the tribal patriarchal order. Moreover, this strict regimen in the realm of sexuality could be imposed owing to the religious injunctions of the Qur'an, which explicitly presents a male-dominated society where women play only a secondary role.

For instance, that the Taliban targeted the minority Persian-speaking, non-Pashtun elite women over their counterparts is a little known fact. Indeed, the Taliban were especially cruel to women in the cities, whereas those in rural areas were left to live a normal life, as they conformed to the pre-modern moral order envisioned by the former. In the urban anonymity of Pakistani cities and adjacent refugee camps, strict codes for women were reinvented in harsher form, to preserve the values suddenly under attack (Kaplan 2000: 69). Therefore, it would be wrong to assume that women did not enjoy the right to a civil identity. Unfortunately, on the Taliban's interpretation, the civil identity of women was restricted to the confines of the home. For it argued:

the world should know that the United Nations and all the other foreign welfare organisations in the name of women's rights are but destroying the society, the culture of the Muslims. Under the veil of 'rights' they want to take away their *purdah*, their veil, and thus dishonour the Muslim women. Their intention is to destroy completely all the Islamic values. (Gohari 2002: 109)

In this context, there clearly existed a fundamental difference between our notions of the 'right to an identity in the feminine mode', which is negotiable, and its exact opposite in an Islamic polity where it is non-negotiable.

True, the Taliban's interpretation of the role of women in society was defined in religio-cultural terms. Yet, the camaraderie that existed among the rank and file of the Taliban forces, and their obsession with misogyny, had both a psychological and a historical explanation. The male brotherhood was a condition of tight military discipline. Gender puritanism was one way of keeping the fighters strictly focused on their goal of military success. Since the Taliban were orphans of war, who in their long hard battle against Soviet occupational forces had little or no encounter with women and their company, they retreated into a male brotherhood compared to the Crusaders of the Middle Ages. In addition, the Taliban imposed strict punitive measures on recruits guilty of deviating from their original path.

The Taliban's marriage of religious orthodoxy and twentieth-century totalitarianism was uniquely vicious. According to Sher Abbas Stanakzai, the Chief Mullah of the Department for the Preservation of Virtue and the Elimination of Vice, 'many of the Taliban's harsh socio-religious restrictions were enforced in order to bring the Afghan people under its control. The regime needed to impose these restrictions to make people learn to obey the government' (Miller 2002: 83–4). It argued, 'purdah (veil) is not the injunction of the Taliban but the order of the almighty Allah (Gohari 2002: 109). Therefore, 'although the Taliban's pronouncements regarding women may be couched in Islamic rhetoric, the web of hidden attitudes governing official actions and colouring public statements was woven of many complexities' (N. H. Dupree 1998: 151).

The same goes for the Taliban's treatment of cities, other repositories of modernity and comfortable living. Both in theory and in practice, the upper echelons of the Taliban despised the forces of modernity. A majority of Taliban warriors grew up in the refugee camps in Pakistan in utter poverty, squalor and minimalist grey desperation. In their destitution, they were encouraged to become wedded to the idea of revenge in countless madrashas sponsored by Saudi Arabia, Pakistan and the CIA.

This indoctrination into radical Islamism, and the psychological and emotional scars incurred during their time as refugees, produced a deep-seated contempt for a normal life-style associated with urban peaceful existence amidst modernity and prosperity. In the opinion of a contemporary observer, the Taliban 'embodied a lethal combination; a primitive tribal creed, a fierce religious ideology and the sheer incompetence, naiveté, and cruelty that are begot by isolation' (Kaplan 2000: 71). Yet there could be other explanations of the Taliban's war against modernity.

Pre-Taliban urban Afghanistan was a world completely interiorized by a non-Pashtun ethnic minority. Its Persian-speaking urban elites lived a life alien to the rest of the populace. Throughout Afghanistan's modern history, this urban elite disdained and was contemptuous of the rural masses, and kept them at a safe distance. During the Communist era, this elite went so far as to direct its energy to persecuting the rural majority. In the tradition of messy tribal politics, the Taliban, which consisted of Pashtun peasants, mountain folk and nomads, pursued a policy of musical chairs when it reclaimed the cities. The elites were slaughtered, their mansions vandalized, their women sentenced to life beneath a *burqua* and condemned to the confines of home. Absolute aggressive puritanism, in other words, became the order of the day.

In the hectic early days of their emergence, the Taliban liberally used various tribal practices to consolidate their position. Consolidation of their authority, however, overburdened it with expectations. Being unable to deliver, they had to engineer chaos in society. In the first phase, they directed the masses looking for action against a fading minority that was well versed in modernity. Having succeeded in fulfilling that objective, they turned the masses against themselves. In classic revolutionary mode, Afghanistan became a country in which everyone was taught to be suspicious and to hate. This attitude can at best be explained as a circular position common to many revolutionary regimes. In this construct, the regime experiences a profound inability to define its objective in clear terms, and pits the society against itself.

Since this inverse revolution is country-, culture- and time-specific, the concerned regime may devise a particular notion of the enemy for public consumption. In circumstances such as these, it may either turn every individual against every other, as was the case during the Khmer Rouge rule in Cambodia, or target a particular class, as was evident during the Maoist Cultural Revolution in China. A new variant of this intramural struggle that has emerged in recent years is a community's direction of extreme hates at a particular sex and such inanimate objects as culture, as exemplified in the case of the Talibanization of Afghanistan (Halliday 1995: 410).[4]

The regime reiterated that it could do little to rebuild the country so long as the fighting continued and subversive elements continued to plague the socio-political process. The aim of the Taliban in this context was the 'purification of Afghanistan'. In the initial years of its consolidation, the Taliban leadership made it absolutely clear that its main goal was to rid the country of 'corrupt elements existing within'. So crucial was this initiative that the paramount leader Mullah Omar set aside the external face of Afghanistan completely, suggesting that we will think about it 'when we have sorted out our own internal affairs' (Marsden 1999: 61).

However, once that inward revolution was complete, the Taliban required new targets to keep the masses occupied. With the coming of Osama bin Laden and his mercenaries, the regime found an enemy in the world outside. The Taliban easily embraced the martyrdom logic of al-Qa'ida ideologues, owing to the parallel understanding of reactionary Islam by both parties. Curiously enough, both found themselves on the margins of the larger society. Whereas the Taliban were isolated and shunned owing to their conservative statecraft, al-Qa'ida members were social rejects and literally homeless.

Hanging on this abstract Archimedean point, both vowed 'to act out, to realise, to practise the faith as an expression of their uncompromised belief'. Unsurprisingly, both quoted the Qur'an randomly to justify their course of action. In this ideological and strategic alliance, they considered the freedom and duty of a true Muslim to be to act according to *hakimiya*, or the sovereignty of God. Since the larger world had rejected them, it was easy for both to see it as *jahiliyat*, a godless world. And, by the same logic, they took upon themselves the task of ending *jahil* (modern) activity, even though this involved terrorist strikes and the killing of innocent civilians.

Islamic consolidation

To assess the role of the Taliban in Afghan politics, it is useful to distinguish between political movements that are genuinely inspired by religion and those that use religion as a convenient legitimation for political agendas based on non-religious interests.[5] Islamic orthodoxy, according to Abd-al Ibn Khaldun, the last great Muslim thinker, is most likely to take root in the periphery of a state. It exists on the margins of a society where there is little or no economic development, where people are destitute, and there is constant fighting among various groups. This is a society that is caught up in itself, where there is widespread resistance from orthodoxy to the logic of modernity.

In such an anarchic condition, orthodox Islam provides a modicum of normality by bringing together an ill assortment of individuals, groups, tribes and communities. Radical Islam, in other words, is a direct outcome of the state's diminished authority. But after having consolidated itself, radical Islam does not necessarily aim to reinstate the authority of the state. Instead, it reiterates that what really matters is not the state, but that complex mechanism of religion-inspired institutions and associations that can act as an alternative to the state.

To this end, the Taliban's goal was the introduction of a theological arrangement that replaced secular order with divine order, the nation-state with an Islamic system, popular representative democracy with an Islamic notion of consultative council, constitutional law and human legislation with Shari'a law and the institutional mechanism of government of the people and by the people with a self-appointed God's representative government on earth.[6] In sum, the Taliban not only committed themselves to these principles, but also strictly imposed these doctrinal recommendations on the overall political and social life of Afghans throughout their rule.

Even critics of the Taliban admit that the movement put a lid on the perpetual banditry, tribal vendettas and sectarian violence, and disarmed much of the mountainous countryside. But the institutional mechanism that was required to keep a society running was largely absent in Afghanistan. Apart from imparting quick and violent justice, creating a sense of fear, and forcing the populace to adhere to extreme religious orthodoxy, the institutions spawned by the Taliban did little. They had virtually no policy programme with regard to such key areas of social regeneration as infrastructure reconstruction, health care, education, sanitation, transport and so on (Goodson 2001: 121). Almost three-quarters of the population lacked a proper job. People survived on subsistence, international aid and through smuggling of arms and drugs. Why the Taliban adopted such policy postures requires a psychoanalytical study.

Like 'radical Islam of the Hamas variety', the Taliban viewed international relations as an 'anarchical state of nature' dominated by independent, self-reliant civilizations struggling for power and prestige in a milieu inimical to co-operation. This condition of perpetual hostility required the followers of the Taliban to arm themselves against all non-Muslim forces competing to undermine them. This consolidation effort led the Taliban to adopt two extreme measures to retain this space: first, holy war, or jihad, against outsiders; second, adoption of a strict self-imposed moral code, which can be viewed as a 'discipline and punish' procedure.

Ironically, although scriptural Islam demands brotherhood among Muslims, there existed very little tolerance towards various sects within the Taliban's version of Islam. The Taliban and their cohorts were essentially truth-tellers from the dark side. The accusation of anarchy, therefore, was not attributed to non-Muslims only, but was liberally used against competing tribes and groups. It is now evident that, although Islam was given pre-eminence in the Afghan po-litical process under the Taliban, the latter frequently perse-cuted other Islamic sects.

This view is shared by many critics. According to Ahmed Rashid, even though the Taliban began as Islamic reformers espousing the notion of jihad, or holy war, against non-Muslim infidels, they soon broadened their scope to target minority Islamic ethnic groups and sects. According to Amnesty International, the Taliban methodically executed between 2,000 to 5,000 civilians, predominantly Shi'ite Muslims in 1998 (Tarock 1999: 812). Although fellow Muslims, the Shi'ite Hazaras who survived this onslaught were told by the Taliban 'either to adopt Sunni Muslim rituals, pay a special tax as non-Muslims, face death or emi-grate to their spiritual homeland Iran' (Cooper 1998: 5).

Unsurprisingly, all non-Pashtun Muslims in Afghanistan felt that the Taliban were 'using *jihad* as a cover to extermi-nate them' (Marsden 1999; Rashid 2000). Though religious by self-definition and inspiration, they were nevertheless overwhelmingly organized according to ethnicity and tribal structure, in this case Pashtun tribal structure. This repre-sented a revival of Pashtun consciousness in a country increasingly absorbed by ethnic self-definition (Garfinkle 1999: 406). Indeed, among the non-Pashtun, the Talibaniza-tion of Afghanistan was interpreted as nothing less than the spread of Pashtun fundamentalism.

Rashid also argues that the Taliban's obtrusive position in the religious realm and their political adventurism were products of 'naiveté, frustration, and ideology' (Rashid 2000: 137). Since the regime was not recognized either by international society or by all fellow Muslim nations, it adopted the mentality of a problem child. The net outcome of this was its persistent defiance of all the conventional international norms. This rejection in turn pushed it to harbour dissidents, meddle in the domestic conflicts of various countries, persecute its own citizenry, and export global terrorism. In fact, many close observers had forewarned that 'continued neglect of the Taliban regime would likely result in Afghanistan remaining a base of operation for some of the most violent terrorists in the world' (Khalilzad and Byman 2000: 71).

Their conquests and their ability to influence radical elements in the larger Islamic world had an intoxicating effect on the Taliban. They overestimated their strength, and by harbouring many 'zealot drifters' they hoped to establish a Federation of Islamic Republics with Afghanistan as its hub and the Afghan cleric as its spiritual and political head. That it revelled in its notoriety was evident when it refused to comply with Washington's repeated extradition demand for the Saudi-born radical Osama bin Laden before 11 September and in the period following. Arguably, the Taliban's continued engagement in such actions was directed at taking revenge on the international community. More precisely, the introduction of religious orthodoxy in the country and the export of terrorism beyond its borders were aimed at injecting the type of self-pride that comes with defiance.

The Taliban and globalization

While the comparative study of the Taliban is not exempt from acerbic criticism by modernists averse to the idea of the radical conservatism that this movement espoused, it is striking that the Taliban was itself a product of modernism and other forces of globalization. The role of external powers is crucial in this matter. Both the United States and the erstwhile Soviet Union, through their rivalry, inadvertently brought a traditional tribal society under the intense scrutiny of global politics. Furthermore, by infusing the mujahidin with radical Islam as a bulwark against the evil Soviet empire, Washington inadvertently became party to the promotion and export of Islamic extremism and a world-wide terrorist network.

Since the events of 11 September 2001, those sympathetic to the Taliban have argued as follows: since their overall attitude to civilization came into conflict with our indulgent lifestyle and morality in the West, we were vindictive in our attitude towards this regime. It is not too far-fetched to suggest that, although various Islamic regimes denounced the Taliban and supported the international campaign against al-Qa'ida, their citizenry were supportive of the Taliban.

Islam, by and large, has difficulty with radical new ideas. The globalization of Western-dominated culture, whose contours are yet to be identified, is naturally viewed with suspicion and scepticism by the followers of Islam. According to Samuel P. Huntington, the failure to respond to globalization by a large constituency of Muslims is itself responsible for fermenting this new conflict between Islam and the West. In his view, when some Muslim societies failed to respond to globalization, it inadvertently led to social problems and political and ideological unrest. In this confusion and the resulting crisis of identity, the anxiety and anger were hastily attributed to the globalization process, which tried to reinforce Western identity at all levels (Huntington 2001: 9–12).

Similarly, globalization in the economic and political spheres and in the realm of communications inevitably challenges many old orthodoxies. Ironically, it was not only the Taliban who adopted a differential treatment of women and made religion the central hub of society. Other contemporary Muslim societies 'find it impossible to contemplate the separation of religion and state, or admit to a changed place in society for women or permit the free exchange of ideas' (Kennedy 2002: 7). Some ten years ago, in one of his provocative essays, Ernest Gellner remarked that 'no secularisation has taken place in the world of Islam: that the hold of Islam over its believers is as strong, and in some ways stronger, now than it was 100 years ago' (Gellner 1992: 2).

Moreover, even when Muslims cease to believe in Islam, they may retain Islamic habits and attitudes (Lewis 1993: 7); this certainly is not helpful to the dissemination of supposed universally held norms and values. Viewed from the perspective of globalization, it is evident that Islamic movements have now largely 'displaced secular nationalist and leftist movements as the primary mobilising force of resistance against real and imagined western political, economic and cultural domination' (Lubeck 2000: 149). Nevertheless, there is another, larger explanation of radical Islam's hostility towards the process of globalization.

Since globalization has been constructed primarily against the backdrop of Western experiences, and overwhelmingly seeks to impose the West's conception of modernity, it has quite naturally been contested in some societies (Beck 2000; Hardt and Negri 2000). Here it might be prudent to ask what Islamic understandings, experiences and interpretations of globalization are. Furthermore, one needs to address another crucial question: namely, what aspects of globalization are offensive to political Islam in the above-mentioned societies?

In the context of globalization, radical Islam, though it draws on 'pre-modern readings of the *Qur'an* and other religious texts, is wholly modern in its revolutionary existentialism' (Ruthven 2001: 4). Radical Islam has its own interpretation of globalization, as is explained in the context of martyrdom. As one critic suggested following the events of 11 September, 'radical Islam is built on the failure of liberalism, communism and nationalism' (Halliday 2001: 18). And each of these schemas captured aspects of reality in Afghanistan. First, it was King Zahir Shah's surreptitious liberalism that helped a home-grown Communist movement, only to be replaced by nationalists.

Second, since nationalism was too alien an ideal in a society divided by ethnic, clan and tribal loyalty, radical Islam was a natural choice to act as a fixture. Third, the non-recognition of the Afghan state by the international community forced the Taliban to give sanctuary to all the radical elements rejected by their own Muslim societies. As in many other underdeveloped states, pressed from outside, corrupt and incompetent within, successive regimes proved unable to defend the national interests of Afghanistan or deliver social and economic justice. Caught in the middle of this malaise, Afghanistan simply choked.

In spite of our general dismissal, the Taliban were commentators on, and critics of, a disappearing state that was Afghanistan. They were a force against the tide, the tide of general decay that had set in in Afghanistan after generations of backwardness and decades of civil war. Of course, their attempt to create an Islamic arcadia was grossly outrageous, but it would be wrong to assume that they did not have a vision. Their world-view was part of what a leading critic has described as 'a fierce, redemptive Islam' (Ajami 2001: 5). Those belonging to the Taliban and the now infamous al-Qa'ida brotherhood clearly felt that Islamic civilization was adrift, and took upon themselves the task of rescuing it from that listless, uncertain voyage. In a somewhat skewed Islamic existential schema, the Taliban argued that there is no essential humanity, and that a Muslim is defined by his or her own actions.

There may be one specific explanation behind Islam's prominence in Afghan socio-political life. Most Afghans clung tenaciously to their Islamic heritage as a defence against all the uncertainties caused by the war. 'Islam quite naturally became the principal medium of political expression against the Soviets and drove people even further toward God, as it was the only thing left to them' (Kaplan 1988: 19). By highlighting the interface of religion and politics, the mujahidin magnified Islam's importance in order to gain victory against 'a godless external enemy'.

In reality, Islam was the only principal institution to have survived the Soviet occupation and the civil war that followed. The Taliban's use of Islam to further their political goals was not unique. They used Islam merely as a vehicle of communication to reach out to the majority of Afghans. Indeed, the leadership of the Taliban had a very good understanding of the Afghan psyche in this regard. Afghanistan, during a decade-long Soviet occupation and a further five years of civil war, witnessed the breakdown of most social institutions. In those desperate years, religion was the only source of hope. Therefore, for the Taliban a strict and rigid interpretation of the rituals and traditions of Islam appeared to be the only mechanism to ward off the absolute anarchy that haunted the society.

Considering the catalogue of errors, misjudgements and reckless policies, the Taliban was a vile regime indeed. But, as one commentator has argued, 'it may be easy and obvious for victims to blame the regime for its egregious crimes, but the social and historical context that contours the Taliban in its own way facilitated the commission of such systemic violence and human rights abuses' (Drumbl 2002: 1129).

Conclusion

In reflecting on the future of Islamic radicalism in Afghanistan, one can draw parallels between Soviet suppression of the mujahidin during their occupation of Afghanistan and the current international campaign to dismantle the Taliban and their cohort, al-Qa'ida. A survey of the Taliban has acquainted us with the diffuse nature of its command structure. As the Allied Campaign demonstrated, its operatives were only loosely connected organizationally. For mujahidin, any setback against the Soviets was merely a battle lost; but the war was far from over. This organizational structure helped them continue their offensive against the Soviets.

The Taliban clearly were not hugely disappointed following their removal from power. And the evidence in this regard is not hard to find. Asked about the future of the Taliban towards the end of the international military campaign, one supporter is reported to have said: 'in the event of death or elimination of Osama bin Laden, Mullah Omar and the rest of the leaders there will be others to take their place, because everyone who works for Osama is like Osama.'[7] This exit strategy of the Taliban demands a fresh probe. As the inner mechanism of the Taliban and its military wing al-Qa'ida begins to unravel, it is apparent that neither believed in national states.

The Taliban's vision of an Islamic entity was not confined to Afghanistan, but stretched all the way from Morocco to Malaysia. On a tactical retreat, its troops either sheepishly surrendered or defected to the advancing non-Taliban force, perhaps to regroup and fight in future. On this trajectory, 'the Taliban's rout in Afghanistan would appear as not defeat but just a withdrawal, which left its armed wing al-Qa'ida to fight another day' (Judah 2002: 12). On that score at least, it would be unwise to conclude that we have seen the last of the Taliban.

Thanks to the old loyalties between Afghan warlords and their counterparts in north-eastern Pakistan, most hard-line leaders of the Taliban and prominent al-Qa'ida members easily escaped to Pakistan. Prior to the international campaign in Afghanistan, al-Qa'ida cells were operational in Pakistan. The bombing campaign and dislodging of the Taliban, which infuriated a good many Pakistanis, have helped create a situation in which Pakistani society is actively supportive of al-Qa'ida extending its network within the country. It would be safe to argue that, with its operations throughout the Islamic world, United States and Europe, al-Qa'ida retains a widespread network and headquarters capable of giving orders and moving its recruits around. Therefore, despite its setbacks in Afghanistan, it is very much active and capable of initiating a long stretch of terrorist combat.

4 Brothers in Arms: Radical Islam and its Followers

Radical Muslims exhibit hostility toward all those who are different, a free-floating rage, and a tradition of violence that favours the appearance of terrorism.

Walter Laqueur, *The New Terrorism*, 2001

Introduction

The state failure during the Taliban's rule was manifested by the rejection of the authority of the state by a segment of the population. In spite of its control over almost 90 per cent of the country's territory, the regime lacked overall legitimacy. Its ability to govern relied on force and terror. While it enjoyed only partial internal legitimacy, the international community overwhelmingly denounced it. Since the Taliban remained an illegitimate government to most of the international community, it was not constrained by international laws or norms of interaction. Isolated, it provided the political space for various radical non-state groups to experiment with their ideas.

The regime in a failed state often favours autonomous armed groups just to stay in power and revel in its notoriety. Terrorists are strongest where states are weakest. A 'viable state' with all the trappings of universal values could not afford to provide safe haven to social, political and ideological rejects from around the world, let alone give them a free hand to experiment with their 'evil designs'. What the likes of Osama bin Laden and his network of terror needed was not a state but the absence of a state (Jacquard 2002; Rotberg 2002b). What they required was a territorial base from which they could carry out certain organizational and operational functions such as indoctrination of recruits, training in guerrilla and terrorist warfare, and work on logistical planning (Kahler 2002: 29–30). In sum, Afghanistan was 'strong enough to provide Osama bin Laden with a convenient safe harbour, but weak enough to depend on him for its financial and military survival' (Radu 2002: 281).

Osama bin Laden and al-Qa'ida found protection in places such as Afghanistan where government and society had collapsed (Straw 2001: 4). In Afghanistan, al-Qa'ida chanced upon the ideal corporate headquarters – weak enough to oppose the designs of non-state actors – but strong enough to provide a security blanket with a veneer of sovereignty that warded off external intervention (Takeyh and Gvosdev 2002: 98). Three factors were key in al-Qa'ida's use of Afghanistan as its base. First, although the regime and the Afghan state were unacceptable to the larger world, the latter did not denounce its spatial sovereignty or the sanctity of Afghanistan's territoriality. Second, to bin Laden and his associates the Taliban were an important ally as they had a shared vision. Third, the West's abandonment of Afghanistan (following the Soviet withdrawal) allowed it to be 'hijacked' by terrorists, warlords and religious fanatics such as Osama bin Laden (Straw 2001: 5).

Why Afghanistan?

The question why Muslims from all over the world went to Afghanistan, first to fight against the Soviets but later to join the radical movement under the Taliban is not hard to discern. The non-Islamic West could see the conflict in Afghanistan as a second uprising against the oppression of Muslims in the twentieth century (Lewis 2003), the first one being the deposition of the Ottoman Turkish Sultan in 1922 under the Treaty of Sevres of 1920. The deposition of the Sultan and the dissolution of the institution of the Caliphate was undertaken by the West in order to end the political power and prestige of a succession of leaders who tradition- ally invoked authority and legitimacy as defenders of Islam from the time of the Prophet Muhammad.[1]

In fact, 'in the premodern and modern periods, the Afghan resistance represents the first case in which Islamic ideology has served as a rallying point for success against an outside, non-Muslim force' (Magnus and Naby 1998: 138). Soviet withdrawal convinced the mujahidin, the Taliban and al-Qa'ida that a force of devoted Muslim believers could defeat any army, even one belonging to a superpower. This new con- fidence in their own ability and strength motivated many mujahidin and al-Qa'ida supporters to take the holy war from the mountains of Afghanistan to their own specific regions and countries. The larger goal, they maintained, was to establish a pan-Islamic Caliphate throughout the world. Since the Islamic world was divided by self-serving regimes, they suggested that the supporters of al-Qa'ida, by working together with other allied Islamic radical groups, must aim to overthrow governments it deemed 'non-Islamic' and take measures to expel Westerners and non-Muslims from the land of Islam.

With the end of the Cold War and the growing influence of the USA throughout the Islamic world, it became impos- sible for renegade Islamic groups to find shelter and sanctu- ary in a Muslim country. Although Iran, owing to its avowed hostility to the West, would have been a natural choice for many, the nature of its religious orientation – that is, Shi'aism, as against the Arab world's professed Sunni beliefs – proved to be a barrier. Other Muslim countries such as Iraq or Syria, which defied the authority of the USA, might have been an alternative. Yet, thanks to the extreme hostility to any kind of orthodox Islam in these two countries, no group even dared entertain the thought of making these their abode. Libya, which for a whole generation nursed a grudge against the West, was unwilling for any such partnership, as it was itself trying to step out of its old image as a terrorist state.

It was at this juncture that veterans of the Afghan war suddenly became 'rebels without a cause', and turned to the defensive and unleashed a campaign against themselves and the world around them. Veterans of Afghan war, the mujahidin were instrumental in destabilizing the political process all over the Islamic world, from Algeria, Egypt and Sudan in Africa to Pakistan, the Philippines, Indonesia and Saudi Arabia in Asia, and such places as Chechnya and Daghestan in the north Caucasus. The umbrella organization under which they would work came to be known as al-Qa'ida.

The emergence and rise of al-Qa'ida

The structural and organizational roots of al-Qa'ida are very much products of Western involvement. The three ideologically inspired radical resistance movements operating from Afghanistan – namely, the mujahidin, the Taliban and al-Qa'ida – owe their very origins to Western organizational and economic support. The United States, its friends and client states provided material, military and economic support to these movements until the 'Embassy bombings' in the year 2000. They also turned a blind eye to the activities of al-Qa'ida and its radical Islamic cohorts throughout the 1980s and 1990s.

Although al-Qa'ida gained international prominence only in the late 1990s, its origins can be traced back to the early years of war in Afghanistan. The Arabic word for 'base', the idea of al-Qa'ida was mooted by a Palestinian academic by the name of Abdallah Azzam, one of the key players in the Afghan resistance movement against the Soviet occupation. The precursor to al-Qa'ida was *Mekhatab al Khidmat*, loosely translated as the Services Organization, which trained Islamic fighters, looked after their well-being, organized funds from various external sources, and maintained offices throughout the world, including the United States. This operation to provide logistics and religious instruction to the fighters came to be known as *al-Qa'ida al Sulabh*, or the 'solid base'.

While Abdallah Azzam provided the early ideological foundations of al-Qa'ida, Osama bin Laden became its chief patron and executioner of policies. They initiated a programme of conscription in the Afghan resistance war. Through *Mekhatab al Khidmat*, they managed to recruit Muslims from all over the world, ready to fight in Afghanistan. During this period, Abdallah Azzam enlisted jihadis throughout the world, including the USA, where he visited 27 states on his recruitment drives. While bin Laden provided the funds for transportation of these new recruits, the Afghans made available land for setting up facilities to train them. Osama bin Laden's al-Qa'ida, which was one of the seven main mujahidin factions at that time, received part of CIA-sponsored $500 million-per-year aid in the form of armaments and cash.

In its formative years, through Osama bin Laden, the loosely structured al-Qa'ida managed to extract sizeable amounts of economic and military assistance from the United States, Saudi Arabia and Pakistan, the three prominent external actors in the war in Afghanistan. These external actors recognized this organization, as it worked to promote their interests. Abdallah Azzam had a vision. He argued that after the defeat of the Soviet forces in Afghanistan, the jihad must extend to other lands that once belonged to Islam. In fact, in his scheme of things the struggle to expel the Communist Red Army from Afghanistan was a prelude to the liberation of Palestine and other 'lost' territories, including Spain (Ruthven 2002b: 33).

Just when the Soviets were pulling out of Afghanistan, however, Abdallah Azzam was killed in a bomb attack in Peshawar, Pakistan, leaving al-Qa'ida without a top leadership. For those associated with al-Qa'ida, the killing of Azzam and Soviet withdrawal from Afghanistan meant the end of their organization and its operation. Disbanding the group was not an easy option, however. The group had to make some hard decisions about the enormous resources it had inherited. Equally important, it had to find alternatives for the expertise of its fighters gained during the war of resistance. It appears that a decision was taken to keep the organization intact and use it to fight for Muslims facing persecution all over the world, and ultimately strive for a purer form of Islam (Elliot 2002: 19).

The loosely structured al-Qa'ida now seized the opportunities of war in other theatres of conflict, such as the Balkans, Chechnya, Kashmir and the Philippines, where Muslims were persecuted by non-Muslims. Throughout the 1990s Afghan mujahidin, through the institutional and economic support of al-Qa'ida, fought wars alongside fellow Muslims in these troubled spots. This is a fact that was known to the United States and its allies. However, al-Qa'ida's activities were ignored, and to some extent tolerated, as the West itself recognized some of these conflicts as wars of resistance. Unlike in Afghanistan, the rhetoric of holy war and the demand for an orthodox Islamic state did not find an audience among Bosnia's Westernized secular Muslims (Ruthven 2002b: 32). With the end of the Balkan conflict and the crackdown on insurgencies in Chechnya, Kashmir and the Philippines, al-Qa'ida suddenly found itself a band of fighters without a cause.

The international brigade of jihad veterans, being outside the control of any state, were suddenly available to serve radical Islamist causes anywhere in the world (Ruthven 2002a: 32). Around this time, it identified new enemies and dedicated itself to wage a war of liberation never witnessed before. As the liberator of oppressed Islamists, al-Qa'ida took upon itself the duty of sending more fighters to fight the kafirs or infidels wherever they threatened Muslims.

In the new phase, al-Qa'ida dedicated itself to further opposing all the governments in Muslim societies that owed their strength and very existence to Western military support. While much of the driving philosophy behind al-Qa'ida was formed during the Afghan war of resistance against the Soviet Union, it felt the philosophy could be used with equal vigour against the United States and its allies. According to the *Declaration of War against the Americans Occupying the Land of Islam*, it stated: 'the latest and the greatest of aggressions, incurred by the Muslims since the death of the Prophet . . . is the occupation of the land of the two Holy Places – the foundation of the house of Islam, the place of the revelation, the source of the message and the place of the noble Ka'ba and Qiblah of all Muslims by the armies of the American Crusaders and their allies' (Miller 2002: 63). By drawing parallels between the Soviet occupation of Afghanistan and the presence of US troops in the Arabian Peninsula, al-Qa'ida Islamized a strategic and political issue. For orthodox interpretation of the Qur'an imposed a compulsory obligation, or *fard'ayn*, on all Muslims wherever non-Muslims, or *kafirs*, occupied Muslim lands. By invoking this classical interpretation, it clearly made an attempt to promote dissent among the general populace in the Islamic world against their specific governments. By fingering some ruling houses and regimes as lackeys of United States, it made them appear non-Islamic, and therefore their claims to power dubious.

This comparison, in effect, delegitimized the right of several governments to govern. This form of Islamic jihad proclaimed by al-Qa'ida has 'a political logic, which feeds off the need for revolutionary transformations in the Islamic world and the failures of existing regimes, whether conservative or nationalist' (Blackburn 2002: 22). Although Muslims did not come out on the streets *en masse* to translate al-Qa'ida's vision into action, the vision did encourage alternative radical thinking among Muslims, and this could have long-term implications.

Some of these governments have since recognized the threat posed by al-Qa'ida to their own regimes and the overall political stability of the region. The Arab League has been at the forefront of devising a common counter-terrorism policy. Since 1998, the 22 member nations of the League have been involved in sharing intelligence and extraditing suspects. This effort has been marred, however, by the large-scale antagonism of the civilian populace, who see such attempts as pro-Western and help militant Muslims escape from the anti-terrorism efforts of the state. To complicate matters further, there exists no commonly agreed definition of al-Qa'ida or a militant terrorist within the Arab world.

Arab states do not consider groups like the Lebanese Hizbollah or Palestinian Hamas to be terrorist groups.

Since there is a very thin line between al-Qa'ida's proclamation of jihad against Jews and Crusaders and Hamas's interpretation of Israeli occupation of Palestine and its armed incursion as acts of 'state terrorism', it is very difficult to discern the one from the other in terms of overall ideological and military commitment. Both proclaim that their jihad is aimed not at expanding the territory of Islam, but restoring it, to recover land rather than conquer it. Overall, this is termed a struggle to regain a lost portion of the territory of Islam (Knapp 2003: 87). Put simply, al-Qa'ida has now penetrated the everyday forms of resistance among Muslims against one form of authority or another throughout the Islamic world. Therefore, although it is 'a terror network of no more than a few thousand men, al-Qa'ida has been able to ignite the resentments and frustrations of tens or even hundreds of millions in the Islamic world' (Blackburn 2002: 4).

In the non-Arab world, the overlapping objectives of al-Qa'ida and several militant resistance movements, like the Islamic Movement of Uzbekistan and Harkat ul-Mujahidin in Kashmir, Abu Saayaf in the Philippines, Jemaah Islamiah in archipelagic south-east Asia, allow legitimacy to al-Qa'ida's influence among the civilian populace in these conflict zones. Since their local supporters see these movements as made up of freedom fighters, they are naturally inclined to welcome any involvement of al-Qa'ida in their liberation struggle. While prepared to work with a variety of Islamic resistance movements, al-Qa'ida has succeeded in forging a global alliance whose prime objective is to oppose all forms of non-Islamic domination of Muslims everywhere in the world.

In spite of our tendency to see al-Qa'ida as a coherent, well-connected superorganism, it remains relatively amorphous. It can best be described as a network of diverse radical Islamic organizations in various parts of the world. While there exists no large-scale co-ordination among al-Qa'ida activists at intra-state or international level, this is amply compensated by an ideological cohesion that helps them work towards a single, unitary goal. The underlying thread that unites them all is the use of terrorism for the attainment of their political goals. Their cogency is evident in terms of their subscription to an agenda whose main priority is the overthrow of infidel or heretic governments in order to replace them with pure Islamic ones.

Possessing fiscal autonomy, able to organize and deploy a significant military force in Afghanistan, its global reach and membership made al-Qa'ida a unique terrorist organization (Radu 2002: 282). From a managerial perspective, al-Qa'ida acts as an umbrella group, financing and subcontracting operations to local radicals such as the Islamic Movement of Uzbekistan and Harkat ul-Mujahidin in Kashmir, the Armed Islamic Group of Algeria (GIA), and the Islamic Brigade in Chechnya, to name a few. To some observers, 'until the US intervention in Afghanistan, al-Qa'ida acted in a manner somewhat resembling a large charity that funded terrorist projects to be conducted by pre-existing or affiliate terrorist groups (Smith 2002: 36). The structural blueprint of the organization is such that individual or group-related activities couldn't be traced directly back to the top leadership. Each group operates independently, with its supporters and members not knowing who the others are. Under this arrangement, if one individual member of a group is identified and arrested, others in the superorganism remain unaffected (Engle 2001: 19). It is because of this diffused command structure that it is often compared to a mutating virus that is impossible to totally grasp or destroy (Erlanger and Hedges 2001: 1). Therefore, it is unsurprising that almost 98 per cent of al-Qa'ida's top leadership were alive and engaged in various militant activities even a year after a continuous international military campaign against it.

The objective

There are almost as many explanations for al-Qa'ida's emergence and growth as there are contemporary analysts who have written on the subject. From a structural perspective, al-Qa'ida flourished in an environment of weak states or quasi-states that were undergoing disruptive economic, political and social transformation (Smith 2002: 38). However, some critics blame the illiberal attitude of the West towards the world of Islam, which created a sense of inferiority among Muslim radicals, who then gave themselves the task of rescuing Islam's lost glory from the evil, self-serving and invidious designs of the United States and its allies (Chomsky 2001; Ali 2002). The strong slant in US policy towards the Israeli–Palestinian conflict is held up to validate this argument. Yet some others hold Islamists responsible for the alleged collapse of the social, economic and political world within some Islamic states, which in turn forced upstanding Muslims towards conservatism and radicalism (Ajami 2001; Kepel 2002).

The exact explanation behind its emergence is both more ambitious and more disturbing. Radical Islamists who operate at a global level tend to blame a Western backlash against efforts at Islamic consolidation. They also unreservedly highlight the inner spiritual and moral bankruptcy within the world of Islam that prompted it to stand up and take stock of the situation. According to one critic, 'Radical Islam represents a long evolving soul searching process in most Islamic countries in reaction to the Western systems of knowledge, which were perceived to be detrimental to Islam and Muslims' self-identification. Those systems' biased ethnocentricity and their damaging impact in terms of traditional institutional decay and value dependency have increasingly become the focus of Islamic resentment and rejection' (Sabet 1995: 59). Like many Western political theorists, al-Qa'ida views the future of international society as a struggle for power and dominance. It is also in sympathy with those who have proposed that all conflicts between societies or cultures in the years ahead will be purely on civilizational terms. To people on both sides of the argument, the events following 11 September 2001 are pointers in that direction. From all parts of the Islamic world, and at all socio-economic levels, there is a refusal to acknowledge any regret for the terrorist strikes in America on 11 September 2001. Now governments all over the Western world have been working out effective ways and means to defend their own socio-economic, political and cultural supremacy. A similar attempt is made by Islamists too. The problem, of course, is to discern the operational strategies of the two.

Al-Qaida's conception of Islamic identity is global in scope (Takeyh and Gvosdev 2002: 97). It unreservedly divides the world into *dar-al Islam*, or the zone of peace, and *dar-al Harb*, the zone of war. Arguably, its campaign against the Soviets during the Afghan war and the establishment of the Taliban government according to Islamic orthodoxy gave al-Qa'ida and its leadership the confidence that they could eventually extend their vision of an Islamic polity not restricted by any boundaries. It unhesitatingly distorted the interpretation of jihad from a defensive individual measure to a communal offensive force, and demanded all those true to Islam to live by this new principle. For 'Islamic fundamentalist belief in God's sovereignty goes hand in hand with the doctrine of jihad as the sixth pillar of Islam. This entails a method of armed struggle, coupled with an assertion of Islam as a religion that has to be ultimately embodied in a totalitarian state' (Choueiri 1996: 21–2). In Afghanistan, through the Taliban, al-Qa'ida posed the question of government in the following terms: 'Do you wish to be ruled by God or by Man?' Their question was an invitation to bestow the ruler with the divine right to oppress the ruled. It was an invitation to authoritarianism in the name of God. By allowing the supreme leader Mullah Mohammed Omar the title of amir al maumin, or the Commander of the Faithful, it established his and the Taliban's undisputed authority as God's representative on earth.

Contrary to popular beliefs, al-Qa'ida is not a homogeneous or monolithic resistance movement spawned by modernist radical Islam. It is but an organization of a small minority of Muslims, and holds an equally minority position along the broad spectrum of Islamic political theology

(Philpott 2002: 86). Yet al-Qa'ida's long-term objective is to establish a pan-Islamic Caliphate in the Muslim world based on Qur'anic principles and according to the laws prescribed in Shari'a. The common perception that dominates our imagination of al-Qa'ida is of a resistance movement spread across the globe that aims to strike against US interests in a resolve to undermine its global domination. Interestingly, it is not only what it regards as the debased West that is the main target of al-Qa'ida. In its resolve to establish a uniform Islamic society, it also aims to overthrow regimes that it deems non-Islamic.

Equally important, al-Qa'ida represents the Sunni sect within the world of Islam. In other words, it either ignores the presence of Shi'a Muslims or condemns their presence within mainstream Islam. Although perplexing, this attitude has a rational justification. 'Unlike the Shi'a minority view, which is explicitly dynastic and authoritarian, the majority Sunni view on Islamic polity falls midway between authoritarianism and democratic ideals' (Ba-Yunus 2002: 105). Similarly, radical Islam as represented by al-Qa'ida and its cohorts prefers to ignore the fact that Islam, like other great world religions, has incorporated a diverse body of thought and practice and has contributed and accommodated itself to ideas of religious tolerance, secular political power and human rights (Held 2002: 85).

The breadth of radical Islam

Though al-Qa'ida has its roots in Afghanistan, investigators and scholars exploring its reach are of the opinion that it is equally potent in Western societies where Muslims represent only a fraction of the total population. Thanks to the spread of ideas of Islamic revolution on the new communication highway and the relative freedom allowed by the liberal West to practise one's own religion without restriction or restraint, there have emerged new converts to al-Qa'ida, born not in the land of Islam but in Islamic communities of Europe and North America. In their voluntary exile, scores of Muslim youth, who have had little or no link to the war in Afghanistan, have embraced the ideology of revolution in exile.

Critics of American foreign policy argue that Washington must dispel the widespread image of al-Qa'ida as 'a ubiquitous, super-organised terror network and call it as it is: a loose collection of groups and individuals that does not even refer to itself as al-Qa'ida'. Since most of the affiliated groups have distinct goals set within a specific geographical terrain, it is a gross over-exaggeration to bundle them together under the label of al-Qa'ida (McCloud and Dolnik 2002: 7). While the above view has some credence, it also has several shortcomings. First, as was evident from the international campaign in Afghanistan, al-Qa'ida is a multinational enterprise. It did not demand the allegiance of dissatisfied radical Islamic groups, but the latter associated voluntarily with the former's vision and took on board its broad objectives to achieve that vision.

Second, al-Qa'ida can also be interpreted as a state of mind that is loosely translated into a world radical Islamist movement. Everyone who is a part of that movement and seeks results from the very grass roots to the international level is a natural participant in al-Qa'ida. Third, thanks to globalization, since there is an intertwining and overlapping American interest in every part of the world, any attack on a particular institutional interest by a disgruntled Islamic group can in fact be treated as an affront to American interests and be logically extended to the workings of al-Qa'ida. But how pervasive is al-Qa'ida in influencing regional and group-specific movements?

Since the late 1990s al-Qa'ida has taken over many small, localized, radical Islamic groups, the most prominent of which was *al jihad*, led by Ayman al-Zawahiri, another prominent Egyptian mujahid of the Afghan war. Although many small groups have joined forces with al-Qa'ida, the latter has allowed complete freedom in matters relating to local organizational structure and, in some instances, to area of operation. Al-Qa'ida is like a superorganism where all units are autonomous but work to achieve the common goal, for the common good. It operates on the basis of a loose

network of local militant groups receiving only token economic but full moral and spiritual support from the radical
leadership.

It is important to notice, however, that the support base of
militant Islam (in this context as al-Qa'ida) is not confined
solely to areas where Islam is dominant. As a matter of fact,
militant Islam is becoming more powerful in regions where
it is in a minority position. This implies that, whatever the
political culture, whatever the demands of the host society,
its structure of rights and obligations, some Muslims living
in it will always contrive to respond to the call of radical
Islam, even if that amounts to waging war on their own
adopted homeland. It is the prospect of the spread of this
mind-set that is most alarming to everyone.

The most worrying of al-Qa'ida's ideological partners is
Takfir wa'l Hijra – a very elusive sect operating from within
the liberal Western societies. Very little is known about this
sect, and our understanding of its operation remains patchy.
It is widely believed that most of its members are second- or
third-generation Muslims in the West. They mostly feel alienated from their adopted, host society. Like other radical
Islamists, the Takfiri hold Western society responsible for the
destitution and apparent humiliation of Muslims within and
outside the world of Islam. Followers of this ideology
consider it their sacred duty to attack Western interests and
institutions whenever a chance presents itself.

The movement originally started in Egypt in the 1960s.
Followers of this sect modelled their behaviour on the
Prophet Muhammad, who renounced the corrupt society of
Mecca and made his *hijra* (migration) in order to set up a
pure society in exile in Medina. Takfir's philosophy is based
on this radical view that Muslims need to *withdraw* from
corrupt secular societies and establish sacred self-sufficient
communities. It has now emerged that the Takfiri were
present in large numbers in Taliban-controlled Afghanistan,
and were responsible for the promotion of many key policy
initiatives.

Just like the Taliban, which viewed all non-radical versions
of Islam as impure, the Takfiri too believe in the religious jus-

tification for subjugating and slaughtering not just *kafirs*, or unbelievers, but also those who do not adopt orthodox Islamic practices. It is this particular notion of 'war against traitors of true Islam' which has been attractive to al-Qa'ida. It is now established that Osama bin Laden and al-Qa'ida harnessed the extreme fanaticism and violent dynamics of Takfir to execute plans from their base in Afghanistan. The Takfir recruits in al-Qa'ida were introduced not only to the latter's *fatwas*, that called for strikes against US and Western interests, but also to those that aimed at exerting violent pressure against Muslim rulers who contradicted the basic tenets of Islam.

Since al-Qa'ida allows incorporation of all radical Islamic movements under its umbrella and under the banner of a 'common Islamic future', Takfir wa'l Hijra's activities have grave implications. The extremist views of Takfir are so severe that they often call on followers to kill fellow Muslims who deviate from their vision of an untainted orthodox Islam. According to Takfir's central tenets, those belonging to this sect and subscribing to its ideals need to go through self-imposed internal exile among the infidels, followed by a vengeful return to a society where all non-Muslims and non-believers will be put to death.

In their voluntary, self-imposed exile, Tafkiri are often allowed to deviate from strict Islamic practices, in order to blend into the host society and so avoid detection. During this exile, they are free to engage in non-Islamic activities under the concept of *taquya*, which implies 'protecting oneself by burrowing underground' or 'making oneself undetectable'. According to Roland Jacquard, a leading French scholar of Islamic terrorism, 'Takfir's are the hard core of the hard core: they are the ones who will be called upon to organise and execute the really big attacks' (Elliot 2002: 17). The goal of Takfiri is to assimilate into host societies in order to plot attacks against them. 'Although the overwhelming majority of Muslims living in Europe (or, for that matter, the United States) are peaceful and law abiding, many European governments worry under their breath about the role of some European Muslims in past and future terrorist attacks – a concern stoked by the discovery of al-Qa'ida cells in Germany, France, Italy, and Britain' (Taspinar 2003: 77).

Well versed in the Western way of life and mannerisms, enjoying the right to travel freely within various political frontiers, Takfiri are virtually impossible to identify or detect. This has an obvious advantage. In the next phase of al-Qa'ida's war against the West and the West's war on terror, the Takfiri are likely to feature prominently. In fact, it appears that one such Takfir, Yasser al-Siri, a leading bookstore and website owner in London, specializing in radical Islam, was the main conspirator behind the assassination of Ahmed Shah Mas'ud, who died days before the events of 11 September 2001.

From an ideological standpoint, Takfir wa'l Hijra and the Taliban appear to be two sides of the same coin. Though they emerged in two distinct geographical settings and were separated by two different time frames, both the Taliban and Takfir wa'l Hijra appear to have gone through a cycle of co-evolution under the patronage of al-Qa'ida, in terms of their ideological orientations and world-views. When it gained popularity and won new converts in Egypt in 1970s, the Takfir demanded that all its followers adhere to the purest form of Islam, the kind practised by the Prophet when he withdrew from Mecca to Medina.

The Taliban and Takfir often had overlapping ideological goals. Both aimed to establish a self-sufficient Islamic community untouched by the so-called impurities of the West, the only difference being while the Taliban had inherited a state from the chaos of a decade and a half-long civil war, the Takfiri were a stateless community. But it was this very statelessness which brought them closer to the Taliban. The Taliban regime saw Takfiri as compatriots in an ongoing ideological struggle, and was happy to provide them with succour and use some of their expertise. The Taliban's notoriety as a Fascist regime had a lot to do with the version of Islamo-fascism promoted by Takfiri. It is likely that Takfiri were instrumental in influencing the Taliban regime to adopt a harsh hard-line policy as far as destruction of Afghanistan's non-Islamic heritage was concerned.

The waves of policy measures that required minority Sikhs and Hindus to wear coloured arm bands and carry identity papers at all times, the destruction of every non-Islamic arte-fact in the country, including the giant Buddhas of Bamian, and the persecution of tribal communities who practised a liberal version of Islam, although initiated by the Taliban, were often physically enforced by Takfiri. It is argued that the frequent assaults against the Shi'ite Hazaras throughout the Taliban's reign was in fact a covert operation of the Takfiri. Since a majority of the Taliban belonged to the Pashtun community and expressed their power relationship with other ethnic groups in the country exclusively in ethnic terms, they were willing accomplices as far as the massacre of Hazaras by their hard-line external mercenaries was concerned.

Takfiri are insurrectionists caught in a no man's land, on the run from their own homelands, but never at home in the West (Ajami 2001: 4). These young radicals, who want to become extraordinary in a very ordinary world, who have great ambitions without having great talents, or who face real external difficulties in the pursuit of their careers, are easily carried away by fundamentalist creeds and myths of heroism. To most of them, the temptation to carry out strikes is doubly rewarding. For not only do they achieve heroic status in their own society, they are assured of a fantastic life after their martyrdom. The new jihad of the Takfir, the Taliban or al-Qa'ida is not only apocalyptic, it is also nihilistic.

The Taliban spokesman's statement that his people love death as much as the Americans love life is an expression of supreme nihilism. The eroticization of death, as evidenced on the one hand by the frequently heard vulgarism about *huris*, the dark-eyed virgins who are to meet the warriors in the afterlife, and on the other hand, and more importantly, by the destruction of one's own body in an act of supreme vio-lence, which dismembers and pulverizes it, is remarkable (Benhabib 2002: 38). Since this form of self-sacrifice is linked to aspects of salvation, there are ready converts to this form of martyrdom (Euben 2002: 7).

Conclusion

According to the State Department, al-Qa'ida opposed the United States for a number of overlapping reasons. It was an enemy state, as it provided both moral and military support to governments that flouted the laws of Islam. On this definition, the ruling regimes of Egypt and Saudi Arabia were treated by al-Qa'ida as enemies, as was the United States. Al-Qa'ida further argued that the United States, owing to its military might, remained as an occupying force in the sacred land of Islam, and therefore it was its sole duty to see to the overthrow of this force.[2]

In spite of the international coalition engaged in dislodging the Taliban and their cohort, al-Qa'ida, the latter may not be a spent force. It would be rash to suggest that the US 'war on terror' has reduced the future possibility of terrorism either globally or against civilians in the West. It is hard to discern what are the long-term objectives of al-Qa'ida, 'but high on its priorities must stand a desire to grab control of one of the moribund Islamic states (with a corrupt regime and restless mass) such as Egypt, Saudi Arabia, or better still closer to Afghanistan a nuclear armed-Pakistan' (Emmot 2002: 26). Some commentators have argued that 'the ability of al-Qa'ida to attract sympathy and support in the Islamic world could certainly be undercut by initiatives favourable to democracy, economic development, self-determination, and respect for the peaceful exercise of religious rites and rights'(Blackburn 2002: 22).

Although it might appear paradoxical, most of the violence perpetrated by radical Islamists in recent years is directed neither against the West nor against Zionists, but is inflicted on their fellow Muslims, as is evident from the civil war situations in Afghanistan, Algeria, Iraq and Pakistan. These societies or nations have been engaged in what might be termed an inverse revolution aimed at self-reformation (Pipes 1994: 84).

The jihad has turned inward, as the radicals have come to believe that evil at home has first to be eradicated before the infidels abroad can be destroyed (Laqueur 2001: 129). If one turns the mirror on Muslims themselves, one realizes that what we are witnessing is not a clash of civilizations between Islam and the West, but 'a battle within Muslim civilization where ultraconservatives compete with moderates and democrats for the soul of the Muslim public' (Heffner 2001). This is indeed a struggle between 'a humane, tolerant, and progressive faith, and a hangman's vision of a punitive God and a humankind defined by prohibitions' (Peters 2002: 5).

One could argue, in this context, that radical Islamists are less interested in Islam as a religion and more keen to endorse a form of extreme nationalism. Followers of this new ideology 'seek to return to what the *Qur'an* calls the "straight path" of Islam through overthrow of their rulers, whom they consider impious, as well as confrontation with non-Muslims whom they regard as infidels' (Piscatori 2002: 147). Furthermore, this radical vision transcends the narrowly defined borders, particular sets of governments, divisions based on wealth and power, and, most important of all, national interest of that specific country. Since it recognizes the trials, tribulations and sufferings of any Muslim in any part of the world, al-Qa'ida's message has found an audience which on occasion has defied and denounced the artificial man-made markers that keep them divided.

> If any government sponsors the outlaws and killers of inno-
> cents they have become outlaws and murderers themselves.
> And they will take that lonely path at their own peril.
>
> George W. Bush, 7 October 2001.

Introduction

The 'failed state' theory suggests that the international
community or a set of countries or even a single power can
intervene in the affairs of a third country with the explicit
objective of regime change and the imposition of order. For
such failed states are a threat not only to themselves but to
the interest of their neighbours, the region and the international community as a whole. Put simply, terrorism is one of
the chief threats that dysfunctional states pose (Mallaby
2002: 3). Hence, it is the responsibility of the international
community to do everything possible to stem this threat.
Viewed within this framework of argument, the US intervention in Afghanistan and the unseating of the Taliban
would appear to have been conducted primarily to stop the
terrorist network operating from Afghanistan.

Although that was the key purpose, the US intervention
in Afghanistan was also an extension of anticipatory self-
defence doctrine found within the annals of international law.
For, according to some critics, 'if "failed states" pose a threat

to international order there is no normative predicament because the great powers are charged specifically with defending international peace and security under Chapter 7 of the UN Charter' (Jackson 1998: 4). This chapter discusses the US 'War on Terror', set against the backdrop of Afghanistan, the Taliban and al-Qa'ida. It throws light on various aspects of this undertaking. Furthermore, it enquires whether the US administration, by recourse to international law and by using the failed state logic against an amorphous enemy, has further widened the division between Muslims and non-Muslims.

'Intervention' in international affairs refers to 'a situation where one actor, a group of actors or an international body interferes in the affairs of another fellow actor'.[1] Intervention differs from diplomatic talk. It also refers to a situation in which oral communication between actors is replaced by some form of external deployment of force in the internal affairs of that particular state. This deployment of force could be in the social, economic, political, religious or military domain. Additionally, this imposition may be deployed against a particular regime, a part of that state's territory, or the society as a whole. Intervention presupposes the existence of a conflict situation, and aims to isolate and eventually resolve that conflict.

However, one needs to bear in mind that conflict-related interventions are not always military in nature. They could involve such steps as 'the provision of aid' to civil war-stricken zones and those affected by such civil war. Supply of humanitarian assistance is also a key feature of non-military intervention. The goal of humanitarian assistance is to help those civilians caught up in the war survive the hostilities between parties to the conflict (Esman 2001). Furthermore, should there be a change in the conflict dynamics in the region, it aims to provide long-term rehabilitation or reconstruction aid to help people rebuild their lives.

Conditions for intervention

Since the civil war in Afghanistan began in 1979, following the Soviet invasion of the country, one could justifiably argue that the scope for intervention existed from that particular period. However, thanks to the Soviet presence in the country and Cold War politics, such action was unthinkable. Following the beginning of Soviet troop withdrawal in 1988, conditions within Afghanistan improved significantly for some form of international intervention.

The first major interventionist effort, through the Geneva Accord of 1988, although it succeeded in providing an exit route out of the conflict for the Soviets and the Americans, failed to offer a power-sharing arrangement on the domestic front. Subsequent attempts by the UN to enforce a settlement in the form of a nationally accepted interim government were unsuccessful, as there was no let-up in the fighting between various rival factions. The focus therefore shifted from political to humanitarian intervention (Rubin 1995a; Ewans 2001). This form of intervention was facilitated mostly by various NGOs and INGOs, including various organs of the United Nations.[2]

The primary focus of intervention in this phase was the eradication of poverty. There was very little opposition to this initiative from the various warring factions within the country, as they came to appreciate the innate nobility of this task (Cordovez and Harrison 1995; Rubin 1995a). However, one has to acknowledge that the poverty eradication initiative and social regeneration often existed side by side, and there was plenty of overlapping. Since there was an all-round social breakdown, many external bodies working in the country employed several policy programmes within a single project. For example, NGOs and INGOs could not countenance social regeneration without the empowerment of women.

In a tradition-bound society, such as Afghanistan, this did not always go down well. Yet most parties to the conflict tolerated international humanitarian intervention, if grudgingly. When the Taliban regime took over power, it viewed international humanitarian intervention in the form of aid and assistance as a direct threat to its conception of the ideal Islamic society. Naturally, one of the first tasks following the consolidation of its authority was to bar the presence of international organizations in the country and those involved in humanitarian work.

We discussed in chapter 3 how the Taliban's outlook and world-view led to the complete breakdown of Afghan society, and the regime's complicity in exporting terror to other regions of the world. It was within this context that the international community realized that the Taliban was not only a threat to Afghans, but also a menace to humanity as a whole. But prior to the events of 11 September 2001, it did not have any clear approach to dealing with Afghanistan. There were some indirect military confrontations, such as an aerial attack by Washington on some targets in Kabul following the US embassy bombings in East Africa. Iran also threatened punitive military action against the Taliban during this period, when several of its diplomats were massacred in Mazar-e Sharif in 1998. In addition, the imposition of an arms embargo was considered, but could not be actively pursued owing to Afghanistan's porous borders with Central Asia and Pakistan.[3]

In sum, the international community resigned itself to a level of non-commitment as the Taliban went about violating one civilizing principle after another. The catalogue of atrocities included the treatment of women as second-class citizens, the expulsion of international agencies, mass persecution of ethnic and religious minorities, gross human rights violations, cultural vandalism in the form of the destruction of the Bamian Buddhas and other artefacts of the country's non-Islamic heritage, promotion of an illicit economy through opium production and, finally, providing a safe haven to international terror networks from which to strike international targets. Following 11 September, the international community found itself in a situation in which military intervention became inevitable, as the scope of the conflict no longer remained confined to Afghanistan but spread to other parts of the world. This development, in effect, provided the ground for a form of 'protective activity' that fell under the rubric of external military intervention as explained by the UN Charter. At its heart it had the following objectives: 'a short-term use of armed force by a government (a group of states) in what otherwise would be a violation of the sovereignty of a foreign State, for the protection from death or grave injury of nationals of the acting State – and, incidentally perhaps, nationals of other States' (Baxter 1973: 53).

A direct military intervention, however, was not the first priority of the international community. Under the leadership of the United States, there were several attempts to persuade the Taliban regime to hand over the suspected terrorists. The Taliban's non-compliance with this request left the UN with little or no choice but to pass a Security Council resolution authorizing a war on terrorism. But the United States, which was most affected by the militants operating from within Afghanistan, succeeded in extending this resolution's scope to the realm of 'self-defence' as prescribed in Article 2, paragraph 2 of the UN Charter. This was a clever manipulation of the principle of intervention. In the first place, the UN became a source of 'collective legitimation' for what could otherwise be interpreted as a unilateral US military intrusion in Afghanistan (Mallaby 2002; Lind 2003). Secondly, it distributed the intervention objectives: the military aspect was appropriated by the USA, while the UN was left to the much more problematic task of the long-term reconstruction of Afghanistan (Keohane 2002: 144).

Much was at stake militarily, but the objectives of intervention in Afghanistan had not been defined coherently (Zisk Marten 2003–37). As the military strikes continued, however, several different projects were unveiled. These were set in an order of primacy, as all objectives were interlinked and sequential in their dynamics (Kennedy 2001; Philpott 2002). The following were considered to be the key to ending the cycle of violence in Afghanistan and helping it emerge as a viable state:

- regime change
- de-escalation of conflict
- post-war reconstruction
- democratization and good governance
- arms decommissioning.

A just intervention?

It is argued that the greatest virtue of intervention lies in its ability to pass judgement on a just war. The just war theory

provides the announced reasons for going to war, the pro-
nounced war aims and the war's conduct, the adopted strategy, the justice of the war, and finally the ability to reconstruct
the society that has undergone internal conflict defined as civil
war, and the external military interventions that were initiated to stop the complete breakdown of the society.[4]

How ought we to proceed in our interpretation of intervention? Opponents of external involvement in the nation-
building process in Afghanistan argue that countries do better
'without interference from outside, that it wastes money and
enriches criminals, and most importantly turns external
soldiers into targets for terrorists (Emmot 2002: 18). The
problem with our 'test case' of Afghanistan is that too many
overlapping and contradictory issues were responsible for the
international community's war efforts in the country. We can
discern two key points that stand out in this context. First,
the intervention in Afghanistan was not a watertight case of
humanitarian intervention. It had elements of national interest built into it. This stand in itself defeats the very ideal of
just war as propounded by St Augustine (AD 354–430) in his
classic work *The City of God* – which, incidentally, forms the
basis of Western humanitarianism and, consequently, intervention in the form of just war.

We continued to ignore the Taliban and the atrocities they
perpetrated on the masses so long as this did not impinge
directly on the national or collective interest of the developed
world. Only when the regime was implicated in the events
of 11 September did we make a resolve to pursue a military
intervention option and project it as conducted in the name
of freeing Afghans from the 'fascist regime'. Second, we conducted the war by taking sides with the Northern Alliance,
whose record of human rights abuse and contribution to
overall anarchy in Afghanistan was equally contemptuous.
Therefore, the claim that the intervention was a 'moral right'
in the case of Afghanistan is thoroughly flawed.

An asymmetric war

The US war against terror can best be described as an asymmetric conflict. This conflict involves two actors who share

polar opposite characters, to say the least. While one is the foremost and only superpower in the world, the other's identity remains amorphous. In terms of conventional symmetrical confrontation, the biggest and most powerful of these two actors is assured of a victory. But in an unconventional and asymmetric conflict – an elusive enemy whose spread is interstate and global in scope and whose methods include catastrophic terrorist interventions – the bigger of the two parties cannot necessarily be assured of a victory.

Victory or relative success or failure of one of these two actors, in this scenario, depends on their 'commitment to the cause'. In the main, the actor with the most resolve wins, regardless of material and military power resources.[5] In fact, this argument has found resonance in a wide spectrum of works, from Aesop's fables to the writings of great strategic thinkers and theorists through the ages.

Andrew Mack, a war theorist writing at the height of the Cold War years, successfully argued that weak actors have as much chance of winning a war as the most powerful ones. There are three key elements to Mack's explanation of asymmetric conflict: (a) relative power explains relative interests; (b) relative interests explain relative vulnerability; and (c) relative vulnerability explains why strong actors lose.[6] In short, a visibly strong actor has an enhanced vulnerability, and is likely to lose more in the event of an asymmetric confrontation, compared to its disorganized, militarily weak and invisible counterpart.

True, 'rules of engagement' in such a conflict are not necessarily accepted by either of the parties. But the weaker of the two is more likely to violate and disobey any 'codes of conduct', in order to further its cause. Terrorist strikes on civilians, depredations against non-combatants (which include abduction and summary execution), use of biological and nuclear materials on an unsuspecting populace, and suicide bombing are some of the preferred techniques of warfare by the weaker of the two.

In Walter Laqueur's view, 'the trouble with terrorism is not that it has always been indefensible but that it has been chosen more often than not as the prima ratio of self-appointed saviours of freedom and justice, of fanatics and madmen, not as the ultima ratio of rebels against real tyranny' (Laqueur 2001: 9–10). According to *Laws of War* (1994), which include the Hague Conventions of 1989 and 1907, the UN Genocide Convention of 1948, the four Geneva Conventions of 1989, and the two Additional Protocols to Geneva Conventions of 1977, the targeting of civilian areas, the use of chemical and biological weapons, and the deliberate destruction of a defender's natural environment are violations.[7] Although radical Islamists have not declared a conventional war against the United States or used all of the above strategies to wreak havoc on the opponent, the indications are that at some point in the future the confrontation could include all of the above.

Thus the international society has been dragged into what could be termed an 'asymmetric war'. In this confrontation, various smaller powers with disparate backgrounds have forged 'asymmetric strategies' to exploit the vulnerabilities of a stronger power. In this scenario, al-Qa'ida and its cohorts may not gain an absolute edge over the United States, its allies or the Western liberal democracies, but they can rupture the peace and stability enjoyed by the latter. From the perspective of alliances and counter-alliances in this new war against terror, the Islamists stand united, closer together than in any other period in history. Osama bin Laden's message that an internal war among Muslims is a fatal error as it will destroy Islam and give advantage to its enemies – that is, the United States and its allies – has undoubtedly reinforced a global Islamic solidarity.

In spite of al-Qa'ida's war games, neither the United States nor the international community could declare a war against this faceless enemy. 'The idea that a democratic nation-state would declare war upon a global network of loosely organised sympathisers of a religious-cum-civilisational cause is an impossible undertaking' (Benhabib 2002: 36). Thus the Allied military campaign in Afghanistan was not preceded by a declaration of war; rather, the US Congress authorized the President to do whatever was necessary to fight the global terror network and to bring the perpetrators to justice

(Benhabib 2002: 36). The Secretary of Defence, Donald Rumsfeld, later explained the US war aims and strategies. According to Rumsfeld, this 'New Kind of War' will not be waged by a grand alliance united for the single purpose of defeating an axis of hostile powers. Instead of such an alliance, in which the USA would have to compromise with allies, there will be 'floating coalitions' adopted or discarded at will by the directing centre: 'Countries will have different roles and contribute in different ways . . . In this war the mission will determine the coalition, not the other way round.' As expected, Washington will define the mission (Rumsfeld 2001: 7; Blackburn 2002: 21).

A misunderstood war?

Although publicly denied, there has emerged a clear consensus among the policy-makers in the West[8] following 11 September, that international relations is all about a clash of cultural mores, ways of life, political process, religiosity and ultimately civilization, as proposed by the American political scientist Samuel P. Huntington. According to Huntington, the most fundamental source of conflict in the new world will be between nations and groups of different civilizations (Huntington 1996: 2). This hypothesis, which has found an audience among scores of individuals in the West, has been unhelpful in building bridges between the world of Islam and the rest.

The most fundamental victim of this mind-set has been trust. What the United States and its allies have been engaged in in their treatment of invisible al-Qa'ida is a systematic macro-politics of psychological warfare. Unfortunately, in the absence of a visible enemy, the whole Muslim world is treated as the enemy by default.[9] A section of the West has come to treat Muslims as evil, waylaid citizens who must be brought back to an honest, law-abiding existence by the imposition of stern discipline and punishment. This tendency to conceive of Islam and Muslims in sweeping civilizational terms, warns a leading scholar, is likely to create further tension and continuing unrest (Geertz 2003: 30).

Following the instigation of the 'war on terrorism', the debate over interconnectedness between nations and states has grown pessimistic. The free flow of ideas, people, currency and information – lauded once – is now understood as providing the very conduits through which nefarious designs of disgruntled individuals travel. Terrorism is now considered an ideological, moral and, most importantly, a strategic challenge to liberal democracy (Boroumand and Boroumand 2002: 5). Naturally, there is now a degree of mutual distrust between the West and the world of Islam. While the war on terrorism is treated as a war of self-defence by liberal democratic powers, disgruntled elements in some quarters of the Islamic world consider it an assault on the very foundation of their identity and existence. The Islamic world now stands alienated from the world dominated by Western nations. The relationship between the two is seen only in terms of power and authority.

The invasion of Afghanistan, the unseating of the Taliban, and the employment of substantial fire-power against those who opposed the US-led campaign did not necessarily create foundations for future peace in the region. They merely increased the widening gap between the secular, multicultural, liberal democratic West and the conservative, inward and in some cases authoritarian world of Islam. They served to reinstate the existing claim that the West is superior in its value systems, treatment of fellow human beings, and sense of justice, fair play and righteousness.

Western military engagements in Afghanistan have come perilously close to achieving what Osama bin Laden probably intended: 'putting pressure on pro-Western governments in Islamic countries and possibly unifying the Islamic world against the West' (Bellamy 2001: 5). His rhetoric on Islamic revolution within the Muslim world in general and the Arab world in particular found a receptive audience (Scott Doran 2002: 23). Unsurprisingly, Islamism has become the primary vehicle and vocabulary of most political discourse throughout the Muslim world (Fuller 2002: 50).

Our commitment against al-Qa'ida can easily be construed as an affront to Islam. The highly evocative 'clash of civilizations' thesis has stripped the younger intelligentsia of any real knowledge of the Islamic world in favour of a theory which can be interpreted as a crass projection of American assumptions and prejudices. Huntington's argument that Christianity and Islam can never coexist sets a dangerous precedent, and completely undermines the nature and future of international relations. To suggest that Islam and the West (Christianity) will always be in opposite camps, and therefore that the West must find ways to subdue Islam or Islamic societies, takes us dangerously close to rhetoric that proposes another global war.

An impassioned observation of the dynamics of this relationship suggests that extreme Islamism or extremist Islam is neither a reaction to US imperialism, as left-wing thinkers like Noam Chomsky or Tariq Ali have argued, nor the result of an inevitable clash between civilizations or religions, as the main advocate of this thesis, Samuel Huntington, would have us believe (Berman 2003). Islam has been a part of Western consciousness and vice versa for centuries. To juxtapose these societies as wholly incompatible civilizations is totally fraudulent and profoundly reckless (Euben 2002; Sacks 2002). Extremist Islam, with its impulse towards totalitarian utopias, is like any other radical political movement. Converts to it suffer from the same anxieties as their obdurate counterparts in political movements espousing extreme left-wing or Fascist ideologies.

As one critic has put it: 'The devoted members of al-Qa'ida display an unsettling willingness to martyr themselves because they feel that, like the Prophet, they are locked in a life-or-death struggle with the forces of unbelief that threaten from all sides. They consider themselves an island of true believers surrounded by a sea of iniquity and think the future of religion and the world depends on them and their battle against unbelievers' (Scott Doran 2002: 26). While the aggressive expansionist urge is common to most world religions (Brooks 2003: 26), it is not necessarily adopted by most in modern times, and exists on an abstract level. This concept, however, is alive in Islam. It is pulled back from the fringes to the mainstream. It had its strongest manifestation in the ideology of the Taliban and since their demise has found a home in the elusive al-Qa'ida. Osama bin Laden's pronouncement that 'the jihad is never over and defeat is only a setback in a holy war' (Bergen 2001; Heller 2002) creates cloudscapes of fear. The war against Islamic radicalism, therefore, is unlikely to bear fruit unless there is a concerted attempt by the West to develop a cogent policy against all forms of Islamic tyranny and corruption. As Malise Ruthven argues, the West is guilty of humbug in acting decisively against the oppressive puritanism of the Taliban, while indulging the all too similar austerities of Saudi Wahabism (Ruthven 2002a: 30–5).

While making a case against American military dominance in the land of Islam, Osama bin Laden has been equally forthcoming in introducing an economic imperialism into the equation. He consistently highlighted that Muslims are starving to death while the United States is stealing their wealth. For a clearer illustration of this fact, bin Laden argued that the price of American wheat has increased threefold, but the price of Arab oil has increased by no more than a few dollars over a period of 24 years – because the USA is relentless in dictating to the Arabs at gunpoint (Jacquard 2002: 221).

Some of his other claims include a statement that the USA has caused Arab nations a total loss of $1,000 billion over the last 13 years. Consequently, it is the sacred duty of all self-respecting Muslim Arabs to redress this wrong (Reeve 1999: 231). Given the breakdown of economic order in several Arab states, such as Algeria, Yemen and Palestine, such messages have found a wide audience, especially among unemployed disillusioned youth. Al-Qa'ida channels their economic anxieties into active political participation.

Osama bin Laden represents two different things. Indeed, each is the direct opposite of the other. In the non-Islamic world he has been accused of being misogynistic, misanthropic and cynically evil. He is also blamed for having spearheaded a new murderous xenophobia against non-Muslims in places where Muslims are in the majority (Ajami 2001: 7). Within the Islamic world, however, he represents something entirely different. His personal piety and willingness to sacrifice worldly comfort and wealth for the cause of Islam has endeared him to his fellows (Calvert 2002: 345). He is regarded as pious, philanthropic, a promoter of Islamic virtues, and above all the defender of a faith that has faced onslaught from a supposedly hostile and self-serving West.

A just war?

Radical Islam does not make any distinction between just and unjust wars (Walzer 1992). It refutes such concepts as Judaeo-Christian inventions, and seeks to go beyond their current scope. It favours a multitude of war strategies, including unlawful warfare. Just as water has no constant shape, so the military force of extremist Islam has no constant contour or formation. It has developed extreme adaptability, according to the adversary's strength and weakness. From Osama bin Laden to the fighters in Chechnya, Kashmiri militants in India, and Palestinian suicide bombers in Israel, all have responded to their own specific enemy and situation with unconventional methods, which can at best be described as barbaric. But the nature of the conflict being asymmetric, such strategies are considered appropriate. For it demands that the weaker strike at the power base of the powerful, attack when they are lax, and do not let the enemy figure out where the next strike is going to be.

How does one effectively combat the war strategies of radical Islamists? Should the principles of a just war be violated in order to successfully counter the threat posed by extremist elements within Islam? Is the threat posed by radical Islamists global in scope, to include all nations, nationalities and humankind? Should there not be a dialogue with the extremist fringe of Islam to find a peaceful solution?

I will address these questions in reverse order. First, a dialogue with Islam is not possible because, contrary to popular assumption, Islam is not a homogeneous political ideology: a majority of Muslims and Islamic regimes denounce those extremists supposedly representing Islam. Conversely, the extremists castigate regimes that are liberal, listen to reason, and seek a compromise with the West. Muslim extremists are concerned only about the fate of their religious compatriots and the larger interest of Islam. Therefore, they are prepared to raise arms and engage in clandestine warfare if their own religious brethren are violated in the religious, political or economic realm. This brings us to the first two concerns: namely, whether the principles of a just war are compromised by a particular power if it justifiably feels threatened by attacks from unsuspecting and invisible enemies.

It is now accepted by the US government that an ideal strategic response in an asymmetric conflict must include (a) preparation of public expectations for a long war despite its own military, economic, political and technological superiority; (b) development and deployment of armed forces specifically equipped and trained for counter-insurgency operations (Arreguin-Toft 2001: 123). But such adventurism brings it dangerously close to the ideological and pragmatic framework of radical Islamists.

In this confrontation, each side dwells within a hermetically sealed ideological framework and given national or communal interest, in which the other side's claims are treated as unjust, illogical and irrational. Unfortunately, the US administration in its commitment to American interests is blind to the extremist Muslim claim that it could be trespassing on Islam's sacred territory and responsible for a form of economic and political enslavement of Muslims. Americans see themselves as a powerful, yet victim community, defending themselves with restraint and reluctance against an overwhelming bigoted, malevolent and fanatical enemy. Therefore, in some circles, the war on terrorism is defined as 'a war of self-defence on the part of liberal democracies' (Howard 2002: 637).

Since conditions outside the United States are either extremely hostile or inimical or at best neutral, it is seen as imperative that the United States engage in an asymmetric war against Islamic extremism. As the campaign in Afghanistan highlighted, the USA became the judge, the jury and the executioner of those whom it regarded as enemies of the American state and its interest. Given this situation, one can predict with glum accuracy that the USA is likely to continue with a policy that is both less transparent and unethical when it comes to a confrontation with world Islamic terrorism.

There is a consensus in the West that al-Qa'ida 'represents the worst that globalisation has to offer' (Smith 2002: 45). Yet, as has been suggested by many scholars, a campaign against al-Qa'ida or global terrorism would be far more likely to succeed if it were genuinely international in character (Blackburn 2002: 23; Žižek 2002: 6). While there is recognition that the United States' perception of threat is credible, its allies are less convinced in terms of its tactics to eliminate those threats. Observers now argue that the 'war against terrorism' is being waged against terrorist networks and states harbouring terrorists, but not against state terrorism – the implication here being that the United States is in fact enforcing its own version of state terrorism. But how far does the international community accept such unilateral actions?

From a European perspective, a threat from extremist Islamists to Western interests exists. But it is not necessarily aimed at European interests. A behavioural audit of European powers – minus Britain – at the height of the US and Allied bombing of Afghanistan and later Iraq was that of prosperous traders with strong neutralist tendencies (Ali 2002; Ray 2003). Although London was fully committed to the war efforts in Afghanistan, the British public were not so forthcoming. Most European statesmen, policy-makers and citizenry agree that European pride and power are economic or cultural, but no longer invested in confrontational war. All other powers of the world are not given to any sense of outrage against militant Muslims unless, of course, the national interest of their country, as is the case of India, Israel, the Philippines and Russia, is directly threatened.

The Bush administration's war against terrorism is destined to be morally unsatisfying, because of the way people think about right and wrong (Byford 2002: 40). Whatever the authoritarian regimes in the Islamic world had to say under intense diplomatic pressure enforced by blunt military threat, the armed strikes against Afghanistan, synchronized with Israeli brutality in Palestine, are easily interpreted by the Islamic community as yet another attack on an Islamic state and, by extension, on Muslims in general and Islam in particular (Al Sayyid 2002: 187).[10]

Predictably, there was a mixed response to the US government's 'worldwide coalition against terror' from Muslim quarters. Apart from Jordan, Pakistan, Turkey and Uzbekistan, few Arab and Muslim governments adopted a position of total support for US military action in Afghanistan (Al Sayyid 2002: 181–2). Saudi Arabia, the staunchest of American allies in the Middle East, refused to allow the al-Kharj military base to be used for the bombing of Afghanistan. Similarly, when the Allied campaign against Iraq was undertaken in March 2003, all Muslim countries (bar Bahrain, Kuwait and Qatar) opposed the war.

As one leading Islamic scholar argued, 'the failure of international legality behind US unilateral military actions under the guise of "war on terror" promotes the cause of militant Islamic radicalism and undermines possibilities of support for international peace and protection of universal human rights in Islamic societies' (An-Na'im 2002: 162). Such insincerity and disregard for international laws and norms, in the opinion of some critics, are enforced by 'men who are democrats at home and dictators abroad. Internationally they rule by brute force. And their global governance is, by all the classic political definitions, tyrannical' (Monbiot 2003: 19). Unfortunately, the eagerness for unilateral intervention in other people's, society's and country's affairs and for wars abroad is potentially very high among these leaders (Lind 2003).

A sense of frustration and outrage has come to inhibit Muslims since the US war efforts in Afghanistan and more recently in Iraq. They see the hypocrisy of the USA and its interference in the everyday politics of Muslims – from Afghanistan to Sudan and Iraq to Chechnya. They have watched in disgust the US support for authoritarian and autocratic regimes well disposed to promoting long-term American interests. An influential international weekly, *Newsweek*, summed up the US foreign policy agenda in the post-Cold War era as 'a policy that favours friendly tyrants and authoritarian military dictatorships to hostile democratic governments'. Prior to 11 September 2001, the United States was in cahoots with several non-democratic regimes throughout the Islamic world.

This policy of containment had only one explicit aim – namely, the furtherance of American interests – and had very little to do with genuine grievances and aspirations of Muslims. Surely, the regrettable antagonism so evident today within the Islamic world against the United States has its origins in this unethical alliance and conspiracy. By underscoring the hegemonic designs of the United States and the repercussions this policy has on the everyday lives of Muslims, bin Laden was able to create a constituency of sympathizers among Islamists. By arguing (in the aftermath of the Iraqi campaign) that the United States is now more than ever committed to 'preserving the status quo (in the guise of "global stability") and ensuring the longevity of morally bankrupt regimes in Egypt, Saudi Arabia, the Persian Gulf, Pakistan, Uzbekistan and elsewhere', bin Laden has succeeded in sustaining an audience receptive to his message (Hoffman 2003: 27).

The outcome

The West was best prepared and best defended when it had a real sense of its enemy. Following the end of the Cold War and the collapse of Communist states, however, the 'Western imagination entered a decade of confusion and inefficiency, looking for suitable schematisation of the enemy' (Ali 2002; Kepel 2002). Communist North Korea and China received bouts of attention, but the growing *rapprochement* in the immediate aftermath of the Cold War with these two powers made it plain that there exists no long-term threat. In the fervent effort to identify threats in this phase, the United States and its allies made *ad hoc* identification of enemies that ranged from warlords to rogue states and even on occasion to pirates on the high seas.

Yet, none could provide an image of the enemy that could be used to shore up US and its allies' defence and, consequently, its permanent military preparedness. As a critic argues, 'only with 11 September did this imagination regain its power by constructing the image of bin Laden, the Islamic fundamentalist, and al-Qa'ida, his invisible network' (Žižek 2002: 6).

It should be borne in mind that Osama bin Laden has never mentioned al-Qa'ida publicly. In the context of the international community's war against bin Laden's terrorist network, the term was imposed externally by Western officials and media sources (McCloud and Dolnik 2002: 5). While the international community has not necessarily been blaming all post-11 September attacks on Western interests on al-Qa'ida, it has passively allowed others to claim themselves as belonging to al-Qa'ida. By elevating an invisible, amorphous enemy to the top brand name of international terrorism, Washington and its allies may have unwittingly allowed the organization with a specific command structure to attain leadership and may possibly have helped it identify and demarcate its future area of operation.

As mentioned earlier, the Bush administration cleverly floated the idea that al-Qa'ida and the Taliban were the same. By this wrong logic it convinced the outside world that an attack on the Taliban was indeed an attack on al-Qa'ida, as both were responsible for targeting American interests. Such reckless generalization, however, did more harm than good. According to one observer, 'the fear of being perceived as weak and indecisive made the Bush administration launch a war in Afghanistan. Like the proverbial drunk looking for his key underneath the street lamp not because he had lost it there but because that is where the light was, the American assault on Afghanistan was more a reflection of what it can do rather than what it ought to do' (Krishna 2002: 70). Although there is some truth in the above argument, one should also bear in mind that the United States was responding in accordance with the precepts of 'reflexive security'. This principle takes on board the fact that the controversial pre-emptive measure against a group, government or state which it fears may pose a threat to American interests. The identification of this 'elusive enemy' and its supposed aims found the clearest manifestation in President George Bush's pronouncement that 'these terrorists kill not merely to end lives but to disrupt and end a way of life. With every atrocity, they hope that America grows fearful, retreating from the world and forsaking our friends. They stand against us, because we stand in their way' (Bush 2001: 27). If we view two positions – namely, those of al-Qa'ida's terrorists and the US response to them – we realize that both have gained strength and live off each other's failures.

It is worth remembering in this context that the United States has exhibited very little appetite for diplomatic solutions to many intractable conflicts. For much of the second half of the twentieth century, the ideology of the US administration has been to ignore some of the pressing demands emanating from a section of Muslims. The latter constituency echoes the over-rehearsed claim that the United States is insensitive to the sufferings of the Palestinians under Israeli occupation. Indeed, there is some truth behind such accusations. Encapsulated by their own logic of victimhood and peddling a self-image as freedom-fighters, some Muslims have gone down the path of terrorism because all other avenues have proved meaningless or remain closed to them. Some strategic thinkers in the West are mindful of the dissent in some Muslim quarters and have envisaged this scenario: 'Where new enemies visit violence on us (i.e. the West) in startling ways; a future in which our cities are among the battlefields and our people are among the targets; a future in which more and more adversaries will possess the capability to bring war to the American homeland; a future where the old methods of deterrence are no longer sufficient – and new strategies and capabilities are needed to ensure peace and security' (Wolfowitz 2001: 4). Perhaps the United States and its allies are being drawn into a conflict of their own making. One could argue that an early intervention to protect suffering Afghans might have hindered the symbiotic growth of al-Qa'ida and the Taliban and, in turn, might have gone some way to preventing the terrorist strikes against US interests in their own homeland (Drumbl 2002: 1121).

If they were to turn the mirror on themselves and make a value judgement, they might realize that the anguish and the anger of a certain section of Muslims are direct results of mismanagement of Muslim affairs by a self-serving West (Said 1997; Midlarsky 1998; Chomsky 2001). There is no denying the fact that al-Qa'ida does not represent the true Islamic voice; but it certainly enjoys widespread sympathy among Muslims (Al Sayyid 2002; Ruthven 2002a). Osama bin Laden appeals to that segment of Muslims disenchanted to the point of hopelessness. Al-Qa'ida's logic of 'defending Islam's honour' is simply inescapable to this particular constituency, especially in the light of the Afghan and, more recently, the Iraqi campaign by the Allied forces.

Destroying the Taliban in Afghanistan – temporarily – will not prevent the emergence of something similar elsewhere (Bellamy 2001: 5). Isolating and defeating al-Qa'ida and its allies will require a political strategy that is willing to disengage from the forces of reaction in the Islamic world, and one that favours 'the forces of enlightenment reform, and democracy' (Blackburn 2002: 6). Since the USA is arrayed against an enemy that draws its populism from that section of the world community that 'sees itself as historically maligned, the importance of diplomacy and propaganda will be crucial for maintaining a global coalition that incorporates the vast internal legitimacy of key states' (Howard 2002: 639).

Conclusion

That al-Qa'ida is committed to a long-drawn-out campaign against the United States and the Western world is without doubt. In a press statement released almost nine months after the attacks on the World Trade Center, an al-Qa'ida spokesman made clear that 'as long as America insists on its unjust and biased policy towards Muslims in favour of Jews and Christians around the world, then . . . we will continue to hit it anywhere in the world'.[11] The succession and magnitude of attacks against Western interests throughout the world make it clear that al-Qa'ida does indeed believe itself to be fighting a war to save the *ummah*, or Islamic community, from the great Satan represented by the West (Scott Doran 2002: 28).

Osama bin Laden, members of al-Qa'ida, and most radical Muslims consider a prolonged conflict with the West as inevitable. Interestingly, a significant proportion of intellectuals and political leaders in Western Europe and the United States share this view. Contemplating the future operations of al-Qa'ida, Oliver Roy, a leading scholar, has predicted that the United States and Western Europe are destined to engage in a mortal incendiary combat in the coming years (Roy 2003: 24). The twin elements that pit radical Islamists and a constituency in the West against each other are their subscription to two entirely different value systems and differing power projections. While radical Muslims appreciate this conflict dynamics, they none the less hold that the asymmetry that exists between the West and the world of Islam is a temporary one.

The success of radical Islam, therefore, is predicated upon a long, arduous struggle and great hardship on the part of its followers – at the end of which their faith will prevail, and Islam will emerge triumphant. Radical Islam is profoundly effective in mounting a protest movement capable of retaliatory actions. As the events following 11 September have shown, radical Islam has no difficulty propping up activists, leaders and martyrs with an absolute commitment to their cause. Given the fact that Islam through the ages had similar experiences of defeat and eventual victory, such a mind-set among certain groups of Muslims is even more terrifying. The conclusion to be drawn here is that there is going to be a long-drawn-out war between radical political Islam and the West for years to come.

6   Poppy Cultivation and the Political Economy of the Civil War

> If we are going to ensure that terrorism is reduced, then we have to make political progress in Afghanistan and we have to give people an opportunity to develop a different way of life and a different way of increasing their living standards than reliance on the drugs trade.
>
> Tony Blair, 31 May 2003

Introduction

One of the less explored dimensions of the civil war in Afghanistan is the role of the 'narco-economy' in fuelling the conflict. One school of thought argues that civil war and state failure are generally accompanied by the prevalence of an economic vacuum. Since state failure coincides with the inability of the institutions of governance to maintain a viable economic structure, actors with non-traditional economic designs step in to fill the void. The underlying motivations of these actors fall into two categories: grievance and greed (Collier and Hoeffler 2000; Sambanis 2001).

In the absence of traditional means of resource accumulation and income regeneration, these new actors introduce and promote a dimension of economic practice considered illegitimate under normal conditions. The profits generated from this illegal economy fuel many contemporary conflicts. Civil war, in other words, provides the perfect environment for an accelerated growth in an 'illegal war economy'. In fact, it encourages participation of individuals at all levels of the society, who contribute to the practice either to settle their economic grievances or purely to satisfy their greed.

Farmers and traders engage in cultivation and production of illegal or banned substances under conditions of the diminished authority of the state. This is an established reality. According to one major study, in the past 20 years all drug-producing countries in the developing world had experienced one or more of the following: *coup d'état*, revolution, tribal tensions, violent ethnic and/or religious conflicts, invasion, intensive guerrilla war, and so on (Jamieson 1992: 11–12). A prolonged civil war produces three key conditions conducive to a rise in the production of narcotics.

First, civil war invariably leads to the destruction of traditional economic arrangements in a society. This forces farmers to engage in alternative cash crops, which require minimum involvement and result in maximum profit. Second, disgruntled groups in civil war may actively encourage or force farmers to shift from traditional modes of farming to coca, marijuana or poppy cultivation in order to contribute to their war efforts. Third, the state itself appears powerless to stop the cultivation and production, as it lacks any control over its disgruntled communities, masses and regions. This is true of several developing countries in the midst of civil wars, like Angola, Mozambique and Sierra Leone, or encountering civil war situations such as Burma, Colombia and Peru.

Afghanistan's ill fame as the largest producer and global exporter of opium is of recent origin. This notoriety developed against a background of the convergence of a complex set of economic, political and geostrategic factors, which have been in place for a long time and eventually led to this repute. However, the country's dependence on narcotics needs to be seen in the wider context of a criminal economy that has dominated Afghan society for centuries. Devoid of any natural resources, historically various rulers sustained their power with revenue drawn from conquests in the adjacent territories/states, notably India.

Both the political stability and economic sophistication of various regimes and the people depended largely on resources generated from loot, plunder, raids and taxes from neighbouring regions (Stobdan 1999: 719–20). When external conditions were unfavourable, Afghans turned against each other and resorted to banditry within the country to sustain themselves. Also, following exposure to a growing international market in narcotics, they resorted to large farming in various illicit plant alkaloids. Involvement in poppy cultivation, drugs peddling and arms smuggling, therefore, do not hold any moral significance for Afghans, but need to be seen as a part of the larger economic process.

Five different factors are crucial in explaining the introduction and expansion of large-scale poppy cultivation in Afghanistan. Of these, three are internal, and two external. However, since Afghanistan's current history is immensely influenced by external factors, it is hard to dissociate the effect of internal factors from that of external ones. First, the Soviet invasion of the country threw the society into chaos, and gave rise to ineffectual governments lacking control over the whole territory. This prompted unscrupulous warlords to take advantage of the situation by encouraging farmers to shift to poppy cultivation.

Second, degradation of agriculture and infrastructure owing to civil war created conditions which required farmers to engage in a cash crop that involved minimum involvement and maximum turnover. Opium poppy, with its short harvesting seasons and ability to survive in arid and semi-arid conditions, proved a life-giver to many farmers struggling to eke out a living. Third, the breakup of the Soviet Union and the emergence of independent Central Asian republics created an anarchical condition in the region conducive to drug traffickers and narcotics cartels.

Fourth, thanks to developments in communication networks, these actors greatly facilitated the export of Afghan narcotics to far-flung regions, thereby providing a continuous source of income to an otherwise destitute farming community. Fifth, rogue regimes unacceptable to the outside world resorted to a policy of active co-operation with poppy farmers and narcotics exporters in order to maintain their governmental structure. In this fragmented and unstable political environment, there emerged direct links between poppy cultivation, opium production, narco-trafficking and arms purchases for various sides in the civil war and, later, al-Qa'ida.

The background

A species of poppy known as *Papaver somniferum*, capable of producing resin in its flower head (known as opium), had been cultivated for centuries in Afghanistan. There is evidence to suggest that poppy farming has been a traditional crop in the country going back to medieval times (L. Dupree 1997; Rashid 2000). However, the level of opium production and export was determined by the nature of government and external demand. Naturally, depending on the nature and character of the internal and external environments, there have been periods of rise and slump in opium production in Afghanistan and, consequently, in the overall political economy of the country.

The Mughal emperor Akbar the Great saw opium as a useful source of revenue, and actively encouraged poppy cultivation among Pashtun subjects living in the north-western fringes of his mighty empire. Opium produced by Pashtuns was exported to neighbouring Persia and the whole of the Central Asian region to fill the Great Mughals' coffers (Moorhouse 1984: 245). In the nineteenth century, the British East India Company became a major patron of poppy farmers in Afghanistan by monopolizing the whole international trade in these narcotics. The British administration in turn depended heavily on the East India Company for channelling Afghan opium to China in its infamous Opium War campaign there.

Although opium has been integral to the country's economy, it would be wrong to assume that Afghans or various regimes have shown little or no respect for the international community's opinion regarding the production of these narcotics. In fact, under the auspices of the League of Nations, Afghanistan did enrol itself as one of the opium-producing countries. Following its admission to the United Nations, in 1945, Afghanistan prohibited the production of opium. Although the government remained committed to the ban, marginal farmers living in far-flung areas and dependent on poppy cultivation for their very survival continued to defy the ban, as the state was unable to provide them with alternative sources of income. To combat this illicit farming and to revive the otherwise poor economy previously dependent on hard currency through opium export, in 1956 the government of Zahir Shah requested the UN Commission on Narcotic Drugs to allow it to produce legally a limited amount of opium for export as a much-needed foreign currency earning.[1]

In the 1960s and until the early 1970s, when Zahir Shah's government was fully committed to economic and political reform, the state's development was hugely dependent on foreign aid.[2] Therefore, securing international economic aid and assistance was largely dependent on controlling poppy cultivation. If cultivation of poppy and production of poppy continued at all during this period, it was solely due to the constraints imposed on the government by the unavailability of resources to enforce the ban effectively. But, most important of all, 'militant tribes' inhabited areas of poppy cultivation in the country where government control was 'purely symbolic'. In the 1960s, the 'hippy trail' that went through Afghanistan provided further incentive to farmers in these areas to return to large-scale poppy farming to meet the growing demand in opium. Pashtuns, for whom 'smuggling had been a way of life', used this opportunity to keep the inter-state trade in narcotics alive.

Soviet occupation saw a massive drop in traditional agricultural practices. Almost half of agricultural farms were abandoned, and between one-half and two-thirds of all villages were bombed, between one-quarter and one-third of the country's irrigation systems were destroyed, and there was a 70 per cent decline in livestock (UNDP 1993: 10–11). This amounted to a loss of government control over the countryside. The rural economy was all but destroyed. These calamities imposed on Afghans created a chain reaction, whose end result was the introduction of a war economy primarily based on large-scale cultivation of poppy and the production of opium. As Barnett Rubin argues, 'as food subsidies were limited to the city dwellers and those in the refugee camps, farmers who were left in the inaccessible mountains and valleys had nowhere to turn to but rely on poppy cultivation' (Rubin 2000: 1791–2).

At this juncture, mujahidin who needed money to finance their war efforts found it extremely convenient to peddle opium (Urban 1988). In terms of purchasing power, opium was equal to gold or diamonds, and could generate the required money to buy armaments. Thus was born the concept of 'drugs for arms' trade in Afghanistan (Roy 1995; Rubin 1995b). As a document produced by the UN highlights, a global ban on opium production in many formal and open economies, Iran's withdrawal from poppy cultivation after the 1979 Islamic revolution, and, finally, a rising demand for opium in the world market provided perfect conditions for Afghanistan to assume the leadership in global opium production (UNDCP 2000: 142).

Throughout the Soviet occupation, poppy cultivation had effectively been included in the livelihood strategies of individual farmers, itinerant labourers and rural communities for a number of reasons. In the period following Soviet withdrawal, there was no noticeable change in the larger political process in terms of conflict between groups, and sporadic localized wars continued unabated. The tenuous central government in Kabul was in no position to maintain its authority throughout the country, let alone to provide food and other forms of economic subsidies which could perhaps have encouraged poppy farmers to abandon the opium harvest (Goodhand 2000: 271–3).

The absence of a peace dividend in this phase reinforced the informal opium economy, and in fact encouraged those involved in it to elevate it to a prime position. Patronage of warlords was another key factor in the post-Soviet withdrawal phase. The occasional interruption of war led only to the government in Kabul printing more paper money to meet its growing budget deficit. This in turn pushed up food prices. Overburdened by decades of famine, war and destitution, peasants had no choice but to depend far more heavily on poppy cultivation to sustain their livelihood.

While it is abundantly evident that civil war in Afghanistan contributed to the wholesale involvement of a substantial number of Afghans in the narco-economy, this also needs to be viewed in the context of poverty, underdevelopment, natural calamities and lack of external aid and investment. In other words, Afghanistan faced the multiple economic uncertainties facing many underdeveloped Third World countries. This had a significant effect on its populace; consequently, Afghans resorted to the production of opium as an alternative survival option. If we exclude the civil war dimension from the equation, from the perspective of destitute peasants, poppy cultivation was a necessary pre-condition for survival for the following interrelated practical reasons.

First, in an agrarian economy in which other cash crops failed to yield an effective return, poppy became the only alternative cash crop. Second, unlike other crops, poppy could be harvested within months, and often twice a year, subject to the availability of water. Third, it is labour-intensive: whole families and clans could find gainful employment in the harvesting. Fourth, unlike many other agricultural products, opium harvested from the poppy fruit could be stored for long periods owing to its non-perishable faculty. Fifth, unlike wheat, maize or other harvests, opium could be transported easily across barely accessible valleys and hazardous terrains. Sixth, in the absence of all other forms of wealth, opium became an easy source of household saving in an economy ravaged by famine and economic breakdown. Seventh, and last, owing to the existence of a continuous demand outside the country and far beyond, peasants could easily gain credit from local money-lenders and traffickers for their day-to-day existence with promises of poppy cultivation under the type of credit known as *salaam*.

Another key factor responsible for the continuation of the narco-economy at this stage was the unwitting acclimatiza-

tion of poppy farmers, labourers, opium producers and ped-
dlers to a trade which was initially a stopgap arrangement.
Their decade-long involvement in the farming, production
and understanding of the market development of an informal
infrastructural network, however, had made them masters of
a sustainable economic practice. As the Soviet withdrawal did
not facilitate peace, and there was no let-up in fighting among
various groups in a new round of civil war, those engaged in
this economy continued their practice (Ali 2002: 215).

Narcotics as weapons of war

The use of narcotics as a weapon of war has its origin in
Asiatic societies. In medieval Persia a Shi'a ruler introduced
the idea of committing individuals to impossible missions
against potential enemies. Soldiers who were high on hashish,
known as *hashisheen*, became death-defying fighters, and
their daring later gave rise to the term 'assassin'.[3] In the nineteenth century, imperial Britain pursued a policy of creating
opium addicts among Chinese in order to quell rebellion
against its incursion; this later came to be known as the
infamous Opium War. In peninsular South-east Asia, in the
region known as Indo-China, the first occupying colonial
force, France, and later the invading Americans resorted to
the introduction and supply of hard drugs and plant-based
narcotics to weaken and demoralize the enemy.[4]

The United States was long aware of the connection
between the warlords engaged in poppy cultivation and their
contribution to the menace of drugs in outlying areas. However, it did not wish to arrest the development: Washington
used the structures of narco-mafia and the narco-traffickers
as a counterweight against the Soviet *status quo* in the
region.

Paradoxical as it may seem, external actors boosted
large-scale poppy cultivation and heroin production in
Afghanistan. During the Soviet occupation of the country, in
a cleverly designed plan, Pakistan's Inter Services Intelligence
(ISI) and its American counterpart, the Central Intelligence

Agency (CIA) produced almost 70 per cent of the world's total supply of heroin in Pakistan to finance mujahidin war efforts against the Soviet occupying force (Bonner 1987; Rashid 2000). Since the long-term rationale was the end of the Soviet occupation, the United States and Pakistani governments consciously ignored the collusion between mujahidin, Pakistani drug traffickers, and elements of the military from the United States and Pakistan side (Rashid 2000: 120). In addition, to settle its own long-standing difference with India, the Pakistani secret service used profits from Afghan opiates to finance a secessionist uprising in Punjab in the 1980s and in Kashmir throughout the 1990s.[5]

The United States, in its opposition to the Soviet occupation of Afghanistan, did entertain the idea of introducing narcotics to open another front in its proxy war against Moscow. In well-documented but unverified studies that have appeared since the Soviet withdrawal, it is argued that Washington toyed with the idea of making Soviet Red Army soldiers drug addicts while they were in Afghanistan. In fact, President Ronald Reagan seriously contemplated this option under Operation Mosquito Initiative. While it is not clear whether this operation officially and deliberately implemented the narcotics clause, it is true that Washington encouraged the Afghan resistance to introduce Soviet to locally produced opium and its derivatives, and even made available other fancy and expensive narcotics from outside the region such as cocaine (Cooley 2000: 161).

Serving in an inhospitable terrain in a mindless war, the occupying Soviet forces were a demoralized lot. To gain temporary respite from the violence and atrocity raging all around them, and for short-term entertainment, some soldiers did indulge in the use of opium, hashish and other plant alkaloids. They became hooked to this habit in no time, and the affliction spread from the rank and file to non-military staff serving in Afghanistan. In a desperate attempt to curb this habit from spreading, Moscow put a ceiling on military personnel's postings in Afghanistan of nine months, but such measures did not stop the raging tide of drug addiction (Harrison 1995; Rashid 2000). Soviet soldiers who returned to their homeland after active service brought back habits that opened up another channel for poppy cultivation in Afghanistan. Many Russians privately argued that the problem of drug addiction among Russian soldiers was so acute that it forced Moscow to rethink its presence in Afghanistan.

Enter the Taliban

Although poppy cultivation in Afghanistan pre-dates the civil war, its steady rise can be attributed to it. The failure of the various warring factions to agree on power sharing after they took over Kabul in 1992 meant continuation of civil war. At this juncture, the United States, which was committed to supplying arms and providing other forms of economic assistance, had withdrawn from the scene, as its objective of Soviet withdrawal from the country was complete and the end of Cold War had begun a new era. Afghans, however, found themselves in the midst of another civil war. Starved of external money and arms, various warlords and political factions became increasingly dependent on the cultivation of poppy and the drugs trade to continue their war campaign.

Those jockeying for power in post-Soviet Afghanistan in the 1990s had to find new means of support to replace the subsidies once plentiful from Moscow or Washington. Without any economic safety network to support them, tens of thousands of Pashtun refugees, who returned from Pakistan when the Taliban took over Afghanistan, immediately engaged in poppy cultivation as the only available source of income (Rashid 2000: 118; Goodhand 2000: 268). Naturally, poppy cultivation received wide-scale attention in this phase and provided succour to the civil war economy. With the dissolution of the Soviet Union, the tightly defended ex-Soviet frontier became porous as newly independent republics lacking resources and a work-force could not defend it well. For the country's impoverished peasants, deep in debt and blighted by drought and internecine civil war, poppy farming was the only means of survival.

Because of international isolation and a need for cash to maintain the structure of its administration, the Taliban needed hard currency. And it had to depend on the drugs trade to finance the run-down economy and fight against those opposing the regime within the country. Although it denied that taxes on opium were sufficient to fund its military campaigns, the regime none the less imposed a 10 per cent levy on poppy cultivation well until the year 2000. It is a well-known fact that the Taliban institutionalized the production and trade in opium and a standardized system of taxation. The income generated from narcotics became the principal source of revenue for the state. According to UNDCP, the tax on drugs brought in between $15 and $27 million to the regime annually. Interestingly, the regime defended its stand on Islamic grounds, by comparing this mode of taxation to *zakat*, the Islamic tax levied for the poor.

The Taliban imposed three separate taxes on opium. Under the traditional system of *ushr,* a 10 per cent tax was levied on the produce, while another 20 per cent was imposed under the clause of *zakat*, or religious tax. But it was in the intra-state transit of opium and heroin that the Taliban derived most of its money, amounting to almost another 50 per cent. According to a World Bank study, the contraband trade in opium and arms in Afghanistan was worth about $2.5 billion – nearly half of the country's estimated GDP for the year 1997 (Rubin 2000: 1802).

Since the Taliban was extremely orthodox in its attitude to the overall working of Afghan society, one legitimately wonders how it could encourage the production of opium – for the Qur'an forbids those faithful to Islam from producing or consuming all forms of narcotics and intoxicants. Throughout its reign in power, the Taliban had an enigmatic attitude towards poppy cultivation. As early as 1997, the regime's chief ideologue and leader, Mullah Mohammed Omar Akhunzadeh, called for restrictions in both cultivation and trade. But others within the top echelons of the Taliban were less committed to this principle, and eventually made Mullah Omar realize the tremendous economic potential for an isolated, cash-starved regime.

Eventually a compromise was reached, and the Taliban came up with a unique way of confronting this dilemma. It banned the cultivation of marijuana and the production of hashish. Furthermore, those who consumed marijuana or were found in possession of the banned substance were severely punished. In fact, the Taliban made the abuse of drugs a criminal offence. However, it turned a blind eye to poppy cultivation and opium production, on the grounds that it was consumed by *kafirs*, or non-Muslims, and therefore the religious injunction did not apply in this case.[6] In the end, the Taliban attitude toward poppy cultivation, opium production and drug trafficking was a curious mix of religious principles, ambiguity and expediency (Cooley 2000: 148).

The Taliban regime had a greater understanding of the long-term effects of poppy cultivation. It recognized that being in the midst of opium production, Afghan society could not insulate itself from becoming its ultimate victims.[7] Equally important, it clearly understood the equation between the power of the warlords and drug production. While declaring the production and consumption of drugs as anti-Islamic, the Taliban sought to achieve two key goals: first, safeguarding society from the evils of narcotics and, second, eventually curtailing the power of the autonomous and semi-autonomous warlords against the central authority, which was directly linked to their involvement in the cultivation and sale of drugs. Indeed, the supreme leader of the Taliban, Mullah Omar, imposed an absolute ban on the cultivation of opium poppies, and enforced the ban most brutally.[8] It proved that the best way forward in terms of eradication was through a government or regime willing to enforce a ban.

While sensitive to the impact of drugs produced in Afghanistan, the Taliban did recognize the social devastation wreaked on their users. The Taliban were not reluctant to impose a ban on poppy cultivation, but they expected a reasonable return for any such step in this direction. It therefore agreed to make the cultivation of poppy illegal subject to recognition of the regime by the international community.

Yet it is argued that the Taliban drug policy toward the outside world was 'double-edged'. In the first place, the

Taliban actively encouraged export of opium and other derivatives to the West, in order to force the latter to come to the negotiating table and thus recognize the regime. The other edge of this policy sword was directed against Iran, which armed the anti-Taliban Shi'ite Muslim factions and the regime's mortal enemy, the Northern Alliance (Cooley 2000: 153). Throughout its reign, large shipments of opium regularly entered Iranian borders from southern Afghanistan. What the Afghans grew, the Iranians smoked or injected.[9]

By 1999, the government in Teheran had openly admitted the growing drugs menace within Iranian society. An otherwise intrepid regime confessed that it was fighting a losing battle against drugs coming from across its eastern frontier. The official figures released by Teheran highlighted the fact that at least 2 million Iranians were addicted to opium, morphine or heroin. Some analysts have since pointed out that the Taliban's apparent resolve to introduce drug addiction into Iranian society aimed at weakening the state there and thereby winning diplomatic recognition from the United States (Allix 1998: 94). Currently, 10 per cent of the total Iranian population are drug addicts.

In spite of its vile image, the Taliban was the first regime in Afghanistan's 300-year-old modern history to stop poppy cultivation. Between the years 1999 and 2001, in areas under Taliban control, poppy cultivation almost came to a halt. The Taliban had real and absolute power to reinforce their dictat in areas under their control. According to the reports produced by the UN Drug Control Program (UNDCP), the Taliban's ban on poppy cultivation reduced the opium harvest from 3,276 tons in 2000 to 185 tons in 2001 – a 96 per cent decline compared to previous years.

While the Taliban were blamed for promoting poppy cultivation, the reality was that almost half the heroin flowing out of Afghanistan was produced in areas controlled by the Northern Alliance (Whitaker 2001: 12). In fact, following the Taliban's ban on poppy cultivation and trade in drugs, the market was taken over by the Northern Alliance. In the months following the international campaign against the

Taliban and its removal from power, the bulk of the drug was being produced in strongholds of the West's putative partner, the Northern Alliance (F. Elliot 2001).

Our approach to comprehending the problem is unidimensional. The international community is as much to be blamed as Afghans for the continuation of narco-economics. The UN Security Council Resolution against the Taliban, passed on 15 November 1999, included among other things the need for the regime to ban poppy cultivation. The recommendations of the UN Drug Control Programme (UNDCP) were made transparent to the Taliban regime. While the regime fulfilled the obligations imposed upon it, the international follow-up was ambiguous and indecisive. While UNDCP aimed to launch projects for alternative farming, there was great reluctance on the part of donors to provide the requisite monetary assistance.

Breach of confidence was a major casualty in this framework. The inability of the UNDCP to assist in any long-term alternative agricultural plan produced a general sense of apathy among Afghans towards any kind of international promise. Farmers were far more demoralized as a result of this new arrangement, and had most to lose, compared to the Taliban or regional warlords. The sanctions came at a time when Afghanistan was experiencing its worst droughts for 25 years. Caught between the Taliban-imposed ban on poppy cultivation and drought, many Afghans simply fled the country.

The external dimension

The cultivation of poppy and the production of various opium derivates in Afghanistan need to be analysed in a wider context. The effect of poppy cultivation in Afghanistan poses a threefold challenge – at local, regional and global levels. First, at the local level it perpetuates the civil war situation by empowering the warlords. At the regional level, it weakens the state by disintegrating legal economies. At the global level, it eats into social relations. To stop communities, societies and states from sliding into this slow anarchical situation requires a sustained engagement with the issue.

In Africa, where illegal mining of diamonds and other precious stones was fuelling the war economy, the West took a stand whereby it bought diamonds produced only under peaceful and democratic conditions. Such simple measures had a widespread impact on conflicts in Sierra Leone, Angola, the Democratic Republic of Congo and Mozambique. But Afghanistan poses a challenge of a different nature. A successful and sustainable policy arrangement, therefore, needs to be multidimensional in its approach.

Under the Afghan Transit Trade Agreement (ATTA), landlocked Afghanistan has access to goods imported from the outside world via the Middle East and Pakistan. In the past, goods destined for Afghanistan were sent from various ports in the Persian Gulf and Pakistani ports in sealed containers. With the onset of civil war, however, a reverse transmission took place, whereby contraband from Afghanistan easily found its way into Pakistan and the Gulf region in sealed containers (Rubin 2000: 1793–5).

According to the UN, opium produced in Afghanistan and destined for the West has created a trail of addiction and social breakdown along the trafficking routes. In Central Asia, through which most of Afghanistan's produce is channelled, there is a substantial rise in drug addiction. Heroin addiction in Central Asia has been the fastest growing in the world since the late 1990s, with more than 300,000 opiate-takers, including children as young as ten.[10] Afghanistan's other immediate neighbours – Pakistan and Tajikistan – face serious security and social problems from trafficking and the vast expansion of drug abuse, which represent serious impediments to peace and development in the region.[11]

Two main routes exist for the opium produced in Afghanistan. The first, the Balkan route that traverses Iran, Turkey and the Balkans before entering Europe, is responsible for growing drug addiction along these transit routes. The second, the so-called Silk Route which follows the ancient caravan track through Central Asia and Russia before entering Europe, has created equally disastrous consequences for those living along it. Currently all the heroin that reaches Russia on its way to Western Europe has its origins in Afghanistan.[12]

The Russian mafia, with ties to Afghanistan established during the Soviet occupation, uses its resources and network to move opiates through Central Asia, Russia, the Baltics and finally into Europe (Rashid 2000: 120). Expanded interdiction efforts by regional and external powers have resulted, however, in low-intensity conflict with drug traffickers, leading to serious human rights violations and the abuse of legal norms. Moreover, tighter border controls to stop the narcotic infiltration have hindered trade in other essential commodities, thereby weakening the already fragile economies of the region.[13]

Afghanistan's resolve to extricate itself from the narco-economy is contingent upon the regional geopolitical situation. Since most or all the neighbouring countries in Central Asia and the Persian Gulf region are undemocratic, possibilities of dissent among disgruntled groups against various regimes will remain high (Misra 2001: 319). To fund their political campaigns, these groups will ultimately turn to Afghanistan to produce opium. Trafficking of drugs produced in Afghanistan is a major source of finance for various disgruntled opposition parties in authoritarian Central Asian republics. Similarly, Islamic radical groups aiming to overthrow existing regimes in the region have consistently resorted to the sale of opium and its derivatives produced in Afghanistan to continue their struggle (Misra 2001; Rumer 2002). A case in point is the Islamic Movement of Uzbekistan (IMU). Juma Namangani, one of its founders, allegedly seeks to control the prime drug transit routes in order to increase his market 'area' and thereby his power.[14]

Political instability, civil unrest and religious and nationalist tensions along the drug-trafficking route of South-west Asia – Europe's principal supply route – will continue to encourage the trading of arms for drugs, as was the case in Afghanistan (Jamieson 1992: 5). So long as the grey border areas of Afghanistan are controlled by restive tribes such as the Pathans, Uzbeks and Turkmen, whose dislocation on both sides of the border guarantees safe passage of drugs across, there will continue to be a market for poppy.

The alternative

According to the British Home Office, Afghanistan is the linch-pin in the illegal trade in opium and its derivatives in Britain.[15] In one of his statements on the opium dimension, British Prime Minister Tony Blair is reported to have remarked that the arms which warlords in Afghanistan were buying were paid for with the lives of young British people buying their drugs on British streets. His solution to the problem was the following: 'What we shall do in helping with the reconstruction of Afghanistan is to make it clear that we want Afghanistan to develop farming of proper agricultural produce, not produce for the drugs trade.'[16] Yet, as long as there is an unmet demand for opiates outside Afghanistan, poppy farmers, warlords and traffickers will have every incentive to continue with their trade. Unfortunately, like any other product or commodity, drugs are also governed by the economics of demand and supply. With the Allied bombing campaign in Afghanistan, there was a rise in the street price of illegal drugs in Britain.

Suggestions that, given United States commitment against drugs in Colombia, it is not going to leave Afghans to return to growing and processing poppies, is rather an ambitious hope (Emmot 2002: 18). While the United States continues to be in the forefront of the war against al-Qa'ida, its initia-tive regarding long-term strategies to deal with Afghanistan's poppy farming has remained rather uneven. Washington's response has been limited in scope, funding, involvement and imagination. As the International Crisis Group argues, Afghan drugs play only a small part in the USA's own nar-cotics problem. The bulk of opium and heroin produced in Afghanistan finds its way to Europe, not the United States (Davenport-Hines 2001). Little wonder there exists a sus-tained reluctance to seriously engage with the issue. However, this 'since it is not directly affecting us it is not our problem' attitude is fast changing.

Traditionally, drug production and trafficking were considered simply a social problem (Pearl 1994; Allix 1998). That definition, however, has been broadened in the wake of 11 September, and it is now regarded as a national security problem by many countries. The US government realizes that most terrorists and their world-wide network survive on resources produced by narco-trafficking. It is now an established fact that al-Qa'ida financed itself through profits derived from poppy cultivation in Afghanistan (Takeyh and Gvosdev 2002: 99). There is a new reckoning in the United States that it simply cannot ignore the issue of Afghan opium production. Following the events of 11 September 2001, the US State Department broadcasts a regular prime-time message on TV. The campaign against narcotics is meant to send a clear message: 'When Americans buy drugs, they provide money for the terrorists.'

Such degrees of patriotism, however, do not exist in the immediate vicinity of Afghanistan and within the European Union, where most of the Afghan opium and its derivatives are consumed. The EU member countries have funded UNDCP programmes, but have not established direct links with the countries of the region – a step which could help to tackle the problem. Moreover, this task is made more difficult by another kind of network. Links between ethnic groups of Asian origin with rights of residence within the European Community are using the cover of their predominantly law-abiding countrymen to run networks of drug-trafficking and money-laundering systems within and beyond EU borders (Jamieson 1992: 8). Furthermore, the future of international efforts to stem drug trafficking in Afghanistan and Central Asia remains uncertain, due to the ongoing military activities in the region and the shifting political alliances (Lubin, Klaits and Barsegian 2002: p. vi).

The production of illicit drugs and illegal mining and lumbering are integral to many civil war situations. These are often key aspects of the political economy of war. It is estimated that the global trade in illegal drugs is as great as the international tourist trade. Similarly, narco-trafficking is a most lucrative business, with returns that exceed those of the legal transactions in oil, and second only to the arms trade. Thanks to globalization, banking deregulation, free-trade agreements, civil wars and nationalist uprisings in various parts of the world, the production and trafficking of drugs is now considered a key resource with which to continue any kind of struggle, nationalist or otherwise.

The UNDCP survey on opium production in Afghanistan for the year 2002 confirmed that there was a huge increase in production. According to its estimates, Afghan farmers produced approximately 3,400 metric tons of opium that year, which is around 18 times higher than the previous year's figure. This statistic reveals two facts: first, the low production for the year 2001 was a result of a strict ban on poppy cultivation imposed by the Taliban in the last year of their rule; second, taking advantage of the power vacuum which preceded the collapse of the Taliban, poverty-stricken farmers and unscrupulous warlords engaged in renewed poppy cultivation and production of opium.[17] Ironically, this bumper crop followed the Afghan Interim Administration's ban on poppy cultivation imposed in January 2002. It goes without saying that absence of a powerful government in Kabul or a strong international presence outside Kabul encourages local warlords to continue with their poppy cultivation.

Afghanistan's central role in the international narcotics trade will continue for years to come. It will be extremely hard to curb the influence of a powerful and flexible network of traffickers, traders, producers and processors operating within and outside Afghanistan. Many of the coalition partners in the interim regime are warlords with a substantial stake in this criminal economy. Persuading them to refrain from this lucrative trade will be extremely hard. Since the very survival of the interim government is dependent on the good will of these warlords, the central executive cannot undertake any unilateral step in this direction.

Any effective campaign would require a massive, sustained infusion of foreign aid, coupled with a strong and equally sustained political will on the part of the current and subsequent regimes. Given the general state of affairs, there is little reason to expect either (Galeotti 2001). In the informal Afghan economy, narcotics have always been regarded as a substitute for any kind of credible currency. Farmers, traders and ordinary people keep narcotics in their homes rather than money, as it is the easiest of products to barter and buy every available recognized monetary unit. Ending Afghans' reliance on this kind of informal economy requires the emergence and promotion of a stable national economy. Without such an environment, it will be very hard to dissuade those involved in the whole process to refrain from their activities. Also, forcing farmers to give up poppy cultivation without providing them with effective alternative sources of income could lead to sporadic uprisings and the emergence of a much stronger local warlord and peasant nexus.

Conclusion

Opium production and the trafficking of its derivatives were and continue to be an important part of the war economy in Afghanistan. As previously stated, Afghan farmers' dependence on poppy cultivation was linked to questions of survival. The breakdown of the state and years of chronic drought meant that the farmers could no longer rely on state subsidies for sustenance. In Afghanistan, there exists a symbiotic relationship between farmers and warlords, both being dependent on poppy cultivation to meet their specific aims.

While the survival aspects were dominant in the case of Afghan farmers opting for poppy cultivation, for the warlords their very war effort was dependent on the production and sale of narcotics. Since warlords and drug traffickers profit from the conditions provided by a 'failed state', they are most likely to reject any attempt to raise the concerned state from its abject situation. As many contemporary studies suggest, profits from this form of trade can provide peace spoilers both the incentive and the ability to independently fund a return to war (Cooper 2002: 941). The opium poppy cartel in Afghanistan, with its extensive terrorist network, not only challenges the integrity of the fledgling new state but also undermines the viability of the new government.

According to some observers, the accumulated power and wealth of the transnational drug industry erodes the democratic foundations of key drug-producing and transit countries (Pearl 1994: 69). This broad characterization, applied to Afghanistan, acquaints us with the fact that although poppy cultivation is a source of livelihood for many Afghan farmers, in the last analysis their activities precipitated the breakdown of order, and ultimately contributed to state failure.

A successful strategy to counter drugs production and trade has to be multi-pronged in its approach. It will be relatively easy to instigate a crop substitution programme if there is a steady flow of external economic aid. While the first is easy in terms of sustained financial assistance, the second is hard to achieve. Law enforcement measures against poppy cultivators would be difficult to implement. It would depend on a variety of factors: namely, the existence of a consensual central government, the end of ethnic rivalry, the absorption of the warlords into the mainstream national political fabric, and a delinking of Afghanistan from external interveners such as drug traffickers, financiers and various intermediaries. A sustainable drug eradication programme will require not just an end to warlordism and a political agreement, but a regional economic transformation that provides alternative forms of livelihood and promises and delivers accountability.

Foreign donors, on whom the country's reconstruction depends, have made it clear that Afghanistan must succeed in eradicating this menace. Otherwise, the only donors left will be Western heroin addicts.[18] Strong words indeed. However, so long as there is a demand outside Afghanistan, and external agents keep enticing Afghan farmers to continue with their poppy cultivation, it will be impossible to put a lid on the problem. Studies conducted by the US State Department show that in Bolivia, where the USA provided millions of dollars to coca farmers to shift to alternative crops, it produced little or no result. The culprits here were external actors. Therefore, reducing the conflict potential within Afghanistan is dependent on cutting down on external demand for opium and its derivatives outside the country. Similarly, continuation of ethno-nationalist struggles in

Central Asia and the Caucasus will go on providing incentives for Afghans to engage in poppy cultivation. Therefore, addressing the problem within Afghanistan necessitates intervention in the wider regional context.

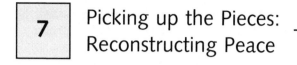

7   Picking up the Pieces: _____
Reconstructing Peace

War in Afghanistan did not begin with the Taliban and it will
not necessarily end with their removal.

International Crisis Group, 2001

Introduction

In Afghanistan, as discussed earlier, successive governments
have failed their citizens, and the citizens in turn have failed
their governments. In order to assess any future peace dividend in the country, it is imperative to make a thorough
examination of the post-war psyche of the citizenry, the attitude of the elites or decision-makers in the society, and finally
the response of the international community to the unfolding
events there. The main advantage of such a multi-modal
approach is that it illustrates every aspect of the conflict
predicated upon a longer rather than a shorter period.

Since Afghan society is structured primarily along ethnic
and tribal lines, because historical grievances are readily
remembered, because spoils of war and disunity are attractive, and because there exists an easy access to a vast cache
of weaponry to project autonomous decision-making, the
potential for continued instability is very high.[1] Indeed,
history tells us that people put more energy into conflict than
they do into peace. Since conditions of anarchy exist in post-

Taliban Afghanistan, chances are that some actors will be motivated 'to tear down whatever institutions and processes of governance exist' (Horf 1996: 25). Under these circumstances, what should be the international society's response to state collapse? What should be its approach to post-war reconstruction in a 'failed state' such as Afghanistan?

A flawed inheritance

A cursory glance at Afghan history in the late twentieth and early twenty-first centuries suggests that the crises that dominated political and economic life in the country between 1979 and 2002 were based on inherited problems that predated the Soviet invasion of 24 December 1979. The implosion of Afghan society during this period was exacerbated by the lack of civil and political rights, the collapsing or nonexisting mechanisms for the peaceful adjudication of disputes, and the inability or unwillingness of various regimes to safeguard and nurture diverse ethnic identities within a given cultural and political system. Furthermore, the pace of social change set by the People's Democratic Party of Afghanistan (PDPA), which gained power in a 1978 *coup* and remained in office until chronic infighting and Soviet displeasure resulted in its demise in May 1986, placed the society on a roller-coaster ride for which it was ill prepared. Reforms were introduced too fast and too soon, leading to a breakdown of order in some parts of the country.

Arguably, conditions within the country worsened in the years following the withdrawal of Soviet forces (Marsden 1999; Nojumi 2002). Sensing the breakdown of order, and motivated by a desire to rescue Afghanistan from internecine civil war, a group of students launched an offensive from the southern town of Kandahar in November 1994. The Taliban's call for an end to warlordism, inefficiency and corruption was welcomed by many local communities, and allowed demoralized local militia to retreat. Within a short length of time, the Taliban had brought more than 75 per cent of the country under its control and introduced a semblance of normality.

Yet the Taliban was just another group heading an already decaying structure. Unable to find remedies to stop the further rotting of state and society (due as much to a flawed inheritance as to external isolation), the Taliban instinctively had recourse to various fundamentalist orthodoxies, and initiated 'internal chaos' in the form of intense radicalism. Not surprisingly, many non-Afghans who were in the country to advance their own radical objectives cleverly exploited this atmosphere, using Afghanistan as a base from which to experiment with their own brand of governance and statecraft through the Taliban regime. Radical Muslims from all over the Islamic world – powerless to rise against their own regimes, which embraced Western concepts and culture – appreciated the sanctuary offered by the Taliban. They succeeded in convincing the Taliban to view the USA and the West as enemies, to enforce public execution, and to treat women as second-class citizens (unheard of in other strict Muslim societies, such as Iran and Pakistan). Additionally, they helped to sustain a polity based on these debased ideas. Ultimately, this led to the collapse of the Afghan state, and left society impaired.

What future is there for such societies? How can peace be reconstructed, and a semblance of normality be returned to the unfortunate masses? As has been stressed above, Afghanistan inherited certain variables that played a part in exacerbating the conflict. Just as important, though, peace efforts were undermined by a 'failure to overcome the much higher hurdle of designing enforceable and credible guarantees on the terms of an agreement – something that is very difficult for the combatants to do without outside assistance' (Walter 1999: 39).

Paul Collier and Anke Hoeffler of the World Bank contend that the risk of a return to civil war is likely to be high in societies or states that have had some experience of the breakdown of the state and the larger society (2001: 563–73). Civil wars always end, but they usually start up again (Bigombe, Collier and Sambanis 2000: 323). Between 1940 and 1990, more than 50 per cent of combatants participating in negotiations around the world were said to be willing to return to war (Walter 1999: 38).

According to the Collier and Hoeffler (2000) thesis, this phenomenon is due to policy-related pre-conflict and structural risk factors. For instance, control of national resources and their ineffective distribution contribute to social inequality. Absence of alternative economic opportunities pushes some young uneducated males to the front lines, while predatory ethnic hegemony (by the majority group) provides the perfect breeding ground for violence. Similarly, in the structural domain, a centre–periphery population divide separates the elite from a significant proportion of the population that is economically backward and lives beyond the immediate limits of the state's authority. This increases the prospect of opposition to the state developing.

Although the larger economic and political situation in Afghanistan was affected by the kind of pre-conflict and structural risk factors noted above, the presence or absence of any sound economic and developmental infrastructure made some groups highly rapacious. This had three major outcomes. First, society became inured to an unending cycle of internal violence. Second, thousands of people fled the country to live as refugees in barely humane conditions elsewhere. Third, an informal, invidious economy came into existence to serve the various minorities and communities that the state wilfully ignored or could not reach.

This section of society became dependent on extreme trade practices, such as arms smuggling and narcotics production, in order to survive. Even now, certain groups and communities continue to rely heavily on such illicit pursuits, as the interim government's post-war reconstruction programme has not been extended beyond the capital. This has created conditions that have allowed some warlords to establish a state within a state. Ismail Khan, for example, runs Herat with his own private militia, and has introduced his own system of justice, economic structure and government.

A society slides into civil war and back again as a result of continued hegemonic control by a particular group. A successful core requires a periphery to sustain it (Horowitz 1985; O'Loughlin 1987). This perpetuates ethnic strife and can eventually lead to civil war. The Afghan reconstruction effort rests on creating a non-predatory economic/political structure that allows everyone a stake. It will remain ineffective, however, unless the citizenry commits to ethnic cohesion. On many occasions, the state or the regime responsible for multicultural governance has been rendered powerless when the majority (in this instance, the Pashtuns) has hijacked the state and unleashed a campaign of terror, undermining a constitution that guarantees the protection of minorities.[2] Similarly, refugees and the displaced populace play an equally important part in designing or destroying order in a war-torn society.

Displacement and anarchy

What role have Afghan refugees played in the larger political process? During the past 25 years, over 5 million Afghans have fled to Pakistan, Iran and India, and over 1 million were displaced internally. According to the United Nations High Commissioner for Refugees (UNHCR) – the main body monitoring the movement of Afghans inside and outside of the country – around 3.5 million are still residing in Iran and Pakistan. Life expectancy in Afghanistan is one of the lowest in the world: Afghan men and women can expect to live to 43 and 44 years of age, respectively. The infant mortality rate is 200 per 1,000 births. Almost a quarter of a century after the start of the protracted displacement, Afghans still hold the unfortunate record of being the single largest refugee group in the world.

From the Soviet occupation until the removal of the Taliban, there were several waves of refugees. In fact, a significant number lived through as many as four episodes of forced migration during this period. Displacement was caused by the arrival of Soviet forces, violence between rival mujahidin factions, the policies of the repressive Taliban regime (combined with the worst droughts for 30 years) and the 2001–2 international military campaign under the aegis of the USA (Schmeidl 2002: 13). Dislocation leaves deep emotional scars; on occasion, it tears at the human identity of a refugee. In Islam, where an individual's position in society is dependent on honour, the situation can lead a person to engage in actions that he or she would otherwise abhor.[3]

Refugees have been at the forefront of any kind of political development in Afghanistan over the past 23 years. At the beginning, it was the Afghan refugees in Pakistan who constituted the bulk of the mujahidin force that resisted the Soviets. Later, most Taliban recruits came from the refugee camps in Pakistan. Notably, the current interim government contains figures who were high-ranking refugees during the Taliban era. And it is the same refugees and émigrés who are engaged in steering the reconstruction initiative, and busy providing insight into the multifaceted character of Afghan society.

It is argued that the 'returning diaspora can puncture the peace process' before the society actually attains a degree of relative normality and calm (Sambanis 2001). Diasporas harbour grievances for longer periods than resident populations. It has been suggested that, since a diaspora does not bear any of the direct costs of conflict, it has a greater incentive to engage in vengeance (Bigombe, Collier and Sambanis 2000: 333–4). Additionally, refugees easily buy into propaganda, rumour and unsubstantiated recollections. In the years following the Soviet withdrawal, returning refugees from Pakistan, along with PDPA sympathizers who remained in the country, launched terror campaigns throughout the land. Subsequently, when they managed to fill the power vacuum in the form of the Taliban, the persecution of minorities continued under the new regime. Some scholars contend that many of those who were displaced (especially those who moved to Pakistan) during the civil war years 'lost the art of compromise' – hence the perpetuation of low levels of ethnic cleansing.

As Collier and Hoeffler highlight, globally displaced, young uneducated males are often the best recruits for civil wars. With little or nothing to lose, they are more likely to enlist with a particular militia leader. Under-educated or uneducated young men and former mujahidin fighters and village mullahs who comprised the Taliban never seemed to be offering any coherent notion of state or society. Their own brand of religious idealism (including the Deobandi, Salafi and Wahabi interpretations of Hanafi Islam), the introduction of an almost medieval political culture, and an overtly hostile attitude to certain universal principles further reversed the growth of the Afghan state after two decades of civil war. In promoting virtue and the abolition of vice, the Taliban and its cohorts jettisoned issues like political rights and the protection of minority cultures.

This situation was not unique in itself. In recent years, several African regimes – such as those of President Robert Mugabe in Zimbabwe and President Charles Taylor in Liberia – have experimented with their own brand of idealism, leading to the regression of the state. Invariably, the collapse of the state establishes conditions of anarchy, which, in turn, create a security dilemma for ethnically divided groups. When combined with the advantages gained by the aggressor through its numerical strength, level of territorial control and historical memory, violence is a 'natural' outcome (Posen 1993; Duffield 1998).

In the absence of governments or regimes assuming responsibility for reintegrating returning refugees and other displaced peoples, there is a greater risk of them acquiring a predatory attitude in war-torn societies. The culture of vengeance that exists among some Afghan factions compounds future conflict potential. Rebuilding Afghanistan does not end with providing the basic minimum to a war-weary populace; nor is the return of refugees a marker for successful reconstruction. Rather, the psychology of vengeance needs to be eradicated from the diaspora, which will eventually constitute a crucial element in the ethno-political and economic fabric.

The civil war involved many aspects of psychological warfare. People were betrayed not only by their leaders, but also by their neighbours. In this climate, the principal casualty was trust. A majority of Afghans continue to see their victims or the victor as a 'continuing threat'. For example, 'land and property issues that typically complicate repatriation after long-term exile were rarely a source of conflict between returnees and the community members who had remained. This pattern, however, may not necessarily continue in future' (Shurke, Strand and Harpviken 2002: 48). In psycho-social terms, individuals who have witnessed absolute horrors are more likely to engage in such acts themselves if they are forced into such a situation. In this Hobbesian-style interregnum, the victimized tend to see the world as dangerous, and those outside their immediate domain as hostile. True, the process of victimization was mutually enforced in most instances in Afghanistan – hardly a consolation. While demands for retribution are present in all conflict-ridden societies, it is particularly difficult for a society governed by tribal rules of vendetta to gloss over past injustices and atrocities.[4] Oppression, as V. S. Naipaul argues, does not make people saintly; it makes them potential killers. All victims are dangerous.

Returning refugees or displaced people have often resorted to the worst possible methods of revenge. The macabre treatment accorded to Najibullah prior to his public execution is a case in point. The mujahidin and the crowd that undertook this act believed that the country was politically impotent, because the leadership was a puppet of the Soviet Union. Equally tragic were the capacity audiences that gathered in Kabul's Olympic stadium to witness public floggings, amputations and executions during the Taliban era. Those who attended these gory spectacles were there to satiate their anger. One Afghan revealed to a non-Afghan friend: 'people went to support it out of a strange kind of "well-at-least-it-is-not-happening-to-me mentality"'. This feeling of security in insecurity can also lead an individual to engage in brutality. From a purely academic perspective, manifestation of such 'personal behavioural violence' is the outcome of a desire to 'discipline' the 'other'.

Unfortunately, politics in Afghanistan operates in accordance with a closed cycle of revenge and counter-revenge. The explicit delight of those who partook in the killing of the Civil Aviation Minister, Abdul Rahman, at Kabul airport on 14 February 2002, for instance, further testifies to the deep-seated psychosis that exists among a section of the citizenry.[5] Even during the traditional Loya Jirgah in June 2002, some delegates cursed and threatened their opponents who were sitting only a few yards away – while the attention of the whole world was focused on the proceedings.[6] One could view the assassination of Vice-President Haji Abdul Qadir on 6 July 2002 in the same light.

In societies emerging from protracted civil war, the general mass not only seek avenues to avenge their past misfortunes (whenever possible); they tend to devalue their victims, believing that they have brought suffering on themselves through their non-nationalistic actions or via gross violation of society at large (Walter 1999). Ironically, the current transitional political alliance is built on the good will of several leaders who themselves have serious wartime criminal records and should be brought to book. Yet, 'with violations widely committed by all parties, holding those responsible will be difficult' (Shurke, Strand and Harpviken 2002: 35) – especially so when some of the culprits have managed to elect themselves to the Loya Jirgah through intimidation; a few even hold positions in the interim administration of President Hamid Karzai.[7]

So, how are trusting relationships built between former enemies? How is compromise to be reached? How can the people be made to live shared lives? Introducing a semblance of 'normal' life when the very existence of individuals has been marred by endless catastrophes is tremendously difficult (Sontag 2003). 'Addressing prior hurts, pain, and violence that the groups have inflicted on each other, and members of the groups assuming responsibility for their group's actions and showing empathy to each other, can be extremely helpful' (Staub 2001: 297). Unfortunately, unlike in the West, where there are a variety of institutional mechanisms for dealing with all kinds of trauma, such facilities are virtually non-existent or unheard of in many conflict zones.

In the Balkans, for example, psycho-social assistance was offered on a large scale to the population as part of the international humanitarian aid package. That all parties in Afghanistan need to go through a similar healing process is not an exaggeration. While there is constant talk among the scores of non-governmental organizations and international agencies present in Afghanistan to provide food assistance and help refugees relocate, there is very little on offer in regard to psycho-social projects like counselling and psychotherapy. Should such services be available to Afghans on a large scale, the potential for inter-ethnic or inter-group violence might be dramatically reduced.

Peacekeeping and civil peace

Post-war reconstruction is a long-term, comprehensive project that requires unremitting effort by the governing regime, the international community, and organizations like the UN. (It should be noted that all post-war reconstruction efforts – with the exception of Western Europe after World War II, under the Marshall Plan – have been failures.[8]) While all of the concerned parties shoulder equal responsibility for successful reconstruction, co-ordination by external actors is crucial. In the past, the UN directed and led such initiatives in the developing world; more recently, the European Union has assumed the task within its territorial sphere, most notably in the former Yugoslavia. The onus to rebuild a state or society, however, is generally on the power (or powers) that intervened in that particular country in the first place. It would be logical to argue, therefore, that the USA should bear the brunt of the responsibility for rebuilding a viable Afghan state. The tendency, though, is to abandon the society or state as soon as the armed intervention has achieved its objective – in this case, 'regime change'.

Within the American foreign policy establishment there has been a sea change in attitude to post-war reconstruction. The 'model of "nation-building" bequeathed by the Clinton administration has been discretely abandoned by the Bush administration' (Gottfried 2002: 156–7). This was evident in Washington's decision to leave state rebuilding in the former Yugoslavia to the Europeans and those who cared about this fractured society. Similarly, US President George W. Bush's administration is equally reluctant to become embroiled in the social and political reconstruction of developing societies unless they pose a direct threat to American interests. Many of the challenges facing Afghanistan might be resolved through greater US-led commitments to peacekeeping and nation-building (Goodson 2003: 95).

The US commitment to post-war reconstruction in Afghanistan, however, is at best humanitarian, and at worst ambiguous. Washington recognizes that financial assistance plays a pivotal role in such efforts, and is generous in that regard (it has provided around $200 million to date). But it has brushed aside any suggestion of involvement in regime reconstruction or nation-building. In August 2002, US Secretary of Defense Donald Rumsfeld stressed that 'it is up to other countries to do more', and 'nation-building is something that Washington is not prepared to undertake'.[9] This is quite a departure from remarks made by US Secretary of State Colin Powell on 29 November 2001: 'The President and everybody in [the] (Bush) Administration are committed to doing what is necessary for the humanitarian relief [of] the suffering Afghans, but beyond that, we will not walk out. We are committed to rebuilding that society and giving all of those people hope – not just hope, but the reality of having a better life for themselves and for their children. This is our commitment.'[10]

The international community cannot afford not to 'engage' in Afghanistan, as it did between 1992 and 2001. It was out of this space that al-Qa'ida and a new form of international terrorism emerged. While it is perhaps too early to spell out the nature of this commitment, a sustained military presence, such as the one at Camp Rhino near Kandahar, to oversee security matters cannot be ruled out. Moreover, the response of Japan, the EU and many other Western actors will, to a significant extent, be dictated by the reaction of Washington.

It is generally believed that a strong external peacekeeping force can help to prevent the escalation of violence in conflict zones. Peacekeeping falls into two key categories. The first involves separating two contending parties, as in Cyprus, Kashmir and on the border between Eritrea and Ethiopia, and having 'blue helmets' present on the ground. The second involves dispatching a mission to an ethnically mixed zone under a single administration, as was the case in Bosnia, the Central African Republic and Sierra Leone. Peacekeeping forces, military police and other authorities can play a significant role in arms decommissioning and in controlling the influx of weapons, and, of course, they can help temper a militant mood and curb vendetta action.

While arms decommissioning or disarmament is vital to the future political stability of Afghanistan, there are serious reservations about the international community's ability and willingness to perform the task. (It is worth pointing out that, despite the best efforts of Western nations, disarmament still remains a distant objective in Macedonia.) Also, it is unclear how peace will return to Afghanistan if the West (especially the UK and the USA) continues to rearm some warlords in order to establish parity among the factions.

Some 60,000 peacekeepers were stationed in Bosnia-Herzegovina, and another 40,000 were earmarked for Kosovo. By contrast, as of September 2002, the International Security Assistance Force (ISAF) comprises around 5,000 personnel, most of whom are confined to Kabul. Yet the interim government demands that the international community provide more troops. How seriously should this call be taken? All parties to the conflict have signed up to the new constitutional arrangements, but the *continuous* presence of foreign troops would be highly sensitive.

What if the larger society is reluctant to accept any kind of authoritarian external intervention in social life? Whether civil, military, political or humanitarian, intervention is a form of interference; by definition, it undermines the sacred autonomy of an individual, society or state. Although the notion of state sovereignty is in steady decline owing to the forces of globalization, the citizenry of various states have not developed a corresponding level of appreciation for universalism or Western values.

An apparently benign resolve to promote good governance in a third country unfortunately smacks of superiority (Žižek 2002: 6). Since democracy and good governance are hard to promote in a country emerging from civil war without some sort of external policing, there is an obvious danger of the whole project being construed as a form of colonialism. As Paul Kennedy suggests, this raises 'an ultimate insidious question: is the very striving for the maintenance of America's place in Afghanistan in particular and the world at large actually desirable?' (Kennedy 2001: 76–7). Throughout the modern history of Afghanistan, leaders have always been scornful about Western involvement in the internal affairs of the state. Irrespective of their ethnic denomination, Afghans are fiercely protective of their sovereignty and independence.

The contention that they are 'guns for hire' and constantly negotiate with the highest bidder has limited applicability. Such alliances in the past were governed by the need to respond to short-term political insecurities, and did not necessarily imply selling out to external bidders. According to one critic, 'two Afghan tribes might fight each other to death for control of power or resources, but the mere presence of an external force in their frontier would weld them together in a common cause i.e. the protection of the Afghan state and its *izzat* or honour'(L. Dupree 1997: 330). The ongoing presence of foreign soldiers will be construed as an occupation. In such an eventuality, trust will be the first casualty, leading to hostile exchanges between the Afghan factions and US and multinational troops.

An overview of some other post-war reconstruction initiatives reinforces such a pessimistic conclusion. In the Balkans, Bosnia-Herzegovina and Kosovo are 'being administered as colonies in all but name by international organizations backed by American and European soldiers' (Ferguson 2001: 123). While opposition to the deployment of some 50,000 North Atlantic Treaty Organization (NATO) troops is muted among local Balkan communities, Afghans are unlikely to display the same tolerance. The very concept of peacekeeping is still alien and confusing to most Afghans. Some question the need for foreign peacekeepers when Afghanistan has millions of men under arms who could do the job.

Peacekeeping missions in underdeveloped countries often undermine the self-worth and pride of local people.[11] The objectives of the operation are compromised if militia or war-lords are sustained by one of the key external actors (Durch 1997; Feil 2002). In the Balkans, Cambodia and various parts of Africa, a parasitic economic relationship developed between locals and multinational forces. For example, peace-keepers were responsible for creating a thriving market for prostitution. A prolonged international troop deployment in Afghanistan could well lead to the same scenario; the back-lash from a conservative Islamic society would be enormous. In such circumstances, the legality of any government that allowed the peacekeepers to remain would be highly con-tested. The assassination in April 2003 of Mullah Jailani (a respected politician, who sheltered Hamid Karzai during the Taliban rule) and Ricardo Munguia, a member of the Inter-national Committee for the Red Cross (ICRC), in the same week aimed at sending an explicit message to the government of President Karzai as to the price it must pay for playing into the hands of outsiders.

Creating a centralized state

Interventions always have political implications. In Somalia, for instance, the initial intervention by the USA favoured one claimant to power (Ali Mahdi Mohamed) over the other (Mohamed Farah Aideed). Unsurprisingly, the US-led peace-keeping force became yet another faction in the conflict. This politicized the original mission of establishing a democratic regime and promoting a viable state (Hirsch and Oakley 1995). Predictably, far from creating the conditions needed to establish a transitional national council by disarming the clans and warlords, these troops were forced to protect their own lives and beat a hasty retreat (Haass 1999: 46). It is argued that 'the military strategy used in Afghanistan pro-duced long-term political ramifications – that is at odds with post-conflict reconstruction' (Goodson 2003: 86).

In Afghanistan, while the initial reliance on the Northern Alliance produced the desired result of ousting the Taliban, it is unlikely to guarantee peace in years to come.[12] In fact, the international community's dependence on local auxiliaries to combat a given regime or ethnic group often generates a permanent climate of conflict. Kosovo is a case in point. In spite of all the hard talk by the interveners, the Kosovo Liberation Army (KLA) remains a potential threat to Serbia's transition to a multi-ethnic polity.[13] Under present conditions, any violence in Afghanistan will be very difficult to bring under control. There is a considerable stockpile of armaments; the interim alliance is shaky; sections of the population, especially unemployed foot soldiers, feel alienated from the existing system of governance; and rival warlords and groups easily and quickly become polarized.[14]

How far can the international community go to produce a patchwork of popularly elected regimes in societies emerging from armed conflict, to impose principles of democracy and human rights, and to create a sense of nationality? 'International interventions may prove necessary but not sufficient to ensure long-term commitments to peaceful relations. Where confidence-building measures fail to overcome ethnic fears, the state can fragment and the international community can become by default the guarantor of last resort for desperate peoples caught up in intense civil wars' (Rothchild and Lake 1998: 224–5). Can the international community remain engaged in Afghanistan if there is a dramatic challenge to the limited peace?

If a state fails to combat the incentives to violence rooted in the strategic interactions of ethnic groups, it is necessary to look to the international community and ask whether external intervention can safeguard minorities and protect the helpless citizenry (Rothchild and Lake 1998: 213). It is a reality that 'failed states lacking control and unwilling to live with the uncertainties of ongoing negotiations ... opt for heavy-handed repression in an effort to compensate for their weakness' (Lapidus and de Nevers 1995: 35). All the regimes in Afghanistan since the overthrow of King Zahir Shah in 1973 have adopted such an approach.

Negotiations to end a civil war are more likely to fail if competing groups are not serious about making concessions. Part of the reason why many peace processes collapse in deeply divided societies has to do with ethnic plurality. Societies relapse into civil war because the partners in the project do not develop a language and mechanism that treat all constituent parties equally. According to Donald Horowitz, 'not all leaders in ethnically divided states want to promote accommodation' (Horowitz 1985: 564). Often they owe their power to 'ethnic' divisions, which they exploit and promote. Perverse as it may seem, without these splits, they would simply lose their power base. For many of these leaders, therefore, pressure to maintain the gulf is enormous.[15] In order to convince people of the peace dividend and to demobilize the factions so that they do not return to violence, it is crucial that combatants surrender power to a single administration. The nature of the central government, however, is crucial to creating an atmosphere of trust. If the new regime is not heterogeneous, or is narrow-minded in its methods, it will be impossible to achieve a viable transition to peace.

Whenever there was a temporary cessation of hostilities in Afghanistan, various regimes tried to impose a centralizing authority. Attempts were feeble, though, owing to a failure to set up a coalition that could rise above ethnic parochialism. Although Pashtuns were the 'state-forming ethnos', they were always reluctant to take on board other ethnic partners in their nation-building ventures.[16]

How does one initiate nation-building in the absence of a single notion of identity? A degree of unity existed in Afghanistan as a result of a common currency, flag, central government and history of foreign aggression. Nevertheless, the state was torn by the logic of ethnic and linguistic belonging. Strategies adopted by various regimes to counter this were varied. The Communists, for instance, promoted the forces of modernist civic nationalism, believing that, once indoctrinated with the trappings of modernity, ethnic groups would abandon their primordial ties. In the post-Taliban era, Afghans need to ask themselves what could infuse a sense of common nationhood among the myriad factions, groups and tribal communities.

The challenge of creating an Afghan state from the grass roots is daunting. Contrary to the views of many observers,

Afghanistan did have a civil society (throughout the Soviet occupation) that was independent of the state.[17] Of course, it had its flaws. A section of the middle class, the Afghan staff of various NGOs and other international bodies, and the indigenous business community remained independent of the predatory state, but their families (the key unit in Afghan society) remained close to it as part of a coping strategy. This divided loyalty often led to activities that could be interpreted as anti-state. In other words, instead of concentrating on peaceful developmental practices, many were forced to improvise and formulate survival strategies based on invidious economic practices, such as poppy cultivation, arms smuggling and banditry.

Owing to the overwhelming tribal character of society and the loyalty of the people to their leaders, a great deal of responsibility for reconciliation lies with the elites. However, Afghanistan's ruling elite is an incoherent, mutually recriminative and hostile grouping of individuals, tribal leaders and warlords whose quarrels and divisions make them incapable of acting as a united political force.[18] Therefore, the elites need to reinvent themselves: many Afghans are frustrated with the relentless warmongering, and genuinely wish to abandon the military adventurism that generates little or no benefit for the wider populace.[19] If these elites could be convinced of a long-term approach that guaranteed advantages to them and their people and simultaneously nurtured the fledgling state, the nation-building task would become much less daunting. Should they fail to commit to reconciliation, it is up to society to instigate a change of political leadership.

Scrutiny of events following the demise of the Taliban and the accession of a broad interim coalition suggests that a new elite may be coming into existence. In a cleverly orchestrated plan, the USA is promoting a new leadership via Karzai, the US Special Envoy to Afghanistan, Zalmay Khalilzad, and the Loya Jirgah. Prior to his assassination in July 2002, Washington blocked the appointment of Haji Qadir – a keen supporter of the US campaign against al-Qa'ida – as Interior Minister because of his reputation as a drugs baron.[20] One could argue that the USA has 'given' the state to the

Panjshiris, and is punishing the Pashtuns for having invited Osama bin Laden to Afghanistan and having hosted and assisted his terrorist network and mission.

The task before Karzai is to begin reconstruction of a largely dilapidated country, enforce law and order in the face of endemic warlordism, and, most importantly, produce a new constitution with the elected members of the Loya Jirgah that will pave the way for constitutional democracy in two years' time. In terms of ethnicity, Karzai's cabinet strikes a balance between Pashtuns and Tajiks, with tacit support from Hazaras.[21] Yet, as the International Crisis Group put it, 'an all consuming concern for short-term stability caused key Afghan and international decision makers to bow to undemocratic demands'.[22] Powerful regional warlords were given key positions, but they have since refrained from expressing their allegiance to the central authority. The paramount concern, of course, is whether Karzai has the 'substance to lead his country towards lasting stability and prosperity' despite recurring violence, ethnic division and an unpredictable group of international financiers and aid agencies.

What role for donors and aid agencies?

The end of the ideological rivalry of the Cold War period has meant that donor countries and foreign aid workers have more room to manoeuvre in conflict zones. Issues like human and minority rights, ethnic plurality and democratization now feature prominently on the agendas of agencies involved in post-war reconstruction. However, the response of donors often comes too late and is motivated by political rather than humanitarian concerns, and often demonstrates a double standard. [23] The best possible example was the launching of a new 'stability pact' for the Balkans in 1999, while Liberia descended into anarchy. This reinforces the claim that humanitarian aid has increasingly become 'politically-driven' rather than 'needs-driven'.

Unfortunately, the Western conception of humanitarianism is culturally specific and has its own biases (Parekh 1997;

Chandler 2002). According to Milton Esman, 'Humility and prudence concerning interventions in societies understood imperfectly have not been prominent in development assistance and stabilisation operations. Yet humility and prudence are precisely what are needed for interventions designed to influence such complex and uncertain subjects as economic institutions and interethnic relations' (Esman 2001: 243).

Given the overwhelming Islamic character of Afghanistan and the perpetual inter-ethnic rivalry in the country, any form of external involvement is precarious. If democracy is applied too hastily, the majority Pashtuns will win the election and take control of government. In fact, proportional representation and universal suffrage can prove to be a politically destabilizing factor. If the Pashtuns gain the upper hand (through this process), the minority ethnic partners will feel alienated. Yet allowing the minorities an equal say in the formulation of policy and the development of the system of governance will mobilize Pashtun opposition – perceiving others to be gaining at their expense. As emphasized earlier, Afghans of all ethnic denominations are fiercely independent and proud people.

Although they have expressed allegiance to several external powers in the past, their commitment to their country's sovereignty and honour remains undisputed. Indeed, over-enthusiasm to make headway on female education, the introduction of Western models of equality, and the practice of secular politics, for instance, in this closed, religiously charged and tradition-bound society is likely to be counterproductive.[24] The international community, therefore, must go slow, develop a sound perspective, make an informed decision on how the situation can be altered, and then prescribe suitable cures.

'A commitment to peace is as important as commitment to war, but it is far more difficult to sustain' (Shawcross 2000: 376). Lack of human and social security and an absence of guarantees can make people suspicious of the long-term objectives of the regime in power and of the state itself. It is argued that 'failures of western development agencies' to complete various developmental initiatives they had undertaken after the Soviet withdrawal led to consolidation of anti-state sentiments and contributed to the continuation of the civil war (Shorthose 2003: 14). Therefore, international aid is the main chance to assert some authority in the current interim government and the elected one that will succeed it. Nevertheless, its hold over a perennially fissiparous state will remain tenuous.

External assistance can go a long way in providing vital guidance. The role of the United Nations Assistance Mission in Afghanistan (UNAMA) in nurturing civil society is worth mentioning.[25] It is co-ordinating a multitude of post-war reconstruction projects, ranging from capacity building to enhancing the operation of Afghanistan's Central Bank, and from the introduction of measles immunization projects in the countryside and cities to the imparting of English education. Similarly, the Asian Development Bank (ADB) has pledged $500 million over two and a half years for farms, power generation, roads and schools. This money will provide a crucial facelift to an almost non-existent infrastructural base, which is critical to sustaining an atmosphere conducive to the development of civil society.

Various NGOs and international agencies have made a concerted effort to merge their resources and expertise in order to introduce multi-pronged social regeneration projects. The Afghanistan Assistance Coordination Authority (AACA), the United Nations Development Program (UNDP), and the Ministry of Rural Construction and Development (MRD) have co-ordinated their strategies and plans of action and established a National Area Based Development Programme (NABDP). The objective of the NABDP is 'to develop the capacity of government at national and local levels to formulate and manage recovery and development strategies through an inclusive process that addresses key socio-economic challenges'.[26]

The viability of such initiatives, though, depends not only on the good will of the people, but also on an unremitting cash flow. Yet it is unlikely that external actors will be prepared to provide continuous assistance for post-war reconstruction. Interim Reconstruction Minister Amin Farhang has stressed that foreign donors are failing his country: 'the pledge of $15 billion investment over a 10–15-year period would return Afghanistan only to where it was before the Soviet invasion 23 years ago'.[27] This sentiment is shared even by Donald Rumsfeld: 'the real problem in Afghanistan emanates from the international community's failure to deliver the level of assistance to President Karzai and his team that is needed'.[28] Too many post-war reconstruction efforts are forgotten as soon as victory is declared.

It remains to be seen how far the Western community will be prepared to go to maintain the spirit behind the reconstruction efforts in Afghanistan. At a time when there is a proliferation of conflicts around the globe, it is sometimes easier to ignore old conflicts rather than do something about them (Holm 2002: 458). This attitude, variously described as 'bystander apathy' or 'compassion fatigue', is likely to affect Afghanistan as post-war reconstruction initiatives are undertaken in earnest in Iraq and Sri Lanka. In the long run, it is likely that the international community will develop inertia *vis-à-vis* Afghanistan. And in the medium term, the developmental initiative has not exactly been a commanding success, either.

According to one observer, post-war reconstruction by the West is carried out not only to benefit Afghans, but also to show 'the larger Islamic world the benefits of co-operation with the West, to justify the coalition's bombing campaign, to stop Afghan support for drug production and international terrorism and to contribute to the wealth and stability of its neighbours' (Stewart 2002: 37). Most likely, we will witness a Bosnia-type situation in Afghanistan. Between 1995 and 2002, around $6 billion of international aid flowed into the country. Bosnians of all ethnic groups claim that much of it vanished as a result of corruption, and underscore that the only industry to have emerged around Sarajevo is the one catering to the needs of the 10,000 or so members of the international community. Interestingly, two years into post-war reconstruction a large portion of what had arrived in Afghanistan – in terms of external aid – has been spent covering the fat salaries of foreign workers and to pay for their fancy and expensive cars.

In sum, giving control to external bodies or launching an indigenous reconstruction effort each has its liabilities. It is a conundrum. Ultimately, however, forging a sense of nationhood will depend on the citizenry. As the constitution of the United Nations Educational, Scientific and Cultural Organization (UNESCO) highlights, 'Since war begins in the minds of men, it must be in the minds of men that the defence of peace must be constructed.'

Many post-war reconstruction programmes do not 'take off, since they do not provide adequate voice to those in whose name they were initiated. Unless the citizenry become the active stakeholder in reconstruction – rather than the passive clients of NGOs, international agencies and bodies like the UN – such efforts will be doomed.'[29] As the General Assembly-appointed International Commission on Intervention and State Sovereignty [ICISS] argues in its report, *The Responsibility to Protect*: '[A] reconstruction and rehabilitation programme which does not take sufficient account of local priorities and does not create space for active local participation . . . could create an unhealthy dependency. . . . The long-term aim of international actors . . . is "to do themselves out of a job".'[30]

Conclusion

Civil wars are distinctly uncivil in their conduct, and rule-bound military interventions will not be able to bring them to closure (Peters 1995: 24–5). As mentioned earlier, the risk of a return to civil war in developing societies is unfortunately very high. What is the future of Afghanistan? The country is on a bumpy ride. Transition from war to peace cannot be assumed in the best of circumstances. Although there are indications that the society is on a 'road to recovery', it has also thrown up incidents and events that suggest an underlying chronic political instability for years to come. Even if the external reconstruction undertaking succeeds in providing a viable economic infrastructure, other irritants, such as ethnicity, tribalism and warlordism, will continue to have a strong bearing on the overall functioning of the state.

Post-conflict situations often 'provide special opportunities for political, legal, economic and administrative reforms to change past systems and structures which may have contributed to economic and political inequities and conflict' (Mehler and Ribaus 2000: 37). The task ahead involves profound transformation amidst challenges at micro, meso and macro levels. An effective post-conflict reconstruction programme 'will provide the ultimate hedge against the return of instability and infighting' (Goodson 2003: 96). Building viable peace in the country will depend on a multi-level transition involving security (from civil war to civil peace) and with political (from 'pariah' to legitimate state), economic (from political economy of war to peace), social (from psychotic revenge to reconciliation) and international (from self-serving international involvement to moral responsibility) aspects.

Conclusion: Confronting the Future

Afghanistan is a nightmare, full stop.

Clare Short, 2001[1]

During the course of our discussion, we found that Afghanistan's travails and tribulations had their origins in both internal and external factors. It also emerged that the crises in Afghanistan were produced and reproduced as part of a 'domino effect' – meaning that one particular event contributed to the next until the state and the society as a whole were engulfed by an ever-widening world of chaos. Perpetuation of this turmoil was also due to the physical location of the country and the nature of Afghan political culture. Because of its rugged topography, which has supported a history of warlordism, Afghanistan was a stranger to successful colonial rule and to effective central government (Kaplan 2003: 47). These combined factors were responsible for state failure in Afghanistan.

An audit of Afghanistan's civil war brought us face to face with the costs in human suffering and the challenges posed by a failed state to the wider international community. As one critic puts it, we study how states fail and collapse in order to learn how to put them back together (Zartman 1995: 267). Our analysis of the conflict aimed at enhancing that knowledge. Simultaneously, our understanding and appreciation of the ongoing political process and unfolding events hold keys to the process of restoring the state and designing order.

Almost two years since the overthrow of the Taliban, it remains hard to make any sure-footed prognosis on Afghanistan's future. The short-term goal of regime change has not produced any long-term vision for Afghanistan. In spite of the international intervention, its ill reputation as the most volatile and poorest country in the world remains unchanged. Precisely what kind of country Afghanistan is to become, and what role Afghans will play in it, are still crucial open questions.[2] To many observers, Afghanistan remains a single bad idea populated by decadent, intolerant, vengeful people who are tortured one day and torturers themselves the next. In its labyrinthine conflict, there exists no scope for reason, 'only the exchange of one group of killers for another' (Pilger 2002: 23).

The conditions that the people and the society live under are a true representation of a failed state – where 'anarchy is fuelled by irrational hatreds and the overall situation is characterised by vicious human rights abuse perpetrated by the mad and the bad' (Cooper 2002: 944). The catalogue of human misfortune in Afghanistan is very long indeed, and is still growing. In the last 25 years of fighting, over 2 million people have been killed in Afghanistan, most of them civilians (Farr 2001: 131). In Afghanistan, history repeats itself within a closed circle.

There is no denying the fact that the modern history of Afghanistan is one of systemic violence. The country witnessed Soviet intervention when its political process fell into chaos. As soon as the Russians retreated, it fell into another round of civil war. During the civil war years, everything operated within a collective and reciprocal circle of revenge and counter-revenge. The cruelty perpetrated by the Taliban was simply part of the violent whole (Drumbl 2002: 1122). Unfortunately, the current scenario is one where violence is always ready to break out. With the overthrow of the Taliban, old animosities have resurfaced. In the view of many analysts, this is likely to push the country into another spell of bloody internal war. Hence, in all likelihood, peace will remain elusive and contingent in Afghanistan for years to come.

This pessimism has its basis in several worrying discoveries. Our analysis of the civil war in Afghanistan acquainted us with the fact that it is an archipelago of competing ethnic groups. We found that the civil war encouraged the already estranged ethnic communities to devise their own law, system of governance, and a parallel economy, which ultimately produced the perfect ground for ethnic infighting and helped indigenous warlords to fill the vacuum where the state had failed. To a large extent the authority of these groups was organized and expressed as in an illegal state, and it remains so in the post-Taliban phase.

In this context it is worth asking: can Afghanistan emerge as a viable state? To make any long-term assessment of the conflict in Afghanistan, we need to concentrate on five key areas: (a) the future of radical Islam, (b) the role of warlords and private militias in the political process, (c) the contribution or intervention of the international community in rebuilding the country, (d) the regeneration of institutional frameworks, and (e) the role of civil society in terms of cross-community peace initiatives. An analysis of the developments in these areas should provide us with the knowledge to make a reasoned appraisal of the ability of the Afghan state to face its future.

The term 'Islam' has a special significance in the context of Afghanistan. It is often seen as a politically potent force. 'In a country like Afghanistan where the concept of the nation has developed but recently, the state is seen as external to society and where people's allegiance is directed primarily towards the local community, the only thing which all Afghans have in common is Islam' (Roy 1986: 30).

Therefore, the temptation to use and abuse Islam for set political purposes is immense. In the past, the common mass, the mujahidin and the Taliban all embraced Islam to achieve their own particular goals. Therefore, it has to be acknowledged that it will be extremely hard for any future Afghan government not to use the potential offered by Islam. The current conservative elements within Afghan society might have wanted to give the impression that they were retreating to a consensual, liberal political culture. But this could be a false dawn.

Almost two years into the regime change, most of the Taliban pronouncements that reduced women to the status of animals are still intact. The all-pervasive *burqa* or *chaddari* still dominates the life-style of most Afghan women. In many areas of the country, local warlords have made it obligatory for women to stay behind closed doors in their houses. Women continue to be used as pawns in political rivalry between warring groups. The victorious Northern Alliance regularly engages in sexual violence against women to suppress dissent among the Pashtuns. Just as various rival mujahidin exchanged girls and boys among themselves to resolve squabbles, women are now exchanged between warlords as payment in the settlement of feuds.[3] The violence against women continues against a backdrop of religious orthodoxies. Regrettably, Afghans remain committed to the version of Islam espoused by the Taliban.

The conservative elements are gauging the mood among Afghans in their apparent resolve to return to mainstream politics. The majority of Afghans in southern Afghanistan still support the Taliban. There are fears of these radical elements regrouping again in this safe haven. The role of some key warlords turned politicians in this regard is worth mentioning. Abdul Rashid Sayaf, a theologian and warlord responsible for destroying much of Kabul after the Soviet withdrawal, has posed the most fundamental question of all: What should be the role of Islam in Afghanistan's political process? Many warlords, clerics and elites who colluded with the Taliban and later contributed to its defeat would like a firm place for Islam in any future political arrangement. Traditionally, religion contributed to their power and strength. They would like to maintain that *status quo*. The growing influence of conservative elites in the interim administration is, therefore, a cause for concern.

The atomization of the warlords who have been the face of Afghanistan's continuous conflict requires a fresh probe. International intervention has not necessarily helped ease the problem associated with warlordism. The international coalition in its fight against the Taliban came to depend on various regional and tribal warlords. The pressure to return the favour is now most intense. Provincial leaders who exercise their authority by dint of their ethnicity and tribal leadership are powerful and often recalcitrant in their attitude towards the central government. The newly created Afghan army is organized along ethnic and regional lines, and justifiably contains threats to central administration and control.

It is instructive to remember that the security situation in Afghanistan in general has deteriorated considerably since the removal of the Taliban. Western aid workers hasten to say: 'leaving aside their vile policies, the Taliban had at least provided a modicum of security throughout nearly all of the country'.[4] Despite its best efforts, the international community has achieved precious little in terms of bringing normalcy in the realm of civil peace, policing, and law and order. The issue of security casts a long shadow over the whole peace process and, indeed, over the whole future of Afghanistan.

Therefore, the idea of establishing a military authority to deal with the internal security problems of a 'failed state' appears very appealing. Using international force to 'police' the militia and the warlords, however, is a complicated process. Given the nature of civil war dynamics in Afghanistan, any such force is likely to be dragged into the quagmire of factional tribal politics and become yet another party to the infighting.

Outside actors should also be realistic about what ideas they can push in the context of a 'failed state' (Hamre and Sullivan 2002: 89). Introduction of Western-style democratic processes such as elections would not necessarily produce the desired results. Elections do not always lead to enduring political stability. Cambodia's disintegration into factional fighting even after years of a carefully planned UN-monitored transition is a case in point. Given the continuous ethnic tension and history of dissent, it is unlikely that either the international community or the interim government in Afghanistan will be able to create peace, prosperity and 'a broad multi-ethnic government respectful of human rights and guided by the rule of law'. Hence, it is the opinion of some scholars that 'peacekeeping should be designed to stave off anarchy, not make a democracy' (Zisk Marten 2003: 50). Yet, retreat from any form of nation-building responsibilities in Afghanistan is fraught with complexities. If the international community were to abandon its democratization initiative, it would be likely to produce the worst possible result: failure to achieve Afghan democracy, yet untold resentment for not trying.

Any broad-based political arrangement will fail the legitimacy test if it is unable to improve the material well-being of the masses. There is a sharply rising popular expectation in Afghanistan following its exposure to the international community. These expectations are mostly economic in nature, and demand for their fulfilment is strong. However, there is precious little to stem the tide. The post-Taliban government is in deep trouble, by most accounts; its economy is a wreck, and unrest is mounting. As the United States and its Western allies contemplate a global anti-terrorist campaign, it is worth asking how long world attention will focus on Afghanistan.

Assessing the Afghan crisis in the mid-1990s, the then UN Secretary General was of the opinion that 'Afghanistan represents one of the world's orphaned conflicts – the ones that the West, selective and promiscuous in its attention, happens to ignore in favour of other conflicts'. Ten years on, this pessimism is still shared by Lakhdar Brahimi, the current UN Special Representative for Afghanistan. In his view, 'in post-conflict situations, would-be promises tend to be forgotten'.[5] He has even conceded that Afghanistan is going to be less of a priority for the international community as time goes by. Given the international community's new concerns in relation to post-conflict reconstruction in Iraq and Sri Lanka, it would be safe to assume that development programmes will remain unfulfilled, and that the economic and social toll of war will linger, feeding social unrest (Weinberger 2002: 267).

Moreover, even if the international community helps Afghanistan with generous aid packages, it is only going to perpetuate the earlier 'rentier model', and that would be unhelpful to the country when it comes to attaining economic self-sufficiency. The key to its recovery, then, is the creation of an independent and indigenous economic base.

A successful transition from civil war to civil peace is dependent on the capacity of the state to extract resources and to allocate those resources equitably (Zartman 1995: 271). Absence of these twin principles, or failure to see them through, can only perpetuate the earlier conditions of disorder. In Afghanistan, the warlords have not only held a vice-like grip on the country's politics for the past ten years, they have also stifled all attempts at meaningful economic development. Throughout the civil war, they pursued a strategy of predatory extraction, securing prudential support by distributing to clients some of the resources which they extracted (Maley 2002: 190).

Following a quarter of a century of internecine conflict, a war economy is now fully entrenched in Afghanistan. While this may sound perverse, the civil war in Afghanistan has actually benefited a whole lot of Afghans. Facilitation and continuation of this war economy have been made possible by people from tribal warlords to foot soldiers. Fearful of losing their profit in a post-war economy, this constituency has been trying hard to destabilize the peace process. Designing a transition from conflict to peace therefore requires introducing these individuals to alternative sources of livelihood. A simple policy undertaking such as land reform may hold the key to a new, self-sufficient, democratic Afghanistan.

Land reform is an unheard-of subject in the country. Most of the arable land is in the control of militias, tribal leaders or warlords. Unless the issue of land reform receives prior attention, all other well-intentioned policy programmes will suffer a setback. A country-wide land reform programme would have a series of knock-on effects for the better. First, it would create a sense of empowerment among millions of Afghans and make them feel custodians of peace and prosperity. Second, it could raise agricultural productivity, and that in turn would allow self-sufficiency in food grains and fruits. Third, many of the poppy farmers are forced to cultivate poppy as the land belongs to the landlord, or in many instances the local warlord. Should the farmers become owners of the land they till, they would not feel compelled to engage in poppy cultivation. Fourth, this new enfranchisement could lead to the breakdown of the tribal feudal relationships and usher in democratization at the grass-roots level.

Most Afghans point out that their state escaped full-scale European colonization in the nineteenth century only to be reinvented as a suitable ground on which to play out superpower rivalry during twentieth century's Cold War. There is no denying the fact that Afghanistan was embraced, maladministered, and then abandoned by neighbours, self-serving international powers and organizations. Indeed, there is some truth in the assertion that 'having been used as tools to expedite the demise of the Soviet Empire, Afghans were left to rot in their ruined country' (Rashid 2000: 208–9).

It is also worth remembering how Afghanistan's neighbours and fellow Islamic countries conveniently exploited its misfortunes and contributed to its ruination. The rich Arab nations poured billions of petro-dollars into the anti-Soviet jihad in Afghanistan, matching the United States dollar for dollar, in the belief that this would work to their advantage in the contest for an alternative Islamic leadership *vis-à-vis* a radicalized Iran and its effort to export its own brand of political Islam (Kepel 2002).

Afghanistan's immediate neighbours, Iran and Pakistan, have longer-term stakes in the future political process in Afghanistan than distant great powers such as Russia, the United States or the United Kingdom. The history of Afghanistan since the Soviet withdrawal in 1989 has proved the fragility of governments agreed by external powers, including Pakistan, the United States, Russia and Saudi Arabia (Chandler 2002: 207). The onus, therefore, is on the international community to make sure that other countries do not meddle in Afghanistan's internal affairs for their own political gain as they did in the past.

While Afghanistan's neighbours can, and have the resources to destabilize events in the country, they also hold the key to any long-term economic development there. The nascent economy of Afghanistan can get the much-needed boost if it is linked to the outside world. Yet, this will only be possible if it has access to seaports. Both Iran and Pakistan can aid Afghanistan on this issue. However, Iran's pariah status in the international community and its linkage to minority Shi'a politics in the country sit ill at ease with Afghanistan's overall goals. This makes Pakistan an obvious choice, by default.

In the regional Economic Co-operation Organisation (ECO), Pakistan has urged the new Afghan administration to facilitate the construction of a pipeline through Afghanistan that will transport gas between Turkmenistan and Pakistan. This pipeline (if built) will bring vital foreign currency reserves into Afghanistan. This would not only allow the state to shrug off dependence on external aid, but also help extract the much-needed revenue and enable it to be allocated for effective socio-economic regeneration.

Reconstruction of peace and stability in Afghanistan cannot be done only with money or external intervention. External intervention may be needed to rebuild some institutional framework. But, as with many other civil war-affected societies, ultimately 'it is the local forces that will be called to the task of putting the state back together' (Zartman 1995: 272). Thus the people of Afghanistan bear an equal amount of responsibility for ending the conflict. The causes of civil war in the country were as much internal as external. The Afghans' own devices are what have ruined the country, turning its towns and villages into a vast killing field.[6] The rather uncharitable remark that 'even if no other nation were involved, it is likely that Afghans would be fighting Afghans' (Edwards 1985: 505) is depressingly true.

Lest we forget, many more Afghans died during the infighting in the 1990s than during the anti-Soviet war of the 1980s or the US bombing campaign in 2001. With a bare infrastructure, Afghanistan has the highest concentration of small and light weapons in the world (most of it in the possession of civilians). The arms-decommissioning programme has been a complete and utter failure, due to lack of civilian commitment. Therefore, 'without a return to law and order, no transitional administration can hope to produce an atmosphere conducive to resuscitation' (Rotberg 2002b: 138). Indeed, with much bad blood from the past, a resurgent Taliban, a weak economy, and warlords and militias operating with apparent immunity across the length and breadth of the country, it is legitimate to wonder whether there could be yet another, new civil war.

Some of the challenges facing the Afghan state are the residues or remnants of past conflict. Although the current atmosphere in Afghanistan is a cause for concern, we should also remember that it is not always easy for a society or state to make a clean break with the past and begin a brand-new chapter in its history devoid of traces from its past. Most civil war-affected societies exhibit some forms of violence, instability and chaos in their transition to peace. But a lot depends on how the population as a whole responds to these irritations. A society has a better chance of attaining success in its post-conflict endeavours if it reflects on these irritants.

The task before the leaders and citizens alike in this interim period is to not only engage in rebuilding the war-scarred country, but also spend time asking what led to the destruction of their society and way of life. The answer to this, of course, is very simple. Since the country was trapped in an existential no man's land, it was easy for external forces to steer its citizens towards issues and ideas which were not entirely beneficial to the country as a whole. If they are to escape any future manipulation and humiliation, Afghans need to do far more to evolve a transparent federal structure of government that guarantees autonomy of groups and regions without sacrificing the notion of a national identity. To restrict the power of warlords and dislodge them from the political process, efforts should be made to favour the autonomy of individuals over autonomy of a particular individual.

A democratic, peaceful Afghanistan has to be an Afghanistan that exists for all its citizens equally, regardless of their race, sectarian belief or regional affiliation. The politicization of ethnicity has had a corrosive effect on the potential for national reconciliation. The identity politics of the past undermined the state and stalled the nation-building process. The current political process, unfortunately, is still a hostage to that old divisive political culture. One of the core problems facing Afghanistan is the increasing alienation of the Pashtun majority from the country's mainstream politics, which are dominated by minority Tajiks.

Rebuilding Afghanistan and facilitating peace in the country, therefore, are subject to the future attitude of the citizenry towards each other. Owing to ethnic, clan and tribal divisions, the Afghans let the best of themselves slip away and become their own enemy. To guard against the recurrence of mutual abuse, Afghans need to develop a concept of statehood that allows all ethnic groups in the country the chance to flourish in harmony. Institutionalization of social discipline has to be endorsed both by the authorities and by the common mass. A strong Afghanistan is crucial to its own internal stability. Only a strong state can ensure freedom and create an environment conducive to all-round growth for its citizenry. In the absence of these conditions, Afghanistan will simply disintegrate and resume its past fate as a reservoir of dissent and an exporter of terror.

Glossary of Terms ————————

al-Qa'ida	The base. The radical Islamic network and its outfit.
amir-ul-muamanin	Commander of the Faithful. An Islamic honorific title.
Barelvi	A school of Islam with origins in India, founded by Syed Ahmed Barelvi (1786–1831).
burqa	Loose garment, with veiled eyeholes, covering the whole body of women in Muslim societies, made compulsory during the Taliban regime.
Caliph	The 'deputy' of God on earth.
chaddari	*Burqa.*
Dari	The Afghan dialect of Persian.
dar ul harb	The land of infidels (*kafirs*) against which Islamists are required to wage holy war, or jihad.
dar ul Islam	Land of Islam, where Islamic rules and injunctions reign supreme.
Deobandi	An Islamic school with origins in India.
fard'ayn	Fighters/mercenaries.
fatwa	An Islamic decree or judgement handed down by a key religious figure such as a qazi, ulema or ayatollah.
Hadith	'Tradition' or report of a saying or action of the Prophet. One of four roots of Islamic law.

hakimiya	The sovereignty of God on earth.
Hazaras	The ethnic group of Mongolian stock, living in central Afghanistan.
hijra	'Migration' refers to migration of the Prophet from Mecca to Medina.
Hizb-i-Wahadat Islami i Afghanistan	The Islamic Unity Party of Afghanistan.
huris	Celestial nymphs.
jahil	Non-traditional modern activity in direct opposition to the precepts of the Qur'an.
jahiliya	Pagan or barbaric period preceding the emergence of Islam in Arabia.
jahiliyat	A godless non-Islamic world.
Jamiat-i-Islami	Islamic Society. One of the seven major mujahidin parties based in Peshawar during the 1980s, Jamiat was composed primarily of northern minorities.
jihad	'Struggle' – to achieve what is right; also holy war; obligation of Muslims to engage in defensive battle against non-Islamic forces or unjust rule.
jirgah	Originally a Pashtu term meaning council or formal gathering to arrive at a communal or national decision.
Jumbeshi-i-Milli-i-Islami	The party led by Uzbek warlord Abdul Rashid Dostum.
kafir	'Unbeliever', or infidel who has rejected the message of the Qur'an.
Khalq	Radical faction of the People's Democratic Party of Afghanistan (PDPA).
khanate	Self-governing Central Asian territory under the leadership of one of the Islamic ruling houses.
Loya Jirgah	Great Council. The traditional conference of tribal elders and chiefs, *ulema* and other influential people to discuss key political issues. Also the primary law-making body in Afghanistan.

madrasha	Islamic school primarily devoted to religious teaching.
mujahid	The Qur'anic interpretation of all those who resist un-Islamic forces, in the Afghan context those who fought against the Soviets.
mujahidin	Plural of mujahid; holy warriors engaged in jihad, or holy war.
mullah	Traditional Islamic leader of prayer at local mosque; also responsible for teaching the Holy Qur'an.
Muslim	One who has submitted to God; a follower of the religion Islam.
Parcham	Moderate faction of People's Democratic Party of Afghanistan (PDPA) led by Babrak Karmal.
Pashtun	The ethnic group inhabiting southern and eastern Afghanistan who are Pashtu speakers.
purdah	Gender segregation.
qaum	A group of individuals related to each other through a common language, blood and history.
Qur'an	The Islamic holy book.
salaam	A form of micro-credit provided by Afghan money-lenders to poppy farmers.
Salafi	A school of Islamic thought characterized by extreme conservatism and rigour.
shar'ia	The canon of Islamic law distilled from the Qur'an, the hadith and traditional jurisprudence.
Shi'a	A heterodox Islamic sect which believes that Ali, son-in-law of the Prophet Muhammad, and Ali's descendants should be rightful leaders of the Islamic community. Shi'as constitute about 15 per cent of Afghanistan's populace.
Tajik	Ethnic group living in northern Afghanistan of Caucasoid and Mongoloid substock.

takfir	Excommunication (*Takfiri*: one who excommunicates other Muslims).
Taliban	(plural of *Taleb*) Seekers of truth. Originally students from religious schools who later assumed political authority over Afghanistan.
taquya	Protecting oneself by lying low.
ulema	Islamic religious scholars.
ummah	The community of all Muslims, the wider Islamic world not constrained by geography or political separation.
ushr	A traditional taxation system reintroduced during the Taliban rule of Afghanistan.
Wahabism	An eighteenth-century conservative Islamic reform movement started by Ibn abd al-Wahab (1703–92). Current Saudi rulers are the promoters of this ideal. Wahabism is fast gaining popularity in Central Asian republics, and a significant number of Arab mujahidin in Afghanistan were followers of this ideology.
zakat	'Purity'; term used for a tax of a fixed proportion of income and capital by Muslims.

Chronology of Events

1747	Afghanistan asserts its independence following the assassination of Emperor Nadir Shah of Iran.
1819–26	Afghanistan is divided into separate fiefdoms with power centres in Kabul, Kandahar and Peshawar.
1839–42	First Anglo-Afghan war.
1872	Treaty signed between British India and Russia guaranteeing Afghanistan's independence.
1878–80	Second Anglo-Afghan war.
1907	The Anglo-Russian Convention of St Petersburg declares Afghanistan a buffer state.
1919	Afghanistan regains independence after third Anglo-Afghan war.
1926	Amanullah proclaims himself the new king of the country. Afghanistan signs neutrality and non-aggression pact with USSR.
1929	Amanullah flees after country-wide civil unrest.
1933–73	King Zahir Shah's reign.
1934	United States recognizes Afghanistan.
1947	Afghanistan becomes a founding member of the United Nations.
1964	Constitutional monarchy introduced.

Constitution of 1964 provides legal equality for men and women, but sets in motion a period of political unrest and growing radicalism.

17 July 1973 — King Zahir Shah is overthrown in a palace *coup* by the country's former Prime Minister Mohammed Daoud, with the Soviet Union's backing.

April 1978 — People's Democratic Party of Afghanistan (PDPA) assumes power through a military *coup*.

24 December 1979 — Soviet troops invade Afghanistan.

1985 — Mujahidin fighters form alliance against Soviet forces.

1986 — Afghanistan, USSR, the United States and Pakistan sign peace accords, and Moscow begins the first phase of troop withdrawal.

14 February 1989 — Soviet troops withdraw from Afghanistan.

19 April 1992 — Mujahidin forces assume power in Kabul.

November 1994 — Kandahar falls to a hitherto unknown militia of religious students, the Taliban, led by Mullah Mohammed Omar, with volunteers from Pakistan.

3 April 1996 — Over 1,000 Islamic clergymen elect Mullah Mohammed Omar as *amir-ul-muamanin*, or Leader of the Faithful.

25 May 1997 — Pakistan recognizes the Taliban regime, followed by similar decisions by Saudi Arabia and the United Arab Emirates.

16 January 2000 — The breakaway republic of Chechnya recognizes the Taliban regime, and opens an embassy in Kabul.

10 July 2000 — The Taliban orders all non-Afghan relief organizations to sack their Afghan female workers.

19 December 2000	UN tightens sanctions, including imposition of an arms embargo, closure of Taliban missions abroad, and travel restrictions on Taliban officials leaving Afghanistan.
3 January 2001	The trial, in absentia, of Osama bin Laden and many others allegedly implicated in the US embassy bombings in Nairobi and Dar-es-Salaam commences in a court in New York.
19 January 2001	UN Security Council passes Resolution 1333 imposing sanctions and an arms embargo against the Taliban regime.
26 February 2001	The supreme leader of Afghanistan, Mullah Omar, orders the destruction of the Bamian Buddhas.
1 March 2001	UN admits that the Taliban have enforced a ban on poppy cultivation.
31 July 2001	UN Security Coucil passes Resolution 1363 setting up monitoring sanctions on the Taliban.
9 September 2001	Northern Alliance leader Ahmad Shah Mas'ud assassinated by Taliban-initiated suicide bombers in Takhar province.
11 September 2001	Radical Islamists strike US interests in New York and Washington, DC.
October 2001	The US and the UK launch air strikes against Afghanistan.
19 November 2001	Opposition forces seize Mazar-e-Sharif and subsequently occupy Kabul and other major cities.
7 November 2001	The Taliban finally give up their last stronghold, Kandahar, but the leadership escapes.
22 December 2001	Pashtun royalist Hamid Karzai is sworn in as head of an interim, power-sharing government.

April 2002	Former king Zahir Shah returns from his exile in Rome, but declines any claim to power.
June 2002	The Loya Jirgah, or Grand Council, elects Hamid Karzai as interim head of state of Afghanistan.
July 2002	Vice-President Haji Abdul Qadir is assassinated by unknown gunmen in Kabul.
September 2002	Hamid Karzai narrowly escapes an assassination attempt in Kandahar.
December 2002	UN Special Representative for Afghanistan, Lakhdar Brahimi, concedes that Afghanistan is going to be less of a priority for the international community as time goes by.
April 2003	Taliban supporters regroup in the country's south and south-east.
May 2003	The USA says that it expects its troops to remain in Afghanistan for years.
7 June 2003	Four German peacekeepers die in a suicide bomb attack in Kabul.
June 2003	Clashes continued throughout the month between resurgent Taliban forces and those loyal to the new government, leaving more than 60 Taliban fighters dead.

Notes

INTRODUCTION

1 Some Afghans contend that 2 million Afghans gave their lives for the freedom that ex-Communist countries throughout Europe now enjoy.
2 For an early discussion and categorization of failed states, see Gros 1996.

CHAPTER 1 THE CURSE OF GEOPOLITICS

1 Some analysts are of the opinion that although US intervention in Afghanistan began in earnest in the 1980s, following the Soviet occupation of the country, the USA had none the less built up a strong support base prior to the 1979 invasion by cultivating a religious opposition to the Communist regime. See Ali 2002: 206.

CHAPTER 2 ETHNIC RIVALRY AND THE DEATH OF THE AFGHAN STATE

1 The political party led by Burhanuddin Rabbani, which dominated many mujahidin-controlled areas of Afghanistan.
2 The Shi'a section of Afghan society formed the united Hizb-i-Wahadat following key financial contributions from Iran.
3 By contrast, only India and Uzbekistan were consistent in their support for Dostum and Jamiat-i-Islami respectively throughout the conflict.

4 Within the framework of the Six Plus Two conference, held in Tashkent, Uzbekistan, in July 1999, the participatory members – China, Iran, Pakistan, Tajikistan, Turkmenistan and Uzbekistan (assisted by Russia, the USA and the UN) – attempted to stop the supply of military aid to the warring factions and to develop a strategy for establishing a broad-based government. The initiative was a failure, however, as the participating (neighbouring) countries followed their own agendas. For a detailed discussion, see Nojumi 2002: 203–4.

CHAPTER 3 RETURN OF THE CONSERVATIVE NATIVES

1 South Asian Islam has three spiritual inheritances: Deobandi, Barelvis and Faranghi Mahal. Of these, Mughal emperor Aurangzeb established the last one in 1694 – in Lucknow. While the Barelvis offered the possibilities of progressive transformation and apparent diversity of choice in terms of worship of tombs, ascription of semi-divine qualities to the Prophet, and intercession of Muslim saints, the Deobandis abhorred this supposed decadence among the Barelvis.

2 The primary objective of this policy programme was arming Third World anti-Communist insurgencies.

3 For a good discussion, see Fisher 1999.

4 Halliday (1995: 410) points out that 'The real danger of Islamisation lies not in its excesses, its random changes of direction, its blind groping, its utter obsolescence, but in the fact that being incapable of setting up a structured historical order, it produces chaos; and this favours the more subversive and sinister elements who loiter in the corridors of powers waiting for their time to come.'

5 I am paraphrasing Peter L. Bergen's (1996/7) comment on the role of religion in international politics.

6 I am using Bassam Tibi's (1998) interpretation of forms of Islamic government here.

7 *The Economist*, 1 December 2001, p. 24.

CHAPTER 4 BROTHERS IN ARMS: RADICAL ISLAM AND ITS FOLLOWERS

1 The Ottoman Sultan, the Sheikh-ul-Islam, issued a *fatwa* that declared a jihad against imperial Britain and its allies. Inter-

estingly, for the first time in its modern history Islam stood united when both Shi'ite and Sunni Muslims responded to this *fatwa*. Muslims from all over the world – including Afghanistan – went to fight for the lost honour of the Caliph. Many liberal Muslims who were outraged by the 'evil designs' of the West also participated in the Caliphate Movement in India that opposed British and European imperial ambitions and demanded the reinstatement of the Caliph and his authority.

2   Congressional Statement, *Federal Bureau of Investigation*, 18 December 2001; *http://www.fbi.gov/congress/congress01/caruso121801.htm*

CHAPTER 5 11 SEPTEMBER AND COMMITMENT AGAINST TERRORISM

1   See Evans and Newham 1990: 198.

2   See the 'Charter of the United Nations', Chapter VII, Articles 41, 42 and 43.

3   In spite of the problems with border control, the Council of the European Union at the end of 1996 imposed an embargo on the delivery of arms, ammunitions and military materials to Afghanistan. But it had little or no effect.

4   For a stimulating discussion, see Gorry 2000.

5   For a fascinating discussion, see Mack 1975.

6   For an interesting assessment of Andrew Mack's theory, see Arreguin-Toft 2001.

7   All of these conventions and clauses are discussed in Michael, Andreopoulos and Shulman 1994.

8   'The West' throughout the text refers to the United States and its allies in Western Europe. However, one should bear in mind that countries such as France and Germany have good relations with several Muslim countries. Similarly, the United States and the UK share good relations with Saudi Arabia, Egypt, Kuwait, the UAE, Qatar, Bahrain, Pakistan and Uzbekistan.

9   We run into difficulty by generalizing Muslims as a composite whole. Similarly, we cannot assign arch-conservative states such as Saudi Arabia and secular Tunisia to one single category. Many politicians and policy-makers in the developed world wilfully ignore these subtleties, however. The free-floating rage expressed against Muslims in general and Islam

in particular by leaders such as George W. Bush and Silvio
Berlusconi in the immediate aftermath of the 11 September
bombings is a case in point.

10 Also, see introduction in *Interventions*, vol. 4, no. 1, p. 2.

11 *http://bbc.co.uk/hi/english/world/middle_east_2062000/
2062253.stm*

CHAPTER 6 POPPY CULTIVATION AND THE POLITICAL ECONOMY OF CIVIL WAR

1 According to one school of thought, the reason why some
countries engage in drug production and trafficking has a
simple economic explanation. Expansion of the drug-trafficking industry has been an accepted form of development for
several Third World states (Pearl 1994; Allix 1998). Starved of
precious foreign currency reserves, many of these countries
take this route and turn a blind eye to the pervasiveness of the
narco-economy in the socio-economic and political process, for
obvious reasons. Since the production of plant-based narcotics
provides increased employment and income to its poverty-
ridden citizenry, there is very little domestic compulsion to
reverse the process.

2 Almost 40 per cent of the national budget of Afghanistan
during this period came from external sources in the form of
aid, assistance or investment.

3 For a larger discussion of the genealogy of this idea, see Lewis,
1967.

4 There exist volumes of well-documented evidence to support
the Vietcong's argument that the CIA and the US occupying
force resorted to large-scale distribution of drugs to 'win the
war by other means' (Rashid 2000; Davenport-Hines 2001).

5 *Le Monde*, 21 October 2001.

6 It has been suggested by the UNDCP (2000) that confiscated
heroin packages arriving from Afghanistan are sometimes
stamped 'Not for use by Muslims'.

7 Although it insisted on a *quid pro quo* with the West on the
banning of poppy cultivation with the recognition of the
regime, the Taliban were very concerned about the rapid
increase of opium and heroin abuse amongst Afghan youth,
which necessitated severe action against poppy cultivation.

8   According to the UNDCP (2000), the ban imposed by the
    Taliban was responsible for a 94 per cent drop in Afghanistan's
    opium production on the previous year, i.e. 1999.
9   *The Economist*, 16 March 2002, p. 68.
10 *The Economist*, 29 March 2003, p. 66.
11 International Crisis Group, *Asia Report*, no. 25, p. i, 26
    November 2001.
12 ITAR-TASS, 21 August 2001.
13 International Crisis Group, *Asia Report*, no. 25, p. i, 26
    November 2001.
14 *Far Eastern Economic Review*, 18 January 2001, p. 23.
15 *The Economist*, 8 June 2002, pp. 27–8.
16 Quoted in F. Elliot 2001, 'US and Britain Plan to Stop Heroin
    Trade by Buying Afghan Opium Crop'.
17 Pam O'Toole, 'Afghanistan's Opium Production Leaps',
    www.news.bbc.co.uk/1/hi/world/south_asia/2361453.stm, 25
    October 2002.
18 *The Economist*, 20 April 2002, p. 66.

CHAPTER 7 PICKING UP THE PIECES: RECONSTRUCTING PEACE

1   I have localized Robert I. Rotberg's general reference to con-
    ditions of anarchy in a failed state. For a detailed discussion,
    see I. Rotberg 2002b: 130.
2   Afghanistan's minorities often speak of Amir Habibullah II,
    who was the only Afghan monarch to hail from a non-Pashtun
    background. He also had the shortest reign (nine months in
    1928). Subsequent Pashtun monarchs and governments have
    maligned his time in power, and have made every effort to erase
    him from Afghan history.
3   Particularly significant is the issue of 'honour' (*ghairat*), which
    is associated with Pashtunwali culture. The emergence of
    'refugee warrior' youths – first in the form of the Mujahidin,
    later the Taliban – from the refugee camps in Pakistan is testi-
    mony to this effect.
4   True, various communities have codes of conduct that limit the
    use of violence and favour reconciliation or mediation over
    conflict. However, the continued presence of warlords and their
    limited commitment to peace in Afghanistan can only heighten
    inter-ethnic rivalry.

5 The mob that killed Rahman thought that, for personal reasons, he was about to divert the plane scheduled to take the Haj pilgrims to Saudi Arabia.

6 B. Moin, 'Afghan Political Healing', *http://news.bbc.co.uk/1/hi/world/south_asia/2055461.stm*.

7 K. Clarke, 'Challenges facing Karzai', *www.news.bbc.co.uk/1/hi/world/south_asia/2045816.stm*.

8 One can cite the post-war reconstruction efforts in Japan and Korea, but the reference here is to societies that underwent civil war owing to internal divisions.

9 N. Childs, 'US Wants More Help for Afghanistan', *www.bbc.co.uk/1/hi/world/south_asia/2196468.stm*, 16 August 2002.

10 See US Department of State press release, *http://usinfo.state.gov/topical/pol/terror/01120411.htm*.

11 Unfortunately, within the Western community there is also talk of introducing a new form of 'benign imperialism' in those developing societies that have witnessed a breakdown of state and society.

12 For instance, the country's defence apparatus is under the control of the Northern Alliance's Tajik commander, General Fahim. This appointment has led to many uncomfortable questions.

13 A fact recognized by the Independent International Commission on Kosovo. See Independent International Commission on Kosovo 2000: 259–79.

14 I have paraphrased Soedjatmoko's interpretation of the causes of instability and insecurity in the developing world. See Soedjatmoko, 'Violence in the Third World', in Vayrynen et al. 1987: 295.

15 The Pashtun demand for making the interim government more ethnically balanced by offsetting the Tajik and Hazara presence is a good example.

16 Historically, the state has been a largely Pashtun entity, but an accommodation was reached with the minority Tajiks, who staffed the ministries and formed the bulk of the bureaucracy.

17 I do not share the dominant view that defines civil society in terms of the absolute commitment of various groups to a humanistic common objective. Survival is often the shared goal in war-torn, underdeveloped, multi-ethnic societies, and various groups may adopt different strategies to achieve that objective. The ideal parity that conservative civil society schol-

arship aims to achieve is almost impossible to attain in the best of circumstances.

18 Tariq Ali, reflecting on the duplicity, hypocrisy and opportunism of Afghan elites and warlords, posits that the same group that assembled in Mecca in 1993 to thank the Almighty Allah for their triumph against the 'infidel' met again in Bonn in 2001 as part of the peace conference. This time they were thanking the 'infidel' for their victory against the 'bad seed of Noah' and 'false Muslims', an obvious reference to Osama bin Laden and the Taliban regime (Ali 2002: 214).

19 A February 2002 survey suggests that the resurgence of local warlords has placed security rather than reconstruction at the top of the new Afghan government's agenda. M. George, 'Afghanistan's Security Nightmare', *http://news.bbc.co.uk/1/hi/world/south_asia/1802350.stm*, 5 February 2002.

20 For a concise analysis, see R. Yusufzai, 'Afghan Killing Raises Awkward Questions', *http://news.bbc.ac.uk/1/hi/world/south_asia/2107440.stm*, 17 June 2002.

21 However, tension is never far away. Uzbeks have yet to join the cabinet. Now 'stung by Haji Qadir's assassination, Pashtun tribal leaders and opinion-makers have renewed their demand for making the government ethnically balanced by reducing the monopoly of Tajiks in the Cabinet', *http://news.bbc.ac.uk/1/hi/world/south_asia/2107440.stm*, 17 June 2002.

22 See P. O'Toole, 'Afghan Assembly Undemocratic', *http://news.bbc.ac.uk/1/hi/world/south_asia/2165049.stm*.

23 See *www.idrc.ca/books/reports/1996/13–01e.html*.

24 Although the percentage of female Members of Parliament in Britain is considerably less, Britons involved in the electoral process in Afghanistan argue for far larger female representation in the future Afghan government.

25 Set up by the UN Security Council on 28 March 2002, UNAMA is headed by Lakhdar Brahimi, the UN's Special Representative for Afghanistan.

26 See *www.aims.org.pk/*.

27 F. Amin, 'Aid Donors 'Failing' Afghanistan', *http://news.bbc.co.uk/1/hi/business/1970941.stm*.

28 J. Mannion, 'Afghan Government Needs More Aid to Get on its Feet', *Agence France Presse*, 15 August 2002.

29 Ashraf Ghani's Afghanistan Assistance Co-ordination Authority (AACA) and Lakhtar Brahimi's Light Footprint initiative are exploring ways of giving Afghans a voice in their own affairs.

30 International Commission on Intervention and State Sovereignty [ICISS], Gareth Evans and Mohamed Sahnoun, co-chairs, *The Responsibility to Protect*, Ottawa: International Development Research Centre, 2001, ch. 5, paras 27–31.

CONCLUSION: CONFRONTING THE FUTURE

1 The full quote is: 'You can't force Afghans to do anything. They are very independent minded. Afghanistan is a nightmare, full stop' (quoted in M. Kite, 'Britain to Have Big Role in Peace Force', *The Times*, 22 October 2001).
2 *The Economist*, 26 October 2002, p. 72.
3 *The Economist*, 16 November 2002, p. 69.
4 *The Economist*, 12 April 2003, pp. 59–60.
5 Kylie Morris, 'Afghanistan: Is Reconstruction Working?', *http://news.bbc.co.uk/1/hi/world/south_asia/2801829.stm*.
6 Comment made by John Simpson, BBC's World Affairs Editor, quoted in Chandler, 2002: 195.

References

Ahmed, Samina (2001) 'The United States and Terrorism in Southwest Asia', *International Security*, vol. 26, no. 3, pp. 79–93.

Ajami, Fouad (2001) 'The Sentry's Solitude', *Foreign Affairs*, vol. 80, no. 6, pp. 2–16.

Al Sayyid, Mustafa (2002) 'Mixed Message: The Arab and Muslim Response to "Terrorism"', *Washington Quarterly*, vol. 25, no. 2, pp. 177–90.

Ali, Tariq (2000) 'Afghanistan: Between Hammer and Anvil', *New Left Review*, no. 2, pp. 132–8.

Ali, Tariq (2002) *The Clash of Fundamentalisms: Crusades, Jihads and Modernity*, London: Verso.

Allix, Stephane (1998) *La Petite Cuillère de Scheherazadem sur la Route de l'Héroïne*, Paris: Editions Ramsay.

An-Na'im, Abdullahi Ahmed (2002) 'Upholding International Legality against Islamic and American Jihad', in Ken Booth and Tim Dunne (eds), *Worlds in Collision: Terror and the Future of Global Order*, Basingstoke: Palgrave.

Anderson, Benedict (1984) *Imagined Communities: Reflections on the Origin and Spread of Nationalism*, London: Verso.

Arreguin-Toft, Ivan (2001) 'How the Weak Win Wars: A Theory of Asymmetric Conflict', *International Security*, vol. 26, no. 1, pp. 93–128.

Atmar, Haneef and Goodhand, Jonathan (2001) 'Coherence or Cooption?: Politics, Aid and Peacebuilding in Afghanistan', *Journal of Humanitarian Assistance*, July, pp. 1–15.

Augustine, St (1985) *The City of God*, Harmondsworth: Penguin.

Barnett, Rubin (1995) *The Search for Peace in Afghanistan: From*

Buffer State to Failed State, New Haven: Yale University Press.

Baxter, S. (1973) 'Legality of Humanitarian Intervention', in J. Lillich (ed.), *Humanitarian Intervention and the United Nations*, Charlottesville, VA: University of Virginia Press, pp. 32–47.

Ba-Yunus, Ilyas (2002) 'Ideological Dimensions of Islam: A Critical Paradigm', in Hastings Donnan (ed.), *Interpreting Islam*, London: Sage, pp. 99–109.

Bearden, Milton (2002) 'Afghanistan, Graveyard of Empires', in Fredrik Logevall (ed.), *Terrorism and 9/11*, Boston: Houghton Mifflin Company, pp. 38–49.

Beck, Ulrich (2000) *What is Globalisation?*, Cambridge: Polity.

Bellamy, Christopher (2001) 'What is War For', *The World Today*, vol. 57, no. 12, pp. 4–6.

Benhabib, Seyla (2002) 'Unholy Wars', *Constellations*, vol. 9, no. 1, pp. 34–45.

Bergen, Peter L. (1996/7) 'Secularism in Retreat', *The National Interest*, vol. 46 (Winter), p. 11–14.

Bergen, Peter L. (2001) *Holy War Inc., Inside the Secret World of Osama bin Laden*, London: Weidenfeld & Nicolson.

Berman, Paul (2003) *Terror and Liberalism*, New York: Norton.

Bigombe, B., Collier, P. and Sambanis, N. (2000) 'Policies for Building Post-Conflict Peace', *Journal of African Economies*, vol. 9, no. 3, pp. 323–48.

Blackburn, Robin (2002) 'The Imperial Presidency, the War on Terrorism, and the Revolutions of Modernity', *Constellations*, vol. 9, no. 1, pp. 3–33.

Bonner, Arthur (1987) *Among the Afghans*, Durham, NC: Duke University Press.

Booth, Ken and Dunne, Tim (eds) (2002) *Worlds in Collision: Terror and the Future of Global Order*, Basingstoke: Palgrave.

Boroumand, Ladan and Boroumand, Roya (2002) 'Terror, Islam, and Democracy', *Journal of Democracy*, vol. 13, no. 2, pp. 5–20.

Brooks, David (2003) 'Kicking the Secularist Habit', *Atlantic Monthly*, vol. 291, no. 2, pp. 26–8.

Brzezinski, Zbgniew (1997) *The Grand Chessboard: American Primacy and its Geostrategic Imperatives*, New York: Basic Books.

Bush, George W. (2001) *State of the Union Address*, Washington, DC: The White House, Office of the Press Secretary.

Bux, Rasul (1994) *War without Winners: Afghanistan's Uncertain Transition after the Cold War*, Karachi: Oxford University Press.

Byford, Grenville (2002) 'The Wrong War', *Foreign Affairs*, vol. 81, no. 4, pp. 34–43.

Byron, Robert (1981) *The Road to Oxiana*, London: Picador.

Calvert, John (2002) 'The Islamist Syndrome of Cultural Confrontation', *Orbis*, vol. 46, no. 2, pp. 333–49.

Centlivres, Pierre and Centlivres-Demont, Micheline (2000) 'State, National Awareness and Levels of Identity in Afghanistan from Monarchy to Islamic State', *Central Asian Survey*, vol. 19, nos. 3 and 4, pp. 419–28.

Chandler, David (2002) *From Kosovo to Kabul: Human Rights and International Intervention*, London: Pluto Press.

Chomsky, Noam (2001) *9/11*, ed. Greg Ruggiero, New York: Seven Stories Press.

Choueiri, Y. (1996) 'The Political Discourse of Contemporary Islamist Movements', in A. S. Sidahmed and A. Ehteshami (eds), *Islamic Fundamentalism*, Boulder, CO: Westview Press, pp. 19–33.

Collier, P. and Hoeffler, A. (2000) 'Greed and Grievance in Civil War', (mimeo), Washington, DC: World Bank.

Collier, P. and Hoeffler, A. (2001) 'On Economic Causes of Civil War', *Oxford Economic Papers*, no. 50.

Cooley, John K. (2000) *Unholy Wars: Afghanistan, America and International Terrorism*, London: Pluto Press.

Cooper, Kenneth J. (1998) 'The Taliban Massacre Based on Ethnicity', *Washington Post*, 28 November.

Cooper, Neil (2002) 'State Collapse as Business: The Role of Conflict Trade and the Emerging Control Agenda', *Development and Change*, vol. 33, no. 5, pp. 935–55.

Davenport-Hines, Richard (2001) *The Pursuit of Oblivion: A Global History of Narcotics 1500–2000*, London: Weidenfeld & Nicolson.

Davis, Anthony (1998) 'How the Taliban Became a Military Force', in William Maley (ed.), *Fundamentalism Reborn? Afghanistan and the Taliban*, London: C. Hurst & Company, pp. 43–71.

Doornbos, Martin (2001) 'Of State Collapse and Fresh Starts', (mimeo), The Hague: Institute of Social Studies.

Drumbl, Mark A. (2002) 'The Taliban's "Other" Crimes', *Third World Quarterly*, vol. 23, no. 6, pp. 1121–31.

Duffield, Mark (1998) 'Post-modern Conflict: Warlords, Post-adjustment States and Private Protection', *Civil Wars*, vol. 1, no. 1, pp. 65–102.

Dupree, Louis (1997) *Afghanistan*, Karachi: Oxford University Press.

Dupree, Nancy Hatch (1998) 'Afghan Women under the Taliban', in William Maley (ed.), *Fundamentalism Reborn? Afghanistan and the Taliban*, London: C. Hurst & Company, pp. 145–66.

Durch, W. J. (ed.) (1997) *UN Peacekeeping, American Politics and Uncivil Wars of the 1990s*, Basingstoke: Macmillan.

Edwards, David B. (1996) *Heroes of the Age: Moral Fault Lines on the Afghan Frontier*, Berkeley: University of California Press.

Edwards, Mike (1985) 'Afghanistan's Troubled Capital', *National Geographic*, vol. 167, no. 4, pp. 494–505.

Elliot, Francis (2001) 'US and Britain Plan to Stop Heroin Trade by Buying Afghan Opium Crop', *Sunday Telegraph*, p. 18.

Elliot, Michael (2002) 'Hate Club: Al Qa'ida's Web of Terror', *Time*, 11 June, pp. 12–14.

Emmot, Bill (2002) 'New World Ahead: A Survey of America', *The Economist*, 29 June, pp. 1–28.

Engle, Richard (2001) 'Inside al-Qaida: A Window into the World of Militant Islam and the Afghan Alumni', *Jane's Defence Weekly*, 28 September, pp. 37–9.

Erlanger, Steven and Hedges, Steve (2001) 'Terror Cells Slip Through Europe', *New York Times*, 28 December.

Esman, M. J. (2001) 'Policy Dimensions: What Can Development Assistance Do?', in M. J. Esman and D. J. Herring (eds), *Carrots, Sticks, and Ethnic Conflict: Rethinking Development Assistance*, Ann Arbor: University of Michigan Press, pp. 235–56.

Euben, Roxanne L. (2002) 'Killing (for) Politics – Jihad, Martyrdom, and Political Action', *Political Theory*, vol. 30, no. 1, pp. 4–35.

Evans, G. and Newham, J. (1990) *Dictionary of World Politics*, New York: Wiley.

Ewans, Martin (2001) *Afghanistan: A New History*, Richmond: Curzon.

Farr, Grant (2001) 'Afghanistan: Displaced in a Devastated Country', in Marc Vincent and Birgitte Refslund Sorensen (eds), *Caught between Borders: Response Strategies of the Internally Displaced*, London: Pluto Press, pp. 117–37.

Feil, Scott (2002) 'Building Better Foundations: Security in Post-conflict Reconstruction', *Washington Quarterly*, vol. 25, no. 4, pp. 97–109.

Ferguson, N. (2001) 'Clashing Civilisations or Mad Mullahs: The United States between Informal and Formal Empire', in S. Talbott and N. Chanda (eds), *The Age of Terror: America and the World after September 11*, Oxford: Perseus Press, pp. 113–41.

Fielden, Matthew and Goodhand, Jonathan (2001). 'Beyond Taliban? The Afghan Conflict and United Nations Peacemaking', *Conflict, Security & Development*, vol. 1, no. 3, pp. 52–75.

Fischer, Benjamin B. (ed.) (1999) *At Cold War's End: US Intelligence on the Soviet Union and Eastern Europe, 1989–1991*, Washington, DC: Government Printing Press.

Fuller, Graham E. (2002) 'The Future of Political Islam', *Foreign Affairs*, vol. 81, no. 2, pp. 48–60.

Galeotti, Mark (2001) 'Afghanistan's Narcotics', *The World Today*, vol. 57, no. 12, pp. 12–13.

Gall, Sandy (1994) 'An Interview with Commander Ahmed Shah Mas'ud', *Asian Affairs*, vol. 25, no. 2, pp. 84–95.

Garfinkle, Adam (1999) 'Afghanistanding', *Orbis*, vol. 45, no. 3, pp. 405–18.

Garthoff, Raymond L. (1994) *Détente and Confrontation: American–Soviet Relations from Nixon to Reagan*, Washington: The Brookings Institute.

Geertz, Clifford (2003), 'Which Way to Mecca?', *New York Review of Books*, vol. 50, no. 10, pp. 27–30.

Gellner, Ernest (1992) 'Islam and Marxism: Some Comparisons', *International Affairs*, vol. 67, no. 1, pp. 1–17.

Giustozzi, Antonio (2000) *War, Politics and Society in Afghanistan 1978–1992*, London: Hurst & Company.

Gohari, M. J. (2002) *The Taliban: Ascent to Power*, New York: Oxford University Press.

Goodhand, Jonathan (2000) 'From Holy War to Opium War', *Central Asian Survey*, vol. 19, no. 2, pp. 265–80.

Goodson, Larry P. (2001) *Afghanistan's Endless War*, Seattle: University of Washington Press.

Goodson, Larry (2003) 'Afghanistan's Long Road to Reconstruction', *Journal of Democracy*, vol. 14, no. 1, pp. 82–99.

Gopalakrishnan, R. (1982) *The Geography and Politics of Afghanistan*, New Delhi: Concept.

Gorry, Jon (2000) ' "Just War" or Just War? The Future(s) of a Tradition', *Politics*, vol. 20, no. 3, pp. 177–83.

Gottfried, P. (2002) 'America and the West: The Multiculturalist International', *Orbis*, vol. 46, no. 1, pp. 145–58.

Griffin, Michael (2001) *Reaping the Whirlwind: The Taliban Movement in Afghanistan*, London: Pluto Press.

Gros, Jean-Germain (1996) 'Towards a Taxonomy of Failed States in the New World Order: Decaying Somalia, Liberia, Rwanda and Haiti', *Third World Quarterly*, vol. 17, no. 3, pp. 455–71.

Haass, R. N. (1999) *Intervention: The Use of American Military Force in the Post-Cold War World*, Washington, DC: Carnegie Institution Press.

Halliday, Fred (1995) 'The Politics of "Islam" – A Second Look', *British Journal of Political Science*, vol. 26, no. 2, pp. 39–52.

Halliday, Fred (2001) 'Islam and the West – Roundtable', *Prospect*, issue 68, pp. 16–21.

Hamre, John J. and Sullivan, Gordon R. (2002) 'Toward Post-conflict Reconstruction', *Washington Quarterly*, vol. 25, no. 4, pp. 85–96.

Hardt, Michael and Negri, Antonio (2000) *Empire*, Cambridge, MA: Harvard University Press.

Harrison, Selig S. (1995) 'Realpolitik Vindicated', in Diego Cordovez and Selig S. Harrison, *Out of Afghanistan: The Inside Story of the Soviet Withdrawal*, New York: Oxford University Press, pp. 245–70.

Hartman, Andrew (2002) ' "The Red Template": US Policy in Soviet-occupied Afghanistan', *Third World Quarterly*, vol. 23, no. 3, pp. 467–89.

Hauner, Milan (1990) *What Is Asia to Us? Russia's Heartland Yesterday and Today*, Boston: Unwin Hyman.

Heffner, Robert W. (2001) 'September 11 and the Struggle for Islam', *http://www.ssrc.org/sept11/essays/hefner.htm*.

Held, David (2002) 'Violence, Law, and Justice in a Global Age', *Constellations*, vol. 9, no. 1, pp. 74–88.

Heller, Agnes (2002) '9/11, or Modernity and Terror', *Constellations*, vol. 9, no. 1, pp. 53–65.

Helman, Gerald B. and Ratner, Steven R. (1993) 'Saving Failed States', *Foreign Policy*, vol. 89, no. 4, pp. 3–17.

Hird, Christopher (1997) 'The Capable State', *Index on Censorship*, vol. 26, no. 3, pp. 59–66.

Hiro, Dilip (1999) 'The Cost of Afghan Victory', *The Nation*, 15 February.

Hirsch, J. L. and Oakley, R. B. (1995) *Somalia and Operation Restore Hope: Reflections on Peacemaking and Peacekeeping*, Washington, DC: United States Institute of Peace Press.

Hoffman, Bruce (2003) 'The Leadership Secrets of Osama bin Laden: The Terrorist as CEO', *Atlantic Monthly*, vol. 291, no. 3, pp. 26–7.

Holm, Hans Henrik (2001) 'Writing the Rules for Disaggregated World Order' (*conference paper*), Florence: European University Institute, pp. 1–19.

Holm, Hans Henrik (2002) 'Failing Failed States: Who Forgets the Forgotten?' *Security Dialogue*, vol. 33, no. 4, pp. 457–71.

Hopkirk, Peter (1984) *Setting the East Ablaze*, London: John Murray.

Hopkirk, Peter (1994) *The Great Game: The Struggle for Empire in Central Asia*, London: John Murray.

Horf, Robert D. (1996) 'Democratisation and Failed States: The Challenge of Governability', *Parameters*, vol. 26, no. 2, pp. 17–31.

Horowitz, Donald (1985) *Ethnic Groups in Conflict*, Berkeley: University of California Press.

Howard, Shawn A. (2002) 'World Eras, Revolution and War: Modern to Postmodern', *Orbis*, vol. 46, no. 4, pp. 623–39.

Huntington, Samuel P. (1996) *The Clash of Civilisations and the Remaking of World Order*, New York: Simon & Schuster.

Huntington, Samuel P. (2001) 'The Age of Muslim Wars', *Newsweek*, 7 December, pp. 12–14.

Independent International Commission on Kosovo (2000) *Kosovo Report*, Oxford: Oxford University Press.

Jackson, Robert H. (1998) 'Surrogate Sovereignty? Great Power Responsibility and "Failed States"', Working Paper no. 25, Vancouver: Institute of International Relations – The University of British Columbia, pp. 1–14.

Jacquard, Roland (2002) *In the Name of Osama bin Laden: Global Terrorism & the Bin Laden Brotherhood*, Durham, NC: Duke University Press.

Jamieson, Alison (1992) *Drug Trafficking after 1992*, Conflict Studies 250, London: Research Institute for the Study of Conflict and Terrorism.

Judah, Tim (2002) 'The Centre of the World', *New York Review of Books*, vol. 49, (17 January) no. 1, pp. 10–14.

Kahler, Miles (2002) 'Networks and Failed States: September 11 and the Long Twentieth Century' (*conference paper*), Boston: American Political Science Association, pp. 1–48.

Kakar, Hasan (1974) 'Trends in Modern Afghan History', in Louis Dupree and Linette Albert (eds), *Afghanistan in the 1970s*, New York: Praeger, pp. 13–33.

Kaplan, Robert D. (1988) 'Driven Toward God', *Atlantic Monthly*, vol. 262, no. 3, pp. 7–23.

Kaplan, Robert D. (1989) 'The Afghanistan Post Mortem', *Atlantic Monthly*, vol. 263, no. 4, pp. 26–33.

Kaplan, Robert D. (1994) 'The Coming Anarchy', *Atlantic Monthly*, vol. 273, no. 2, pp. 44–76.

Kaplan, Robert D. (2000) 'The Lawless Frontier', *Atlantic Monthly*, vol. 286, no. 3, pp. 66–80.

Kaplan, Robert D. (2001) *Soldiers of God: With Islamic Warriors in Afghanistan and Pakistan*, New York: Vintage Books.

Kaplan, Robert D. (2003) 'A Tale of Two Colonies', *Atlantic Monthly*, vol. 291, no. 3, pp. 46–54.

Kapuściński, Ryszard (1985) *The Shah of Shahs*, London: Picador.

Kapuściński, Ryszard (1990) *The Soccer War*, London: Granta.

Keegan, John (1985) 'The Ordeal of Afghanistan', *Atlantic Monthly*, vol. 256, no. 5, pp. 94–105.

Kennedy, Paul (2001) 'Maintaining American Power: From Injury to Recovery', in S. Talbott and N. Chanda (eds), *The Age of Terror: America and the World after September 11*, Oxford: Perseus Press, pp. 53–79.

Kennedy, Paul (2002) 'Bernard Lewis Asks What Went Wrong?', *New York Times*, 27 January.

Keohane, Robert O. (2002) 'The Public Delegitimation of Terrorism and Coalition Politics', in Ken Booth and Tim Dunne (eds), *Worlds in Collision: Terror and the Future of Global Order*, Basingstoke: Palgrave, pp. 141–51.

Kepel, Giles (2002) *Jihad: The Trail of Political Islam*, London: I. B. Tauris.

Khalilzad, Zalmay and Byman, Daniel (2000) 'Afghanistan: The Consolidation of a Rogue State', *Washington Quarterly*, vol. 23, no. 1, pp. 65–78.

Khan, Sultan Mohammad (ed.) (1900) *The Life of Abdur Rahman: The Amir of Afghanistan*, vol. 2, London: John Murray.

Klass, Rosanne (ed.) (1990) *Afghanistan: The Great Game Revisited*, New York: Freedom House.

Knapp, Michael G. (2003) 'The Concept and Practice of Jihad in Islam', *Parameters*, vol. 33, no. 1, pp. 82–94.

Krakowski, Ellie (1990) 'Afghanistan: The Geopolitical Implications of Soviet Control', in Rosanne Klass (ed.), *Afghanistan: The Great Game Revisited*, New York: Freedom House, pp. 161–85.

Krishna, Sankaran (2002) 'An Inarticulate Imperialism: Dubya, Afghanistan and the American Century', *Alternatives: Turkish Journal of International Relations*, vol. 1, no. 2, pp. 69–80.

Lapidus, G. W. and de Nevers, R. (eds) (1995) *Nationalism, Ethnic Identity and Conflict Management in Russia Today*, Stanford: Stanford University Centre for International Security and Arms Control.

Laqueur, Walter (2001) *The New Terrorism: Fanaticism and the Arms of Mass Destruction*, London: Phoenix Press.

Lewis, Bernard (1967) *Assassins*, London: Weidenfeld & Nicolson.

Lewis, Bernard (1993) *Islam in History*, La Salle, IL: Open Court.

Lewis, Bernard (2003) *The Crisis of Islam: Holy War and Unholy Terror*, New York: Modern Library.

Lieven, Anatol (2002) 'Afghan Statecraft', *Prospect*, issue 70, pp. 24–9.

Lind, Michael (2003) 'The Texas Nexus', *Prospect*, issue 85, pp. 30–5.

Logevall, Fredrik (ed.) (2002) *Terrorism and 9/11: A Reader*, Boston: Houghton Mifflin Company.

Lubeck, Paul M. (2000) 'The Islamic Revival: Antinomies of Islamic Movements under Globalization', in Robin Cohen and Shirin M. Rai (eds), *Global Social Movements*, London: Athlone Press, pp. 146–64.

Lubin, Nancy, Klaits, Alex, and Barsegian, Igor (2002) *Narcotics Interdiction in Afghanistan and Central Asia*, New York: Central Eurasia Project.

Mack, Andrew J. R. (1975) 'Why Big Nations Lose Small Wars: The Politics of Asymmetric Conflict', *World Politics*, vol. 27, no. 2 (January), pp. 175–200.

Magnus, Ralph H. and Naby, Eden (eds) (1998) *Afghanistan: Mullah, Marx, and Mujahid*, Boulder, CO: Westview Press.

Maley, William (ed.) (1998) *Fundamentalism Reborn? Afghanistan and the Taliban*, London: C. Hurst & Co.

Maley, William (2002) 'The Reconstruction of Afghanistan', in Ken Booth and Tim Dunne (eds), *Worlds in Collision: Terror and the Future of Global Order*, Basingstoke: Palgrave.

Mallaby, Sebastian (2002) 'The Reluctant Imperialist: Terrorism, Failed States, and the Case for American Empire', *Foreign Affairs*, vol. 81, no. 2, pp. 2–7.

Marsden, Peter (1999) *The Taliban: War, Religion and the New Order in Afghanistan*, London: Zed Books.

McCloud, Kimberly A. and Dolnik, Adam (2002) 'Debunk the Myth of Al Qaeda', *Christian Science Monitor*, 23 May, pp. 11–12.

Mehler, Andreas and Ribaus, Claude (2000) *Crisis Prevention and Conflict Management: An Overview of National and International Debate*, Berlin: Univerrum Verlagsanstalt.

Meyer, Karl E. and Brysac, Shareen Blair (2000) *Tournament of Shadows: The Great Game and the Race for Empire in Central Asia*, Washington, DC: Counterpoint.

Michael, Havard, Andreopoulos, George J., and Shulman, Mark R. (eds) (1994) *The Laws of War: Constraints on Warfare in the Western World*, New Haven: Yale University Press.

Midlarsky, Manus I. (1998) 'Democracy and Islam: Implications of Civilisational Conflict and the Democratic Peace', *International Studies Quarterly*, vol. 42, no. 2, pp. 485–511.

Miller, John (2002) 'Osama bin Laden: An Interview', in Fredrik Logevall (ed.), *Terrorism and 9/11: A Reader*, Boston, MA: Houghton Mifflin Company, pp. 61–72.

Mishra, Pankaj (2001) 'The Making of Afghanistan', *New York Review of Books*, vol. 48, no. 18, pp. 18–22.

Misra, Amalendu (2001) 'Shanghai 5 and the Emerging Alliance in Central Asia: The Closed Society and its Enemies', *Central Asian Survey*, vol. 20, no. 3, pp. 305–21.

Monbiot, George (2003) 'Out of the Wreckage', *Guardian*, 25 February.

Moorhouse, Geoffrey (1984) *To the Frontier*, London: Phoenix Press.

Naipaul, V. S. (1971) *In A Free State*, London: Hamish Hamilton.

Newby, Eric (1981) *A Short Walk in the Hindu Kush*, London: Picador.

Nojumi, Neamatollah (2002) *The Rise of the Taliban in Afghanistan*, New York: Palgrave.

Nugent, Nicholas (2002) 'Waiting for War Again', *The World Today*, vol. 58, no. 10, pp. 14–15.

O'Loughlin, J. (1987) 'Spatial Models of International Conflict: Extending Current Theories of War Behavior', *Annals of the Association of American Geographers*, vol. 76, no. 2, pp. 63–80.

Olson, William J. (1993) 'The New World Disorder: Governability and Development', in Max G. Manwaring (ed.), *Gray Area Phenomena: Confronting the New World Disorder*, Boulder, CO: Westview Press, pp. 37–74.

Parekh, Bhikhu (1997) 'Rethinking Humanitarian Intervention', *International Political Science Review*, vol. 18, no. 1, pp. 49–67.

Pearl, Raphael F. (ed.) (1994) *Drugs and Foreign Policy: A Critical Review*, Boulder, CO: Westview Press.

Peters, Ralph (1995) 'The Culture of Future Conflict', *Parameters*, vol. 25, no. 4, pp. 18–27.

Peters, Ralph (2002) 'Rolling Back Radical Islam', *Parameters*, vol. 32, no. 3, pp. 4–16.

Philpott, Daniel (2002) 'The Challenge of September 11 to Secularism in International Relations', *World Politics*, vol. 55, no. 1, pp. 66–95.

Piacentini, Valeria F. (1996) 'The Afghan Puzzle', *Iranian Journal of International Affairs*, vol. 8, no. 3, pp. 23–42.

Pilger, John (2002) 'An Unconscionable Threat to Humanity', in

Phil Scraton (ed.), *Beyond September 11: An Anthology of Dissent*, London: Pluto Press, pp. 19–30.

Pipes, Daniel (1994) 'Islam's Intramural Struggle', *The National Interest*, no. 35, pp. 84–6.

Piscatori, James (2002) 'The Turmoil Within: The Struggle for the Future of the Islamic World', *Foreign Affairs*, vol. 81, no. 3, pp. 145–50.

Posen, B. R. (1993) 'The Security Dilemma and Ethnic Conflict', in M. E. Brown (ed.), *Ethnic Conflict in International Politics*, Princeton: Princeton University Press, pp. 79–97.

Poullada, Leon B. (1974) 'The Search for National Unity', in Louis Dupree and Linette Albert (eds), *Afghanistan in the 1970s*, New York: Praeger, pp. 34–49.

Poullada, Leon B. (1990) 'The Road to Crisis, 1919–1980', in Rosanne Klass (ed.), *Afghanistan: The Great Game Revisited*, New York: Freedom House, pp. 37–69.

Radu, Michael (2002) 'Terrorism after the Cold War: Trends and Challenges', *Orbis*, vol. 46, no. 2, pp. 275–87.

Rashid, Abdul (1990) 'The Afghan Resistance: Its Background, its Nature, and the Problem of Unity', in Rosanne Klass (ed.), *Afghanistan: The Great Game Revisited*, New York: Freedom House, pp. 203–27.

Rashid, Ahmed (2000) *Taliban: The Story of Afghan Warlords*, London: Pan Books.

Record, Jeffrey (2002) 'Collapsed Countries, Casualty Dread, and the New American Way of War', *Parameters*, vol. 32, no. 2, pp. 4–23.

Reeve, Simon (1999) *The New Jackals: Ramzi Yousef, Osama bin Laden and the Future of Terrorism*, London: André Deutsch.

Rotberg, Robert I. (2002a) 'The New Nature of Nation State Failure', *Washington Quarterly*, vol. 25, no. 3, pp. 85–96.

Rotberg, Robert I. (2002b) 'Failed States in a World of Terror', *Foreign Affairs*, vol. 81, no. 4, pp. 127–40.

Rotberg, Robert I. (ed.) (2003) *State Failure and State Weakness in a Time of Terror*, Washington, DC: Brookings Institution Press.

Rothchild, D. and Lake, D. A. (1998) 'Containing Fear: The Management of Transnational Ethnic Conflict', in D. A. Lake and D. Rothchild (eds), *The International Spread of Ethnic Conflict*, Princeton: Princeton University Press, pp. 203–26.

Roy, Oliver (1986) *Islam and Resistance in Afghanistan*, Cambridge: Cambridge University Press.

Roy, Oliver (1995) *Afghanistan: From Holy War to Civil War*, New Haven, CT: Yale University Press.

Roy, Oliver (2003) 'Euro-Islam: The Jihad Within?' *The National Interest*, Spring, pp. 59–74.

Rubin, Barnett R. (1995a) *The Fragmentation of Afghanistan: State Formation and Collapse in the International System*, New Haven: Yale University Press.

Rubin, Barnett R. (1995b) *The Search for Peace in Afghanistan: From Buffer State to Failed State*, New Haven: Yale University Press.

Rubin, Barnett R. (1997) 'Arab Islamists in Afghanistan', in John L. Esposito (ed.), *Political Islam: Revolution, Radicalism or Reform*, Boulder, CO: Lynne Rienner, pp. 179–206.

Rubin, Barnett R. (2000) 'The Political Economy of War and Peace in Afghanistan', *World Development*, vol. 28, no. 10, pp. 1791–812.

Rumer, Boris (2002) *Central Asia: A Gathering Storm?*, London: M. E. Sharpe.

Rumsfeld, Donald (2001) 'A New Kind of War', *New York Times*, 27 September.

Ruthven, Malise (2001) 'Signposts on the Road: The Nature of al-Qaeda and the Parochialism of Western Intelligence', *Times Literary Supplement*, 7 December, pp. 3–5.

Ruthven, Malise (2002a) *A Fury for God: The Islamist Attack on America*, London: Granta.

Ruthven, Malise (2002b) 'Radical Islam's Failure', *Prospect*, issue 76, pp. 30–5.

Sabet, A. (1995) 'Interpreting Radical Islam', *Iranian Journal of International Affairs*, vol. 7, no. 1, pp. 41–63.

Sacks, Jonathan (2002) 'The Dignity of Difference: How to Avoid the Clash of Civilisations', *Orbis*, vol. 46, no. 4, pp. 601–9.

Said, Edward (1997) *Covering Islam: How the Media and the Experts Determine How We See the Rest of the World*, London: Vintage.

Saikal, Amin (1998) 'Afghanistan's Ethnic Conflict', *Survival*, vol. 40, no. 2, pp. 114–26.

Sambanis, N. (2001) 'Do Ethnic and Non-ethnic Civil Wars have the Same Causes? A Theoretical and Empirical Inquiry (part 1)', *Journal of Conflict Resolution*, vol. 45, no. 3, pp. 259–82.

Schmeidl, Susanne (2002) '(Human) Security Dilemmas: Long-term Implications of the Afghan Refugee Crisis', *Third World Quarterly*, vol. 23, no. 1, pp. 7–29.

Scott Doran, Michael (2002) 'Somebody Else's Civil War', *Foreign Affairs*, vol. 81, no. 1, pp. 22–42.

Senghaas, Dieter (1987) 'Transcending Collective Violence and Civilising Process and the Peace Problem', in Raimo Vayrynen (ed.), *The Quest for Peace*, London: Sage, pp. 3–14.

Shawcross, William (2000) *Deliver Us from Evil: Warlords and Peacekeepers in a World of Endless Conflict*, London: Bloomsbury.

Shorthose, Jim (2003) 'Unlawful Instruments and Goods: Afghanistan, Culture and the Taliban', *Capital & Class*, issue 79, pp. 9–16.

Shurke, A., Strand, A. and Harpviken, K. B. (2002) *Peace-building Strategies for Afghanistan*, Oslo: Norwegian Ministry of Foreign Affairs.

Smith, Paul J. (2002) 'Transnational Terrorism and the al-Qa'ida Model: Confronting New Realities', *Parameters*, vol. 32, no. 2, pp. 33–46.

Sontag, Susan (2003) *Regarding the Pain of Others*, New York: Farrar, Straus and Giroux.

Staub, E. (2001) 'Ethnopolitical and Other Group Violence: Origins and Prevention', in D. Chirot and M. E. P. Seligman (eds), *Ethnopolitical Warfare: Causes, Consequences, and Possible Solutions*, Washington, DC: American Psychological Association, pp. 289–304.

Stern, Jessica (2000) 'Pakistan's Jihad Culture', *Foreign Affairs*, vol. 79, no. 6, pp. 116–26.

Stewart, Rory (2002) 'Diary', *London Review of Books*, vol. 24, no. 13, pp. 36–7.

Stobdan, P. (1999) 'The Afghan Conflict and Regional Security', *Strategic Analysis*, vol. 23, no. 5, pp. 719–47.

Straw, Jack (2001) "West Must Help Rebuild 'Failed States'", *Guardian*, 22 October.

Takeyh, Ray and Gvosdev, Nikolas (2002) 'Do Terrorist Networks Need a Home?' *Washington Quarterly*, vol. 25, no. 3, pp. 97–108.

Tarock, Adam (1999) 'The Politics of the Pipeline: The Iran and Afghanistan Conflict', *Third World Quarterly*, vol. 20, no. 4, pp. 801–20.

Taspinar, Omer (2003) 'Europe's Muslim Street', *Foreign Policy*, Mar.–Apr., pp. 76–7.

Tibi, Bassam (1998) *The Challenge of Fundamentalism: Political Islam and the New World Order*, Berkeley: University of California Press.

UNDP (1993) *Afghanistan Rehabilitation Strategy: Action Plan for Immediate Rehabilitation*, vol. 4, Kabul: UNDP.

UNDCP (2000) *World Drug Report 2000*, Oxford: Oxford University Press.

Urban, Mark (1988) *War in Afghanistan*, London: Macmillan.

van de Goor, Luc and van Leeuwen, Mathijs (2000) *Netherlands and Afghanistan: Dutch Policies and Interventions with Regard to the Civil War in Afghanistan*, The Hague: Clingendael.

Vayrynen, R., Senghas, D., and Schmidt, C. (eds) (1987) *The Quest for Peace: Transcending Collective Violence and War among Societies, Cultures and States*, London: Sage.

Vincent, M. and Sorensen, Birgitte Refslund (eds) (2002) *Caught between Borders: Response Strategies of the Internally Displaced*, London: Pluto Press.

Vincent, R. J. and Wilson P. (1993) 'Beyond Non-Intervention', in I. Forbes and S. Hoffman (eds), *Political Theory, International Relations, and the Ethics of Intervention*, Basingstoke: Macmillan, pp. 112–39.

Walter, Barbara (1999) 'Designing Transitions from Civil War', in Barbara Walter and Jack Snyder (eds), *Civil Wars, Insecurity, and Intervention*, New York: Columbia University Press, pp. 38–69.

Walzer, Michael (1992) *Just and Unjust Wars: A Moral Argument with Historical Illustrations*, New York: Basic Books.

Weinberger, Naomi (2002) 'Civil–Military Coordination in Peacebuilding: The Challenge in Afghanistan', *Journal of International Affairs*, vol. 55, no. 2, pp. 245–74.

Whitaker, Raymond (2001) 'US and Britain Accused of Creating Heroin Trail', *Independent*, 6 October, p. 12.

Wirsing, Robert G. (1991) *Pakistan's Security under Zia 1977–88: The Policy Imperatives of a Peripheral Asian State*, London: Macmillan.

Wolfowitz, Paul (2001) *Building a Military for the 21st Century*, Washington, DC: Department of Defence.

Wriggins, Howard (1984) 'Pakistan's Search for a Foreign Policy after the Invasion of Afghanistan', *Pacific Affairs*, vol. 57, no. 2, pp. 284–303.

Yapp, Malcolm (1980) *Strategies of British India: Britain, Iran and Afghanistan, 1798–1850*, Oxford: Clarendon Press.

Zartman, I. William (1995) 'Posing the Problem of State Collapse', in William I. Zartman (ed.), *Collapsed States: The Disintegration and Restoration of Legitimate Authority*, Boulder, CO: Lynne Rienner.

Zisk Marten, Kimberly (2003) 'Defending against Anarchy: From War to Peacekeeping in Afghanistan', *Washington Quarterly*, vol. 26, no. 1, pp. 35–52.

Žižek, Slavoj (2002) 'Are We in War? Do We Have an Enemy?' *London Review of Books*, vol. 24, no. 10 (23 May), pp. 3–6.

Index